Colonial Ports, Global Trade, and tł
(1700–1776)

Library of Economic History

General Editors

Peer Vries (*International Institute of Social History, Amsterdam*)
Jeroen Touwen (*Leiden University*)

VOLUME 18

The titles published in this series are listed at *brill.com/lehi*

Colonial Ports, Global Trade, and the Roots of the American Revolution (1700–1776)

By

Jeremy Land

BRILL

LEIDEN | BOSTON

Cover illustration: Port of New York in the early 19th Century.

The editorial work related to this book has been carried out by Professor Maarten Prak and Professor Jan Luiten van Zanden. The author and the publisher are grateful to them for the editorial support and trust in the project.

The Library of Congress Cataloging-in-Publication Data is available online at https://catalog.loc.gov
LC record available at https://lccn.loc.gov/2023940852

Typeface for the Latin, Greek, and Cyrillic scripts: "Brill". See and download: brill.com/brill-typeface.

ISSN 1877-3206
ISBN 978-90-04-54269-3 (hardback)
ISBN 978-90-04-54270-9 (e-book)

Copyright 2023 by Jeremy Land. Published by Koninklijke Brill NV, Leiden, The Netherlands.
Koninklijke Brill NV incorporates the imprints Brill, Brill Nijhoff, Brill Hotei, Brill Schöningh, Brill Fink, Brill mentis, Vandenhoeck & Ruprecht, Böhlau, V&R unipress and Wageningen Academic.
Koninklijke Brill NV reserves the right to protect this publication against unauthorized use. Requests for re-use and/or translations must be addressed to Koninklijke Brill NV via brill.com or copyright.com.

This book is printed on acid-free paper and produced in a sustainable manner.

For Taylor and Elliot

Contents

Acknowledgments IX
List of Tables and Figures XII
Abbreviations XIV

Introduction 1
1   Historical Background   8
2   Outline   12

1 **The Port Complex of Boston, New York, and Philadelphia**   15
   1   The Regional Complex of Boston, New York, and Philadelphia   17
   2   Complementarity and Competition   27
   3   Imperial Constraints and Limits   30
   4   Conclusion   33

2 **Merchants and Mercantile Networks**   35
   1   Merchants and Communities   38
   2   Local Capital Investment in Trade   45
   3   Networks and the Regional Complex   51
   4   Mechanisms of Trade   54
   5   Merchants and the Political Economy   66
   6   Conclusion   69

3 **Trade and Commodities**   70
   1   Imports   72
   2   East Asian Goods   81
   3   Exports   84
   4   Sugar   91
   5   Mechanisms of Consumption and Demand   94
   6   Conclusion   99

4 **Inter-colonial Trade**   100
   1   Quantifying and Defining Inter-colonial Trade   100
   2   Coastal and North American Trade   105
   3   West Indies Trade   111
   4   Conclusion   117

5 **Trans-imperial Trade** 120
   1   Defining Trans-imperial Trade 121
   2   Legal(?) Trade 123
   3   Smuggling 127
   4   Supplying Demand for East Asian Goods 131
   5   Transcending Imperial Borders in the Colonial Arena 137
   6   Lisbon–Philadelphia Trade 148
   7   Conclusion 150

6 **"Salutary Neglect" and the Origins of Independence** 151
   1   "Salutary Neglect" and Imperial Control 152
   2   Colonial Merchants as Competitors with English Merchants 158
   3   The Seven Years' War and the 1760s 165
   4   Economic Implications of Renewed Imperial Control 167
   5   Regional Merchants and Collective Resistance 175
   6   Britain's Military Occupation of Boston and the Sparks of War 177
   7   Conclusion 180

Conclusion: Revolution or a Battle for Free Trade? 181

Appendices 185
Bibliography 217
Index 230

Acknowledgments

There is no such thing as a single-author book. This author owes a huge debt of gratitude to the many people who, both directly and indirectly, have assisted in its formation, production, and refinement. Though I try, I will be unable to adequately express my gratitude to those mentioned below and those I am unable to list here. One of the perks of being able to organize both small and large conferences is meeting hundreds if not thousands of people who, like me, find enormous value and pride in researching the history of human economic activity, each with their own approaches and topics. The scholars I am privileged to talk to at these conferences have influenced this book in subtle, yet profound ways that are hard to quantify and explain. Nevertheless, I treasure these conversations and opportunities to continue learning. Still, there are a number of people and institutions that I want to highlight, as they have had a disproportionate impact on this book and my career.

First, I want to thank my PhD supervisor Ghulam Nadri and the Georgia State University Department of History. Ghulam directed the dissertation that forms the basis for this book, and I was fortunate to have had his guidance and steadfast support in my studies and subsequent career. Good advisors are rare, and he is a great one. The GSU history department was an extremely welcoming environment and home, providing both resources and the freedom to pursue my research, especially with guidance and support from Ian Fletcher, Julia Gaffield, and Denise Davidson, to name just a few. Of course, the book would not exist without the many archives and institutions that maintain the records that are at its core. The archival staffs of the Historical Society of Pennsylvania, the Library Company of Philadelphia, and especially the staff at the Massachusetts Historical Society were fantastic and extraordinarily helpful and welcoming. Researchers cannot and could not conduct research without the world's archives and their staff. It is essential we expand funding and support to these archives, not just maintain the status quo. I want to thank the editors of the Brill series on Global Economic History, Maarten Prak and Jan Luiten van Zanden, and the anonymous reviewers of the book for their guidance and support in the production of this volume. I am grateful to the editors of the Library of Economic History, Peer Vries and Jeroen Touwen, for including this volume in the series. I also want to thank Tim Page my copyeditor for his helpful edits and watchful eye for the tiniest of mistakes, and I am especially grateful to Wendel Scholma and Alessandra Gilberto at Brill for shepherding this volume across the finish line. Any remaining errors are the fault of the author, and the author alone.

As mentioned above, the communities of scholars in economic history and other disciplines have been a lifeline to my career and growth as a scholar. In particular, the scholars that regularly attend the meetings of the Economic History Association (EHA) and the Economic and Business History Society continue to influence my research in only the best of ways. Just some of those that have been important to my development and to this book include Billy Frank, John Wallis, Leigh Gardner, Eline Poelmans, Jason Taylor, Dan Giedeman, John Moore, Olli Turunen, and Simon Mollan. However, there are a few who deserve special mention. Anne McCants, who hired me as conference manager and directed the organization of the 18th World Economic History Congress in Boston, has continued to be supportive of both my career and my research, often providing a place to sleep and food to eat during my long weeks in the archives. Price Fishback wrote letters on my behalf and openly supported my research on many occasions even though I was never a student. Mike Haupert has also been very supportive of my career and my efforts to organize the annual meetings of the EHA. Henric Häggqvist has been a close friend and collaborator for years and likely for years to come. Helping me to create the maps in the book, Eric Oakley has also been a great addition to my network of collaborators, and I look forward to working more together. Last, but certainly not least of these, is Rodrigo Dominguez. A cherished friend and frequent co-author, his work in the Portuguese archives contributed directly to the research found in this book.

When I moved to Finland in late 2020, I was extremely fortunate to have the support and scholarly community of economic and social historians in both Jyväskylä and Helsinki, not to mention the great connections with scholars in other Nordic countries. For the last quarter of 2020, Jari Ojala and the Department of History and Ethnology at the University of Jyväskylä hosted me and my family and provided a home where I could start revising the book you see here. In 2021–2022, the Economic and Social History Unit of the Faculty of Social Sciences at the University of Helsinki was my home. The entire unit has been enormously supportive, especially Hanna Kuusi and Laura Ekholm, but I must extend my most heartfelt gratitude to Jari Eloranta, who has not only been my supervisor in both the distant past and in the last two years but is also a very close friend. He and his partner Charlene have been supportive not only of my career but also of my family. Words will never be enough to express my appreciation. I also want to thank the Unit for Economic History at the University of Gothenburg, including Svante Prado, Susanna Fellman, and Christopher Absell, for providing me with a new opportunity and support for finishing this book and moving to Sweden when I joined the unit at the beginning of 2023.

I also wish to thank my family for their unwavering support for me and my academic career. First, I want to thank my mom and dad, Sharon and James Land, for being wonderful parents and excellent teachers. I would not be here without their love and support. I also want to thank my grandparents, Bob and Brenda Bridges, who have always been supportive and proud of my accomplishments, no matter how minor. They are exactly what any grandparent ought to be. I also want to thank the late Phyllis Land, who was in many ways an additional parent while she lived with us, and while she did not live to see the printing of this book, she would most certainly have insisted to anyone who came to see her, no matter how briefly, that they should buy it. She is missed.

Most importantly, I want to thank my partner and wife, Taylor Land. She is without a doubt everything that matters to me in this world. While this book is an important achievement in my life, the joy of having her as my guide and support far outweighs anything else. She is both an amazing partner and an amazing mother to our wonderful little boy Elliot. I also want to thank Elliot for his daily reminders that no matter how much I must do, spending time together with him and with Taylor is far more valuable than any book, article, or conference. To them, I dedicate this book. To all the others that I failed to mention, I am sorry, but you are not forgotten. Thanks also to the reader for taking the time to read and process this book. I truly appreciate both your time and your interest.

Tables and Figures

Tables

1. Population growth of Boston, New York, and Philadelphia   10
2. Entrances and clearances from Boston and Salem, April–December 1720   18
3. Tonnage clearing Boston, New York, and Philadelphia annually for selected years, 1750–72   28
4. Estimates of currency in circulation in Pennsylvania 1735–75   33
5. Ownership of vessels trading between British ports and colonial ports on the North American Continent, 1770   47
6. The sources of capital invested in the shipping industry of Colonial Philadelphia, 1726–29 and 1770–75   48
7. Value of colonial imports in 1744–48 and 1754–58   74
8. Yearly average commodity imports by New England and the Middle Colonies, 1768–72   75
9. Official values of colonial imports from Britain, 1768–72   77
10. Selected English exports to British America, 1770   79
11. Tea imported from England by American Colonies, 1761–75   83
12. Average annual quantities and values of overseas exports of specified commodities by Boston, New York, and Philadelphia, 1768–72   86
13. Estimates of gross income per capita, 1700–74   98
14. Shares of tonnage clearing for various destinations from Boston, New York, and Philadelphia by selected time periods   106
15. Average annual values of selected commodities in the coastal trade, 1768–72   107
16. Distribution of Philadelphia tobacco exports, 1704–9   114
17. Imports of rum into Philadelphia (Gallons)   116
18. Reexports of West Indian rum to North America (Gallons)   116
19. Origins and destinations of entries and clearances of Boston and Philadelphia for selected years   118
20. Entries and clearances in Boston Gazette, 1739   139
21. Breakdown of entries and clearances in Boston, New York, and Philadelphia in 1740 and 1770   144
22. Fishing vessels entering and clearing bilbao, Spain, 1763–75   145
23. Ten-yearly average values of english imports into colonies by decade   159
24. Percentage of ship tonnage entering and clearing colonial ports owned by colonial residents in overseas trade, 1768–72   160

25   Estimated shipping profits, 1768–72   162
26   Imperial taxes collected under selected British revenue laws, 1765–74   170
27   Tax collected under the Sugar Act of 1766 at four major ports   171

Figures

1   Forelands of Boston, New York and Philadelphia   17
2   Boston's port complex   19
3   New York's port complex   23
4   Philadelphia's port complex   25
5   Overlapping hinterlands   26
6   Exports of bread and flour from Philadelphia, 1768–1772   115
7   Philadelphia cargo entries into Lisbon   150

Abbreviations

BMP   *The Beekman Mercantile Papers, 1746–1799*, ed. Philip L. White, 3 vols. (New York: New York Historical Society, 1956)
HSP   Historical Society of Pennsylvania, Philadelphia, PA
LCP   Library Company of Philadelphia, Philadelphia, PA
LGC   *Letterbook of Greg and Cunningham, 1756–57: Merchants of New York and Belfast*, ed. Thomas M. Truxes (Oxford: Oxford University Press, 2001)
MHS   Massachusetts Historical Society, Boston, MA
NYHS   New York Historical Society, New York

Introduction

In October 1768, British naval ships entered Boston's harbor to transport nearly five thousand British soldiers to occupy and suppress a series of major and sometimes violent protests against newly installed revenue acts and trade restrictions, such as the infamous Stamp Act of 1765. These efforts to control and tax the trade of the British American colonies were met with intense resistance from the merchants and consumers in America, especially in the three largest port cities in North America: Boston, New York, and Philadelphia. The presence of large numbers of soldiers and sailors only caused more friction between colonists and the British Empire, leaving many looking for alternatives to British rule. The occupation of Boston continued until 1775, when, after the Battles of Lexington and Concord, the American Revolutionary War began between thirteen of Britain's North American colonies and Britain. While the American army was able to push the British out of Boston in 1775, New York City was subsequently attacked and occupied for the remainder of the war. Philadelphia, much like the other two ports, remained under constant pressure and attack, and for nine months in 1777–78, the British army also occupied it as it did the other two ports.

Resistance to British efforts to control American trade were also centered in the same three cities, and political dissidents from those ports were able to persuade thirteen colonies to join in their efforts to first resist British imperial edicts and then ultimately rebel. Why did Britain focus its efforts to rein in British America in the cities of Boston, New York, and Philadelphia, and why were merchants and consumers in those cities so vehemently opposed to those efforts? This question is at the core of the following pages that examine the preceding century of economic exchange and commerce that flowed through the ports of Boston, New York, and Philadelphia. What made these cities so important to the economies of British America and the Atlantic community, and in what ways did the global flow of goods influence the development of all three cities?

This book seeks to revise our understanding of colonial American trade within the global economy through the lens of a British Empire that lacked the capacity to fully support and constrain its far-flung peripheries in the eighteenth century. Much has been written on the role of the British trade with its colonies in North America, but little attention has been paid to the American merchants and their role in the global economy prior to independence from Britain. I provide a new approach to understanding how global maritime trade influenced the economic development of the port complex of Boston,

New York, and Philadelphia. Often discussed separately or divided into different regions, these three cities functioned largely the same in their maritime trade. While at times they competed, merchants in these three cities more often complemented and cooperated with one another, creating intricate networks of credit, business, and trade. These shared economic activities gradually tied these three ports and their respective hinterlands into a cohesive port complex. By the 1770s, these economic ties became political as they sought to confront Britain's growing efforts to place and enforce limits and taxes on colonial American trade.

Through a comparative analysis of these cities' intra-imperial and trans-imperial trade, this book pursues a greater appreciation of the nature and significance of British imperial presence—or absence—for the region's commercial economy. Drawing on the existing literature and utilizing archival records and published primary sources, this study reexamines the economic history of British North America in two major ways. First, it argues that Boston, New York, and Philadelphia served as the chief ports within their own port complexes, and then treats them as parts of one large port complex playing the role of a nodal center in the British imperial and Atlantic trade. Second, this study moves away from the framework that examines the economy of this region primarily through exchange of goods and capital between the colonies and the metropolis. This research, while paying attention to the scale and importance of colonial trade, underscores the significance of trans-imperial trade networks, which connected these colonial port cities with non-British ports on both American and European shores of the Atlantic Ocean. It shows that the region was economically less oriented toward Britain than to the rest of the world, which was a constant source of tension between the colony and metropole. As Boston, New York, and Philadelphia carried out a substantial trade with ports and places outside of the British Empire, colonial merchants in these cities resisted mercantilist policies of the British Empire that sought to restrict access to global markets. Their resistance, either by circumventing the imperial policies or disregarding them altogether, continued throughout the eighteenth century and culminated in the war for independence between the fledgling United States and the British Empire.

Always in the background, the British Empire created laws and enforcement mechanisms to constrain American economic activity. However, Britain was rarely able, if ever, to enforce those rules and regulations effectively, leaving the colonists largely on their own in the global economy. Imperial capacity, or lack thereof, was always a specter in the daily lives of American merchants, but they rarely followed imperial rules regarding economic activity. Left to their own devices whether intentionally or not, American merchants in Boston,

New York, and Philadelphia expanded their networks beyond the confines of the British Empire to find the goods and consumers they required to make the profits that made daily life possible. Over time, these merchants found that membership in the British Empire, especially following renewed efforts to enforce imperial constraints in the 1760s, was not worth the effort and sought to find avenues to either autonomy or independence.

This book uses an Atlantic and global approach to the subject, alongside interdisciplinary methodologies, literature, and basic quantitative analysis, to dig deeper into the origins of American independence beyond the political and rhetorical arguments that define the field of early American history. Atlantic World historiography has been prevalent for several decades now, having become its own field of study. An Atlantic approach situates the Atlantic Ocean at the center of any scholarship, even if the focus is on a specific location or commodity.[1] Central to the development of an Atlantic World was commercial exchange and imperial competition, with many European empires jostling for preeminence within the Atlantic arena. Yet at the same time, transimperial exchange was an important component in facilitating coherence within the Atlantic economy, and smuggling may have been just as common as legal trade.[2] This book is situated precisely between these areas of discussion of both illicit commerce and imperial competition, asking how the people living at the edges of empires were influenced by the larger Atlantic and global economies.

In framing this study, I borrow the concept of a nodal center from Thomas Metcalf, who examined the role of India within the Indian Ocean World and the global British Empire.[3] For Metcalf, a nodal center is where economic and political power does not go directly through the metropole. Instead, certain locations, such as India, became economically and politically essential to the larger empire's survival. Unlike Metcalf's discussion of India, however, the nodal center of Boston, New York, and Philadelphia did not serve solely as a center for the British Empire but also as a key entrepôt for the Atlantic and

---

1 Bernard Bailyn, *Atlantic History: Concept and Contours* (Cambridge, MA: Harvard University Press, 2005); David Armitage, "Three Concepts of Atlantic History," in *The British Atlantic World, 1500–1800*, ed. David Armitage and Michal J. Braddock (New York: Palgrave Macmillan, 2002); David Hancock, *Oceans of Wine: Madeira and the Emergence of American Trade and Taste* (New Haven: Yale University Press, 2009).
2 Wim Klooster, "Inter-imperial Smuggling in the Americas, 1600–1800," in *Soundings in Atlantic History: Latent Structures and Intellectual Currents, 1500–1830*, ed. Bernard Bailyn and Patricia L. Denault (Cambridge, MA: Harvard University Press, 2009).
3 Thomas R. Metcalf, *Imperial Connections: India in the Indian Ocean Arena, 1860–1920* (Berkeley: University of California Press, 2007).

global economies. Regional economic networks were centered in these locations, providing significant political power and importance, which limited the larger empire's hegemony over these nodal centers. By using a global approach to study the mercantile networks of these three cities, I describe how they developed into competitors with English merchants and the English mercantilist agenda.

Most scholarship on British America has placed Boston, New York, and Philadelphia in two separate regional categories. Largely as a result of the intense historical focus on the United States, scholars divide the thirteen colonies that declared independence from Britain in 1776 into four regions: New England (New Hampshire, Connecticut, Rhode Island, and Massachusetts); the Middle Colonies (New York, New Jersey, Delaware, and Pennsylvania); Upper South (Maryland, Virginia, and North Carolina); and Lower South (South Carolina and Georgia).[4] Boston is considered part of New England, and New York and Philadelphia are within the Middle Colonies. Rather than separate these three cities into different regions, I emphasize the pronounced similarities between Boston, New York, and Philadelphia and treat them as parts of a larger port complex in which each was related to the other in a relationship of competition and complementarity. In so doing, their connection to the global economy of the period is easier to understand.

Whether or not the eighteenth-century world could be described as a globalized economy continues to be subject to debate. Beginning with Immanuel Wallerstein and his "world-systems" theory, discussion has continued to rage among global economic historians about when exactly the global economy became globalized. Wallerstein's theory placed the core of the modern world economic system in Europe and claims that the system emerged in the late fifteenth and early sixteenth centuries when European empires began their rapid accumulation of territory and wealth.[5] Others have challenged this view and

---

4 These regional divisions are found in nearly any study of British America, and especially those on its economy. For economic historians, one of the most cited books on the economy of British America is James F. Shepherd and Gary M. Walton, *Shipping, Maritime Trade and the Economic Development of Colonial North America* (Cambridge: Cambridge University Press, 1972). Later historians use the same divisions, though with a few minor changes, such as John J. McCusker and Russell R. Menard, *The Economy of British America, 1607–1789* (Chapel Hill: University of North Carolina Press, 1985) and Peter H. Lindert and Jeffrey G. Williamson, *Unequal Gains: American Growth and Inequality since 1700* (Princeton: Princeton University Press, 2016). I have yet to find an example of any scholar who considers Boston, New York, and Philadelphia as part of the same region.
5 Immanuel Wallerstein, *The Modern World System*, 3 vols. (New York: Academic Press, 1974, 1980, 1989).

INTRODUCTION 5

suggested that the world-system may have existed long before Wallerstein's suggestion of the early modern period.[6] Nevertheless, the conceptualization of the world composed of cores and peripheries remains a useful tool in describing the world economy.

More recently, however, scholars have wondered whether globalization truly occurred prior to the nineteenth century. According to Kevin O'Rourke and Jeffrey Williamson, globalization cannot occur without declining transaction costs and convergent prices across the globe. Therefore, they argue that globalization did not occur before the 1820s.[7] This definition of globalization differs from that offered by Dennis Flynn and Arturo Giráldez, who, in direct response to O'Rourke and Williamson, instead suggest that globalization began in 1571 when the Spanish founded Manila.[8] It was then that the global loop was closed, and all inhabited regions of the world were connected in some way or other.

The debate continues to this day, but for this book, the view of Pim de Zwart and Jan Luiten van Zanden is more instructive in that globalization is a continuing process. The eighteenth century was an era in which the world's economies were transformed and continued to evolve as trade expanded to all parts of the world. While at times some places witnessed price convergence and other earmarks of the modern globalized economy, trade continued to bring the world closer together.[9] Though it is unclear if the global economy of the eighteenth century was truly one defined by globalization, the world that Boston, New York, and Philadelphia inhabited was certainly in the process of globalizing, and all three cities were connected to the global flow of goods that defined the eighteenth-century world. American merchants were participants in that global flow, and they helped to shape and bend the global economy as much as global trade shaped their development.

---

6   Janet Abu-Lughod, *Before European Hegemony: The World System A.D. 1250–1350* (Oxford: Oxford University Press, 1989); Andre Gunder Frank and Barry K. Gills, "The Five Thousand Year World System: An Interdisciplinary Introduction," *Humboldt Journal of Social Relations* 18, no. 1, World-Systems Analysis (1992): 1–79.
7   Kevin H. O'Rourke and Jeffrey G. Williamson, "When Did Globalization Begin?," *European Review of Economic History* 6, no. 1 (2002): 1–18.
8   Dennis O. Flynn and Arturo Giráldez, "Path Dependence, Time Lags and the Birth of Globalization: A Critique of O'Rourke and Williamson," *European Review of Economic History* 8, no. 1 (2004): 81–108.
9   Pim de Zwart and Jan Luiten van Zanden, *The Origins of Globalization: World Trade in the Making of the Global Economy* (Cambridge: Cambridge University Press, 2018), 2–24.

Throughout the colonial period in North America, the British attempted to create a mercantilist empire without enough fiscal and state capacity to fully implement the various rules and regulations on colonial commerce. Britain failed to provide enough currency and specie to the colonies at the edge of empire, especially in Boston, New York, and Philadelphia, where major cash crops failed to materialize to increase specie flow into the pockets of colonial merchants. This forced colonial merchants to find alternative methods to conduct business and increase their connections with merchants and destinations that were more willing to conduct barter exchanges for the goods they had available. Though not in any way intentional, the inability of the British to enforce their mercantilist laws prohibiting direct foreign trade between the colonies and the rest of the world created the liminal spaces between which colonial merchants traded with non-British merchants and destinations, gaining access to both goods and profits that overcame the constant shortage of currency that plagued the colonial American economy. As a result, Britain's limited imperial capacity simultaneously created both a disadvantage that colonial merchants needed to overcome and an opportunity to work at the edges of empire, expanding their trade outside of the legal frameworks imposed on them by the British state.

State capacity and its importance in historical development has received significant attention in the first two decades of the twenty-first century. State capacity has traditionally been viewed as the ability to extract taxes and build armies, meaning that warfare and the development of a state were interrelated.[10] Financial extraction was a key component in the growth of the state and the economy, as the institutional turn in economic history has emphasized the value and importance of institutions in determining the development of a society.[11] More recently, scholars such as Mark Dincecco have continued to show that warfare in the early modern world led to the development of centralized fiscal systems that facilitated further growth in the economy and the state's ability to wage war.[12]

---

10   Charles Tilly, *Coercion, Capital, and European States, AD 990–1990* (Cambridge, MA: Basil Blackwell, 1990).

11   Much has been written on this, but a few examples are: Douglass C. North, John J. Wallis, and Barry R. Weingast, *Violence and Social Orders: A Conceptual Framework for Interpreting Recorded Human History* (Cambridge: Cambridge University Press, 2009); Daron Acemoglu and James A. Robinson, *Why Nations Fail: The Origins of Power, Prosperity and Poverty* (New York: Crown Publishers, 2012); and Philip T. Hoffman, *Why Did Europe Conquer the World?* (Princeton: Princeton University Press, 2015).

12   Mark Dincecco, *Political Transformations and Public Finances: Europe 1650–1913* (Cambridge: Cambridge University Press, 2011).

But European empires in the eighteenth century were built at the same time as states transitioned to centralized fiscal systems, leaving colonies and peripheries with limited financial and military support. Precisely because managing an empire was expensive, many European empires, and especially the British Empire, largely avoided those costs by passing on the responsibilities for governance, military protection, and fiscal needs to their colonial subjects via a mix of public administration and private companies.[13] However, these limitations to imperial capacity also created problems when the need arose to increase protection at the edges of empire. The British Empire, known as the premier superpower on the ocean due to its massive and effective navy, was unable to adequately protect merchant shipping from pirates and privateers throughout the eighteenth century. When the British government wished to embark on a campaign to eliminate the threat of pirates in the 1710s and 1720s, the navy found itself with nowhere near the capacity it needed to adequately patrol the Caribbean, Atlantic, and Indian Oceans. Instead, it relied on colonial governments, joint-stock companies, and privately funded ships based in the colonies to eventually suppress piracy, at least in times of peace between European empires.[14]

Clearly, the British Empire failed to provide enough support for its colonies, and this provided both an obstacle to overcome and an opportunity for developing colonial state capacity. While not the focus of this book, colonial governments also confronted the virtual absence of the British state, and each attempted to create their own state capacity via militia training and organization and currency creation. British America was not alone in its need to develop its own capacity, as many British colonies, even those in Africa in the late nineteenth and early twentieth centuries, were left largely to their own devices in supporting trade and defense, which helped facilitate state development in the wake of independence.[15] What follows, however, is an exploration of how merchants and merchant networks developed in the relative absence of the British state.

---

13 De Zwart and van Zanden, *Origins of Globalization*, 25.
14 David Wilson, *Suppressing Piracy in the Early Eighteenth Century: Pirates, Merchants and British Imperial Authority in the Atlantic and Indian Oceans* (Woodbridge: Boydell Press, 2021).
15 Leigh A. Gardner, *Taxing Colonial Africa: The Political Economy of British Imperialism* (Oxford: Oxford University Press, 2012).

1   Historical Background

One of the first port cities to develop in the British Atlantic was Boston. Settlement in the area began with the fabled Pilgrims on Plymouth Rock in the 1620s, but by the 1630s, Boston had become the primary center of political and economic activity for the Massachusetts Bay Colony. Situated where the Charles River and Massachusetts Bay meet, Boston was well protected from the often-violent North Atlantic Nor'easters that ravaged the northeastern coast of North America. Eventually, Boston became the primary base for thousands of cod fishermen, providing a major export from nearly the moment of founding.

While the initial impetus for settling the Massachusetts Bay region was religious freedom, the region was well suited to fishing, shipbuilding, and trade. First, the Atlantic Ocean provided substantial advantages to Massachusetts Bay and Boston as the ocean currents from the North Atlantic filtered down from Nova Scotia toward Boston, but the Gulf Stream current moved toward Europe, allowing fishermen to fish the waters off the coast of Canada, transport and process their catches in Boston, and ship salted cod to Europe and the West Indies. Essentially, Boston and Massachusetts Bay sat at the end of one major current and within easy access to the largest and most important shipping lane in the Atlantic Ocean. While Boston was the primary recipient of the favorable currents, New York and Philadelphia benefited as well, especially as the Middle Colonies of New York and Philadelphia, being farther south, were capable of greater agricultural production.

Wealthy financiers in England understood the value that Massachusetts Bay had to offer, and a few dozen merchants and English Puritans saw the opportunity to increase their own profits and establish a religious refuge in the New World. Between 1630 and 1640, some twenty thousand English settlers arrived in New England, which included the colonies of Massachusetts, Rhode Island, Connecticut, and New Hampshire. Most of these were funded by companies seeking to develop their newly acquired lands in America. Most of the financing came from merchants who had been successful in the East India trade, such as Matthew Cradock, and others who were well established in major European ports, such as Simon Whetcome, who maintained commercial offices in London and Dorset.[16]

In the first Massachusetts Charter, the objective of developing a profitable colony is clearly stated. One of the key provisions stipulates that settlers in the

---

16   Bernard Bailyn, *The New England Merchants in the Seventeenth Century* (Cambridge, MA: Harvard University Press, 1979), 16–18.

colony will be allowed to "take, leade, carry, and transport" goods to and from any part of the British Empire and beyond. The charter provided the settlers and landowners in the colony an exemption from imperial taxes for seven years. Furthermore, the charter also provided exemption to merchants from import and export duties for twenty-one years. This meant that early Massachusetts colonists did not pay any duties on trade with England and invested their capital in ships, docks, and other types of infrastructure.[17] As a result, the population of New England, especially Boston, expanded quickly from its founding in large part due to the expansion of maritime commerce. As the eighteenth century approached, trade sparked further growth as Boston grew into a center of commerce and fishing, attracting merchants, sailors, and day laborers from around the region. By the beginning of the 1700s, Boston was the largest city in British America with an estimated 6,700 inhabitants (see Table 1).

Originally founded by Dutch traders in the 1620s as New Amsterdam, New York developed from a small trading outpost on Manhattan into a great commercial hub by the 1770s. Situated on a long, thin island off the mainland of what became the colony of New York, Dutch merchants sought to create a port to trade with Native Americans for beaver pelts and to take advantage of the region's rivers that provided access to French Canada and the Great Lakes. The Dutch West India Company attempted to find settlers who wished to develop plantations and grow cash crops, but the occupants of New Amsterdam were far more interested in commercial ventures than in farming or craft production. Consequently, New Amsterdam emerged as a major port for fur trading and, eventually, a commercial hub in the Atlantic, where the Dutch imported manufactured goods from the United Provinces and then re-exported them to the West Indies, Virginia, and the northeastern coast of South America.[18]

By 1664, the English had assumed control over the port from the Dutch and renamed it as New York. While the same difficulty in getting settlers to focus on local agricultural and real estate development continued until the end of the seventeenth century, the English applied the economic model of Virginia and Massachusetts, colonies that were successful in establishing locally sustainable populations while still able to produce goods that were profitable

---

17 *First Massachusetts Charter (4 Mar 1629)*, printed in *Settlements to Society, 1607–1763: A Documentary History of Colonial America*, ed. Jack P. Greene (New York: W. W. Norton and Co., 1975), 20–24.

18 Cathy Matson, *Merchants & Empire: Trading in Colonial New York* (Baltimore, MD: Johns Hopkins University Press, 1998), 15–17; Leonard Blussé, *Visible Cities: Canton, Nagasaki, and Batavia and the Coming of the Americans* (Cambridge, MA: Harvard University Press, 2008), 5.

TABLE 1   Population growth of Boston, New York, and Philadelphia

Year	Boston	New York	Philadelphia
1630		300	
1640	1,200	400	
1650	2,000	1,000	
1660	3,000	2,400	
1680	4,500	3,200	
1690	7,000	3,900	4,000
1700	6,700	5,000	5,000
1710	9,000	5,700	6,500
1720	12,000	7,000	10,000
1730	13,000	8,622	11,500
1742	16,382	11,000	13,000
1760	15,631	18,000	23,750
1775	16,000	25,000	40,000

SOURCE: CARL BRIDENBAUGH, *CITIES IN THE WILDERNESS: THE FIRST CENTURY OF URBAN LIFE IN AMERICA, 1625–1742* (LONDON: OXFORD UNIVERSITY PRESS, 1938), 6, 143, 303; BRIDENBAUGH, *CITIES IN REVOLT: URBAN LIFE IN AMERICA, 1743–1776* (LONDON: OXFORD UNIVERSITY PRESS, 1955), 5, 216

in the larger Atlantic economy.[19] New York benefited from London's rise as a global emporium, overtaking Amsterdam as the largest port of call in the North Atlantic at the beginning of the eighteenth century. With that rise, New York merchants came to have access to massive Atlantic networks in both the English and Dutch Empires. This meant that New York merchants could access goods from nearly every corner of the globe via London and Amsterdam.[20] Even though Britain's mercantilist policies made direct trade with the Dutch Empire illegal, many merchants continued to trade with Dutch colonies even at the risk of legal troubles.[21]

---

19   Matson, *Merchants & Empire*, 34–37.
20   Matson, *Merchants & Empire*, 37–38; for a greater understanding of London's rise as a global center of trade, see Nuala Zahedieh, *The Capital and the Colonies: London and the Atlantic Economy, 1660–1700* (Cambridge: Cambridge University Press, 2010).
21   See Christian J. Koot, *Empire at the Periphery: British Colonists, Anglo-Dutch Trade, and the Development of the British Atlantic, 1621–1713* (New York: New York University Press, 2011).

Founded in 1682, Philadelphia quickly grew into a major port for the Middle Colonies, serving as an ideal location to export wheat and other agricultural products from what eventually became the breadbasket of British America. When establishing the colony of Pennsylvania, William Penn realized that maritime commerce would be central to the venture's success. Therefore, he sought to find an ideal location for a port that could service the needs of a large region of agriculturally productive land. That port needed to be able to grow with the colony and its changing economic needs. His choice of location for the port of Philadelphia allowed it not only to become a place where surplus agricultural products could find a home but also to develop into a bustling center of economic activity. Its location on the banks of a river away from the coast gave it access to most of Pennsylvania, where agricultural production remained the primary economic activity throughout the colonial period. Thus, grain and other agricultural products became Philadelphia's main exports to the world market. In fact, being located on the major waterway into the interior of Pennsylvania made agricultural expansion into the frontier economically feasible and desirable.[22]

One of the first structures built in Philadelphia was a wharf that could accommodate a ship up to five hundred tons, indicating a desire to engage in maritime trade beyond small coastal schooners.[23] The city government

---

22   Arthur L. Jensen, *The Maritime Commerce of Colonial Philadelphia* (Madison: State Historical Society of Wisconsin, 1963), 2–3. Scholars differ on the question of whether farmers in Pennsylvania produced for market or for subsistence. Some historians have suggested that subsistence was the main effort of colonial producers and farmers, and exports were a small percentage of colonial incomes. Lindert and Williamson, *Unequal Gains*, 47–50. In their effort to estimate national and per capita income and wealth for colonial America, Lindert and Williamson insist that export was not a priority for landowners and farmers. In their estimation, only 10 percent of national income was foreign trade. This may have been true, but it does not appear that coastal and inter-colonial trade was a part of Lindert and Williamson's estimates. Furthermore, international trade within the modern US economy is only 20–22 percent of the economy, and few would challenge the importance of trade to the modern US economy. However, Winifred Rothenberg, in her study of rare daybooks and journals of New England farmers, noticed that farmers were paying regular attention to market prices and weather conditions on the coast. New England farmers were also loyal subscribers to newspapers from major ports, such as Boston, which published daily arrivals and departures of ships and their cargoes. Furthermore, merchant advertisements soliciting agricultural products from farmers were quite common in those same newspapers. Winifred Rothenberg, *From Market-Places to a Market Economy: The Transformation of Rural Massachusetts, 1750–1850* (Chicago: University of Chicago Press, 1992). Farmers, especially those within reach of the Delaware River and its estuaries, kept tabs on market prices in order to sell their surpluses or choose which crops to sow.

23   Jensen, *Maritime Commerce of Colonial Philadelphia*, 2.

maintained the port's infrastructure, and members of the Common Council of Philadelphia were responsible for the maintenance of wharves, marketplaces, and public warehouses. The earliest laws and regulations were aimed at ensuring fair business practices (such as truthful weights for bakers and grain merchants) and protection of the public wharves (such as prohibiting the production of tar on a dock or within twenty feet of a building). The Common Council quickly raised funds, through taxes and rents for marketplace stalls, for building new and maintaining existing maritime infrastructure.[24]

Clearly, all three cities were founded facing the ocean and the global economy. Each developed their own spheres of influence and port complexes, but by the eighteenth century, all three cities serviced overlapping hinterlands and developed trade relationships with many of the same ports and destinations in large parts of the Atlantic Ocean and beyond. More importantly, the three cities provided access to global goods from Chinese tea and silks to Portuguese salt and wine, becoming an important nodal center for North America and the Caribbean. However, the cities developed this importance despite the British imperial state not because of it, and this book seeks to refine our understanding of the importance of British America within the global economy and show how this growing significance placed it in direct conflict with its imperial master. What follows then is an exploration of the roots of what became known as the American Revolution.

2   Outline

The book consists of six chapters, each examining a particular theme. Following this introduction, the first chapter provides a basic overview of each city's smaller port complexes. The chapter then argues that the three cities functioned as a single, regional port complex that should be considered together rather than separate from one another, unlike previous scholarship on the three cities or colonial America in general. It shows how the hinterlands and forelands of all three cities overlapped. While each city jostled for preeminence in the region, merchants in all three cities developed close ties with one another, often cooperating in joint enterprises. The chapter concludes with a quick overview of the imperial and economic constraints that the region's

---

24   *Minutes of the Common Council of the City of Philadelphia, 1704 to 1776* (Philadelphia: Crissy and Markley, Printers, 1847), 10–15.

merchants faced, such as Britain's Navigation Acts and the chronic shortage of specie in British America.

In the next two chapters, I explore the region's merchant and commodity networks, including the various mechanisms that facilitated commerce between individuals and destinations. The second chapter explores the merchants and merchant networks of all three cities and examines the importance of maritime trade to the region's population. It describes how the merchant communities of each city formed and the ways one could become a merchant. It also explains the mechanisms of mercantile exchange, detailing the various accounting and communication methods that facilitated network formation. It also explores the sources and magnitude of capital investment, showing how regional merchants were largely in control of the ships and goods involved in the region's trade. Similarly, Chapter 3 describes the commodities and commodity networks that flowed through the ports of Boston, New York, and Philadelphia. The chapter details the primary imports and exports, explaining why certain goods were in high demand while others were less important. Sugar products are highlighted, as the region served as a nodal center for both the consumption and production of goods like molasses and rum. The chapter concludes with a short discussion of how consumers communicated demand for certain products and how merchants met that demand.

Chapters 4 and 5 explore the proportions and destinations of commerce with the rest of the world. Chapter 4 shows the importance and mechanics of the inter-colonial trade of Boston, New York, and Philadelphia and their hinterlands. Trade to and from North America and the Caribbean was the largest sector of the region's total tonnage and voyages, far exceeding direct trade with the British Isles. Most of this commerce was also owned and controlled by merchants in and around the three cities, which is also briefly described in Chapter 2. Trans-imperial trade is the subject of Chapter 5, which describes how and to what extent the region conducted trade outside of the British Empire's borders. Much of the chapter is devoted to understanding how merchants were able to circumvent British prohibitions against direct commerce between British colonies and non-British holdings, like Portugal, France, and other European colonies such as Suriname and Honduras. The chapter compares the amount of trans-imperial trade of the region with trade going directly to the British Isles. As much of this trade was considered illegal by the British Empire, smuggling was a key mechanism for trans-imperial exchange. It also discusses the importance of East Asian goods in encouraging trans-imperial trade, and the chapter concludes with a case study of Philadelphia's trade with Portugal, highlighting the amount of trade that is often hidden from posterity.

In the sixth and final chapter, I explore how colonial merchants grew increasingly frustrated with the British Empire and its limits on their trade. It begins with a discussion of British efforts to control colonial trade and how merchants and colonial governments continued to subvert and disregard the imperial agenda of mercantilism, highlighting how imperial capacity was never strong enough to fully support and control colonial trade. I then discuss the role of the Seven Years' War in escalating the conflict between colonial merchants and the British imperial structure, resulting in cooperative movements to end mercantilist policies meant to limit the economic power of colonial merchants. Following the discussion of colony–metropolitan interactions, the British military occupation of Boston and its subsequent fallout concludes the chapter by showing how the century-long struggle for equal access to global markets culminated in a violent war for political and economic independence.

Serving as a natural bookend, the American Revolution and its consequences effectively ended British control over American merchants and commerce. American merchants responded to this freedom by expanding their networks into the Indian and Pacific Oceans, seeking ways to cut out the European middlemen that made Asian goods more expensive to import. Almost all of these early expeditions were funded and carried out by merchants in Boston, New York, and Philadelphia.[25] Nevertheless, their efforts following independence were no different from their efforts before 1775. Rather than being a new period of American commercial expansion, post-Revolution excursions to Asia represent the continued growth of the global maritime power of Boston, New York, and Philadelphia.

---

25   See James R. Fichter, *So Great a Proffit: How the East Indies Trade Transformed Anglo-American Capitalism* (Cambridge, MA: Harvard University Press, 2010), and Eric Oakley, "Columbia at Sea: America Enters the Pacific, 1787–1793" (PhD diss., University of North Carolina at Greensboro, 2017).

CHAPTER 1

The Port Complex of Boston, New York, and Philadelphia

Boston, New York, and Philadelphia played a prominent role in the political economy of North America's eastern seaboard in much of the colonial and post-colonial periods. Each of these three cities functioned as a gateway to the extensive hinterlands and as a port from where ships would embark on voyages to numerous ports throughout the world's oceans, which constituted the forelands. Each city developed and dominated their own smaller, often overlapping port complexes (or port systems). Most ports develop a region of influence, or complex, which includes both the hinterland (continental interior) and the foreland (sea/ocean). Ports served as gateways to and from the hinterland and the foreland. Throughout the eighteenth century, the hinterland continued to move deeper and deeper into the interior, usually following the numerous rivers into the frontier as more farmers and landowners ventured inland. Conversely, the foreland continued to grow larger as Boston, New York, and Philadelphia expanded their geographic reach farther south into the Atlantic, east into Europe, and southeast to Africa. While each city maintained their own smaller complexes, these port cities also functioned as a larger, nodal center of the Atlantic economy, in essence creating a regional port complex that played a major role in the Atlantic and global maritime economies.

In most cases, major ports are situated, geographically and/or economically, among several smaller ports. The larger the main port, the greater the likelihood that substantial numbers of auxiliary or feeder ports will develop. These feeder ports tend to be tied, directly or indirectly, to the main port in a variety of ways. For example, the port of Salem, before 1775, served as a smaller port that accommodated smaller fleets of cod fishermen that, more often than not, were owned by cod merchants based in Boston or sold their catches to Boston merchants. Some smaller ports served as overflow locations in times of plenty. Other ways in which feeder ports are dependent on the main port city tend to be geographic and/or environmental, as sea lanes and routes tend to follow sea currents and winds. This means that many fantastic harbors and possible port locations tend to sit empty or are underused because trade routes did not come close enough.¹ Some ports were initially quite successful, but changing economic and geographic realities make it difficult to sustain that success without significant public and private investments.²

Hinterlands play an enormous role in shaping how ports function, and ports are essential in facilitating transportation of goods from the hinterland. This is especially true in the modern world with intermodal transportation and supply chains, but early modern ports, like Boston, New York, and Philadelphia, also contributed in similar ways with public wharves, storage facilities, and container industries (i.e., barrel and crate production).³ The interplay between hinterland and foreland was focused in and around ports throughout the world. In eighteenth-century India, the region of Gujarat was an essential component within the global economy where textiles and indigo, produced in its hinterland, were traded throughout the world for new world silver. Like Boston, New York, and Philadelphia, Gujarat was composed of several major ports, all vying for supremacy with one another, yet all functioned as a regional complex.⁴ Similarly, settlement and hinterland development directly influenced the development of the ports of Boston, New York, and Philadelphia. Whereas the colonies to the south filtered farther inland and developed major plantations of cash crops, the settlers in the northeast stayed close to rivers and the shoreline, ensuring easy access to the forelands of the Atlantic Ocean.⁵

As outlined below, Boston, New York, and Philadelphia were situated in prime locations with access to extensive hinterlands while maintaining strong ties to the forelands of Atlantic trade routes. Therefore, merchants in each city were able to connect ever-growing networks of Atlantic trade and increasingly productive populations in their hinterlands who needed access to goods and consumers in the forelands of the Atlantic. Being key ports in their respective port complexes, Boston, New York, and Philadelphia developed strong

---

1   Atiya Habeeb Kidwai, "Conceptual and Methodological Issues: Ports, Port Cities and Port-Hinterlands," in *Ports and Their Hinterlands in India (1700–1950)*, ed. Indu Banga (New Delhi: Manohar, 1992), 9–18.
2   See the case of Bristol in Anthony G. Hoare, "British Ports and Their Export Hinterlands: A Rapidly Changing Geography," *Geografiska Annaler: Series B, Human Geography* 68, no. 1 (August 2017): 29–40.
3   Adolf K. Y. Ng et al., "Port Geography at the Crossroads with Human Geography: Between Flows and Spaces," *Journal of Transport Geography* 41 (2014): 84–96.
4   Ghulam A. Nadri, "The Dynamics of Port–Hinterland Relationships in Eighteenth-Century Gujarat," in *Hinterlands and Commodities: Place, Space, Time and the Political Economic Development of Asia over the Long Eighteenth Century*, ed. Tsukasa Mizushima, George Bryan Souza, and Dennis O. Flynn (Leiden: Brill, 2015), 83–101.
5   John H. Andrews, "Anglo-American Trade in the Early Eighteenth Century," *Geographical Review* 45, no. 1 (January 1955): 99–110.

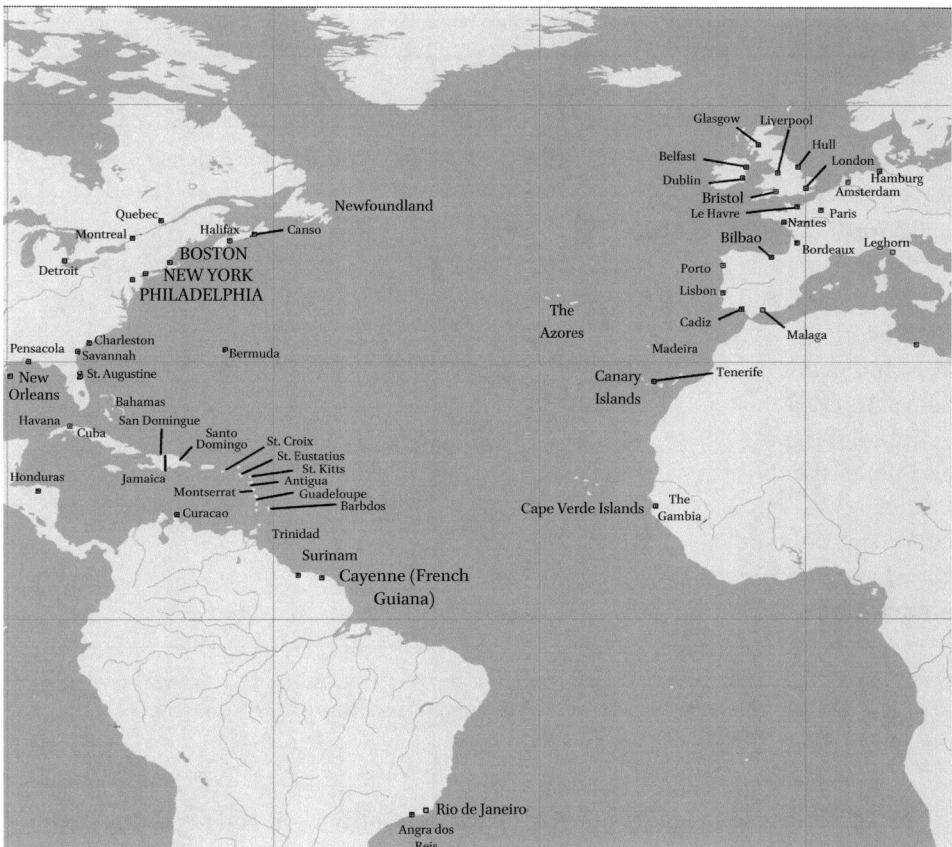

FIGURE 1   Forelands of Boston, New York and Philadelphia

commercial ties and exchanged commodities with each other. Merchants in all three cities created extensive networks of credit, trade, and communications that contributed to the commercial success of all three port cities. In effect, the three cities operated as a coherent core for the northwestern Atlantic economy, growing into continental powers in British America and beyond and strengthening the economic and, eventually, political ties between each other.

1   The Regional Complex of Boston, New York, and Philadelphia

Boston's population and trade continued to grow throughout the century, but the official statistics belie the growth of its hinterland and feeder ports. For

TABLE 2 Entrances and clearances from Boston and Salem, April–December 1720

Destination	Boston Entrances	Boston Clearances	Salem Entrances	Salem Clearances	Combined Total
Coastal (North America)	245	206	5	21	477
Long Distance					
Newfoundland and Nova Scotia	32	30	0	0	62
West Indies and South America	95	135	8	16	254
Southern Europe and Wine Islands	15	17	4	22	58
Britain	21	19	0	0	40
Other Transatlantic	20	12	1	3	36
Total Long Distance	*183*	*213*	*13*	*41*	*450*
Combined Total	428	419	18	62	927

SOURCE: *BOSTON GAZETTE*, APRIL 18, 1720–JANUARY 5, 1721; AS COMPILED BY PHYLLIS WHITMAN HUNTER, *PURCHASING IDENTITY IN THE ATLANTIC WORLD: MASSACHUSETTS MERCHANTS, 1670–1780* (ITHACA, NY: CORNELL UNIVERSITY PRESS, 2001), 79

example, in 1720 the *Boston Gazette* listed ships arriving in and departing from Boston and Salem. Boston outnumbered Salem in the number of entries, but Salem did receive and send a substantial number of ships during that period. In Table 2, Salem comprised just under 10 percent of the combined total of entrances and clearances. Salem's clearances far outweighed its entrances, indicating Boston's dominant role in controlling imports into the region. Salem was one of many smaller ports in the region, and auxiliary ports such as Newport, Newburyport, and others contributed similar numbers and proportions of ships to the overall region's economy. However, Salem and others were dependent on Boston's well-being, as much of the capital and credit available to merchants was centered in Boston. Some merchants, such as Timothy Orne in Salem, were instrumental in adding to Boston's hinterland, providing additional capital and networks for Boston's merchants to utilize.[6] In 1705, Boston

---

6   Phyllis Whitman Hunter, *Purchasing Identity in the Atlantic World: Massachusetts Merchants, 1670–1780* (Ithaca, NY: Cornell University Press, 2001), 124–25.

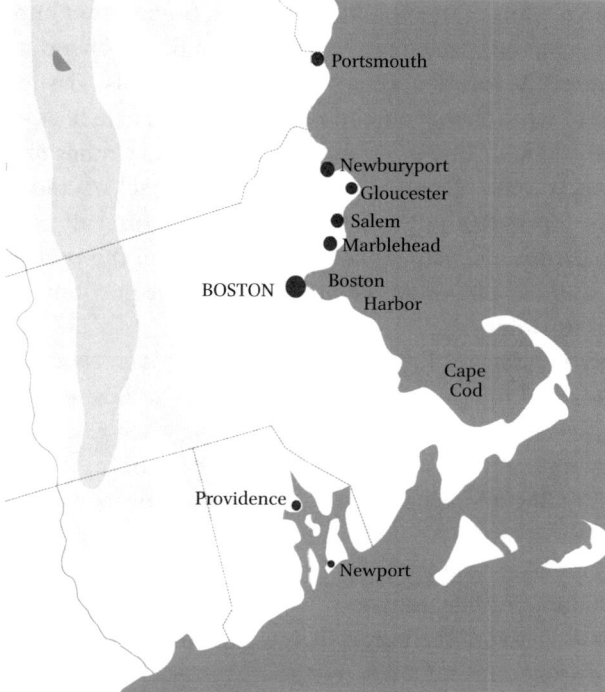

FIGURE 2   Boston's port complex

owned about 95 percent of the total tonnage registered in Massachusetts, but as early as 1714, the rest of Massachusetts increased their share of ownership by 5 percent, leaving Boston with around 90 percent of total tonnage in the colony.[7] While Boston remained the primary engine that increased Massachusetts's position within the Atlantic economy, the ports within its complex capitalized on Boston's success.

As Boston developed its networks outward into the Atlantic, inland Massachusetts experienced substantial growth as more and more grains, wood, and livestock were needed to fill the orders and ships of merchants in Boston. Towns such as Concord and Medfield, founded in 1635 and 1651 respectively, were established in the wake of multiple land grabs that saw greater numbers of settlers and landowners move farther and farther inland, keeping close to main roads and waterways. Some of the earliest merchant account

---

7 Bernard Bailyn and Lotte Bailyn, *Massachusetts Shipping, 1697–1714: A Statistical Study* (Cambridge, MA: Harvard University Press, 1959), 98–99.

books in the 1720s contain records of merchants purchasing timber from lumberjacks, usually remarking on the costs to cart the timber (or float, depending on method of transportation). Most often, small transactions were listed, such as small amounts of meat or wheat being purchased from farmers who needed to sell surplus products to trade or buy other necessities such as clothes and cookware. Much of these account books are merely lists to keep track of credits and debits as currency was in short supply, leaving barter as a natural alternative.[8] These account books indicate a strong connection between the port of Boston and its hinterland to not only obtain commodities for export but for distribution of goods into the interior.

By the 1730s and 1740s, Boston had drawn most of Massachusetts, Connecticut, and Rhode Island into its hinterland. Merchants in Boston regularly listed accounts with merchants in Newburyport, Gloucester, Concord, Lexington, Providence, New London, and New Haven (see Figure 2). These smaller ports, while conducting a small amount of trade on their own, were dependent on Boston and its larger Atlantic networks and often provided insurance for the various shipments. Some feeder ports like Newburyport, Salem, and New London had smaller vessels and boats, which transported goods to Boston for larger ships sailing across the ocean. These port towns also served as auxiliary and secondary locations for ships that sought to avoid the prying eyes of British customs officials. Many rich Boston merchants had secondary offices and agents or consignees in these towns for procuring export goods and for sale and distribution of imports as well as for offloading smuggled goods.[9] By the 1760s and 1770s, Boston's hinterland extended over one hundred miles and reached as far west as Springfield, as far north as Portland, in what is now Maine, and as far south as Long Island and New York.[10] Boston's importance in the region cannot be overstated. In Connecticut, a group of farmers and dealers created the New London Society United for Trade and Commerce in 1732 in an effort to limit their dependence on Boston for access to transatlantic markets and goods. Even with eighty individuals as members, the society could purchase just two small vessels. The venture ultimately failed as one ship was captured by Spanish privateers, and the other sank along the coastline, ending

---

8   Samuel Davenport Account Book, 1724–83, MHS.
9   Samuel Davenport Account Book, 1724–83; Account Book by Boston Merchant, 1736–41; Benjamin Dolbeare Letterbook and Invoice Book, 1739–1811, vol. 1; Amory Family Papers, 1697–1894, MHS. These are just a few examples. More details on the role and function of smuggling can be found in Chapter 6.
10 Amory Family Papers, vol. 4, MHS.

any hope for Connecticut merchants and farmers to challenge the primacy of Boston.[11]

From the beginning, Boston maintained access to a large foreland. Even though London was Boston's primary trading partner by 1700, Boston merchants had developed commercial relationships with British and non-British ports throughout the Atlantic. Trade with non-British locations in Europe, such as Lisbon, Cádiz, and Amsterdam, was established and possibly expanded. As early as 1708, the Jeffries family of merchants established a direct trade with Porto, shipping rum, timber, and cod to Portugal in exchange for port wine and salt.[12]

Merchants from Boston were particularly interested in trade with Catholic nations as a market for Boston's salted cod. They supplied cod, which was in high demand in Spain and Portugal (still an essential part of the cuisine in Iberia), and imported salt and wine.[13] In addition, Boston ships sailed to Cádiz and Málaga for wine and East Asian goods as well.[14] In fact, trade was so common to both Portugal and Spain that regular reports of prices in Lisbon, Gibraltar, and Cádiz were sent to Boston merchants by Iberian merchants and friends.[15] Even the Netherlands received frequent shipments of goods from Boston. One ship in 1738 carried a load of lumber and wood products to Amsterdam, a port that offered higher prices for wood than England.[16]

Cod fisheries were at once part of Boston's hinterland and foreland. Situated off the coast of Maine, Newfoundland, and Nova Scotia, Massachusetts fishermen were given rights to fish off the coast of Canada throughout the eighteenth century. So integral to New England's economy were the cod fisheries of the North Atlantic that they were key line items in the 1783 Treaty of Paris that formally ended the American Revolution. Boston was able to ship merchandise to various small hamlets and towns along the Canadian coasts while at the same time capitalizing on the massive cod fisheries, in the same way as Philadelphia exploited its fertile hinterland for grain production. As a result, the cod fisheries functioned more like a hinterland which produced commodities for export,

11   Hunter, *Purchasing Identity in the Atlantic World*, 9.
12   Jeffries Family Papers, vol. 14, MHS. Collections containing trade records, such the Amory Family Papers, Caleb Davis Papers, Dalton Family Papers, Dolbeare Family Papers, held in the Massachusetts Historical Society, point to Boston's substantial trans-imperial trade. For further details, see Chapter 6.
13   Daniel Vickers, *Farmers and Fishermen: Two Centuries of Work in Essex County, Massachusetts, 1630–1850* (Chapel Hill: University of North Carolina Press, 1994), 86–87.
14   Caleb Davis Papers, Box 7, January 1774; Jeffries Family Papers, vol. 18, 1725, MHS.
15   Caleb Davis Papers, Box 7, December 1774, MHS.
16   Jeffries Family Papers, vol. 15, 1738, MHS.

but it also provided a marketplace for Boston exports, like a foreland. To capitalize on this fact, Boston maintained the largest and most profitable fishing fleets in the North Atlantic, outpacing the English fleets in the same area, as it built, sold, and operated new fishing vessels at a far higher clip than any other region in the North Atlantic.[17]

While transoceanic trade with Europe was profitable, the largest and most lucrative part of Boston's foreland was the West Indies. Sugar, rum, and molasses were in high demand in Boston throughout the eighteenth century. As a result of its large-scale imports of sugar and molasses from the West Indies, Boston developed its own rum industry, eventually competing with its trade partners in the Caribbean. West Indies trade made up 25–40 percent of total exports from Boston, with coastal trade with North America being the only region that was larger than the West Indies.[18] Salted cod was the main export to the West Indies. Lesser grades of salted cod were traded to plantation owners on the sugar islands in the Caribbean to help feed the massive number of slaves working sugar fields.[19]

However, Boston's foreland did not consist merely of Europe and the Caribbean. Early in the eighteenth century, at least one merchant attempted to establish a trading post and office in Brazil, seeking to capitalize on the burgeoning sugar plantations of the Portuguese colony. While it was ultimately unsuccessful, there are many examples of direct trade with Dutch colonies along the northwestern coast of South America.[20] By the 1760s, Boston was using its large rum industry to directly trade with European outposts on the coast of West Africa. Boston's foreland greatly expanded in the eighteenth century, coming to encompass three continents and most of the Atlantic Ocean coastline.[21]

By the beginning of the eighteenth century, New York's hinterland included much of the Hudson River valley and its estuaries as far inland as Montreal in French Canada. This is not surprising as pelt was the primary export from New York to Europe in the seventeenth century and into the first few decades of the eighteenth century. However, by the middle of the century, New York's local trade zone expanded deeper into the more fertile regions of New York, Massachusetts, and New Jersey. While pelt or fur trade continued to thrive, agricultural products also became important as New York's hinterland reached

---

17   Vickers, *Farmers and Fishermen*, 90–98.
18   McCusker and Menard, *Economy of British America*, 196.
19   Vickers, *Farmers and Fishermen*, 99.
20   Nicholas Oursel Account Book, Amory Family Papers, MHS.
21   British North American Customs Papers, 1765–74, MHS.

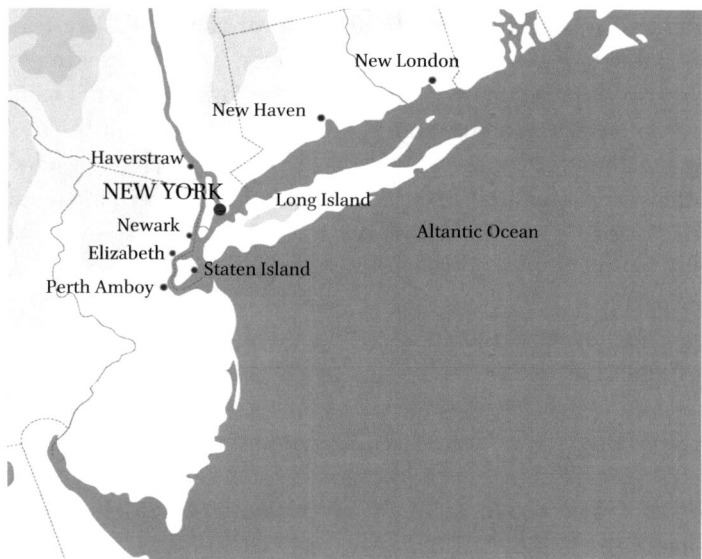

FIGURE 3   New York's port complex

nearly a hundred miles to the west, sparking the development of towns and cities that kept New York supplied with grain and other merchandise. Towns like Albany, New Haven, Hartford, Kingston, and others found their way into New York's orbit (see Figure 3). Montreal remained an important trade partner as it was well connected by the Hudson River, adding a variety of goods moving between both cities.[22]

Being located along the coast and at the mouth of the Hudson River, New York sat at the center of several feeder ports. Many of the feeder ports, such as Elizabeth and Haverstraw, were situated along the Hudson River and provided an easy place for merchants to land their goods away from customs houses and acquire commodities for export. Long Island, similarly, provided ample locations where one could conduct trade. Perth Amboy and Newark, both in New Jersey, were also within the influence of New York, as merchants regularly received prices, agricultural news, and market conditions from Perth Amboy and Newark.[23] New York dominated an area filled with smaller ports and towns, which only continued to grow in number as New York's trade expanded.

22   Matson, *Merchants & Empire*, 97, 226.
23   Philip L. White, *The Beekman Mercantile Papers, 3 Volumes* (New York: New York Historical Society, 1956).

While its hinterland was substantial, the foreland of New York, like that of Boston, spanned much of the Atlantic Ocean. Though it served as a major port of call for British imports into the colonies, New York merchants were well connected with non-British actors and conducted trade with nearly every major port in the northern half of the Atlantic.[24] New York merchants traded with the West Indies, often sending ships as far south as French Guiana and Suriname. As well as trading with British islands in the West Indies, New York ships and merchandise could be found in Dutch Curaçao, Spanish Hispaniola, and French New Orleans.[25]

Across the Atlantic, New York's foreland included London and other ports in England, Amsterdam, Lisbon, Paris, and many other non-British port cities. New York merchants maintained trade with many islands off the coast of Africa, going as far south as Cape Verde.[26] Without doubt, New York's foreland was as extensive as Boston's, but New York maintained a more robust trade with Britain than did Boston and Philadelphia, as the share of its total exports indicates (see appendix A, Table A.1).[27]

Philadelphia largely dominated the Pennsylvania farmlands along and within reach of the Delaware River. Philadelphia merchants were already right in the middle of some of the most productive grain regions. As merchants were able to expand their trade networks, so too did the hinterlands of Philadelphia. In a self-perpetuating cycle, higher grain yields led to greater exports, which led to a higher demand for grain, and so on. In the middle of the eighteenth century, this cycle resulted in a growth in the milling industry and the appearance of middlemen or intermediary merchants, who purchased wheat and flour from farmers to then send or sell to merchants in Philadelphia. Philadelphia's reach was quite expansive, as it immediately began moving goods to and from Fort Pitt following its capture in the 1760s from the French during the Seven Years' War.[28] Still, Philadelphia's hinterland overlapped with that of New York, not surprising considering the great number of mercantile connections between the two (Figure 5).

24　In this book, the Caribbean or West Indies exists in the northern half of the Atlantic Ocean, as it was above the equator, though in many ways, the West Indies region extends into the southern half of the Atlantic with its close relationship with eastern South America.

25　White, *Beekman Mercantile Papers*.

26　The sources indicate that some merchants participated in the African slave trade. Matson, *Merchants & Empire*, 202–3.

27　McCusker and Menard, *Economy of British America*, 196.

28　Daniel Clark Letter and Invoice Book, HSP.

THE PORT COMPLEX OF BOSTON, NEW YORK, AND PHILADELPHIA 25

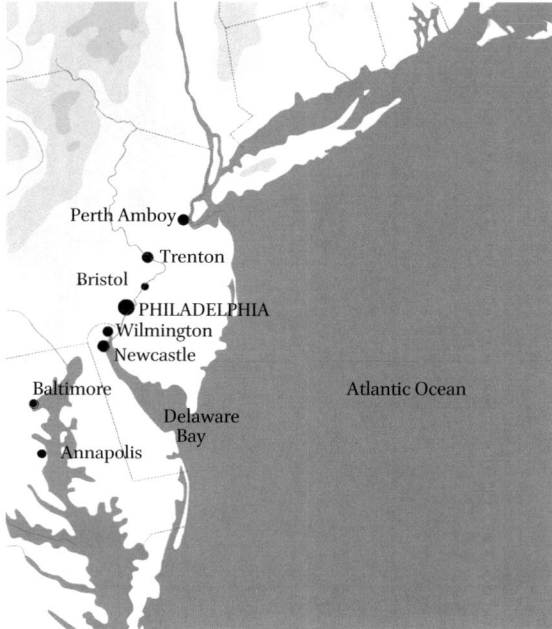

FIGURE 4   Philadelphia's port complex

Like Boston and New York, Philadelphia's port complex grew substantially in the eighteenth century (See Figure 4). Newcastle, Annapolis, and Perth Amboy (in New Jersey) were major feeder ports serving Philadelphia, though a number of smaller harbors and towns along the coast and the Delaware River served as convenient places to load and offload goods. Maryland ports, in particular, profited from their proximity to Philadelphia. Annapolis and Baltimore became important feeder and auxiliary ports to Philadelphia. After 1763, Annapolis experienced a major boom in urbanization thanks to traders and ships looking for ports within reach of Philadelphia that were beyond the prying eyes of customs officials.[29] Baltimore's merchants also benefited from the rise of Philadelphia and British enforcement of the Navigation Acts after 1763. Merchants in Boston had agents in Baltimore to procure grain and other agricultural products for West Indian and other Atlantic Ocean ports as well as to facilitate the sale and distribution of imports into the hinterlands.[30]

---

29   Edward C. Papenfuse, *In Pursuit of Profit: The Annapolis Merchants in the Era of the American Revolution, 1763–1805* (Baltimore, MD: Johns Hopkins University Press, 1975), 6–24.
30   Caleb Davis Papers, Box 5, April 1771–June 1771, MHS.

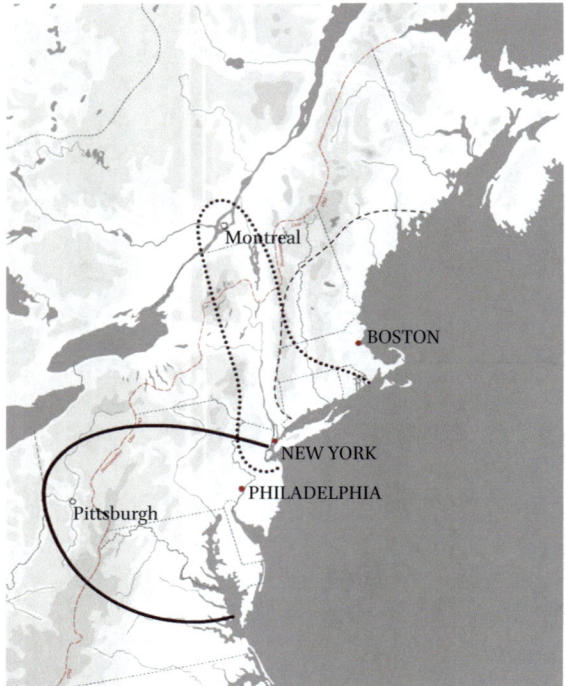

FIGURE 5   Overlapping hinterlands

Philadelphia maintained strong commercial connections with Southern Europe, and its relationship with Iberian ports was particularly strong. It became a primary source of grain for the Portuguese.[31] In fact, by the 1770s, nearly all of Philadelphia's exports of flour went to Southern European ports such as Lisbon.[32] Not only did colonial merchants take advantage of this Philadelphia–Lisbon grain trade but ships owned and crewed by French merchants also made commercial voyages between the two cities.[33] In much the same way as Boston and New York did, Philadelphia conducted regular trade with Amsterdam, Cádiz, London, and most of the West Indies. It also traded

---

31   Arquivo Municipal de Lisboa-Arquivo Histórico, Colecção Impostos, Fundo Marco dos Navios, Livro de Entradas do Marco dos Navios, cota (Lisbon Municipal Archive, Historical Archive, Collection "Taxes," Tonnage Tax Fund, Tonnage Tax Book of Entries), refs. AML-AH-MN 63, 1770, f. 22ᵛ.
32   Jensen, *Maritime Commerce*, 293.
33   Lisbon Municipal Archive, AML-AH-MN 63, f. 22ᵛ, 1770. While the legality of Philadelphia–Lisbon trade by colonial merchants is unclear, it was certainly illegal for French ships to trade between the two ports.

with ports in the Mediterranean, such as Genoa, Marseille, and Barcelona. Like New York and Boston following the British victory at the end of the Seven Years' War, Philadelphia established strong trade with Quebec and Halifax in Canada.[34]

2 Complementarity and Competition

Though their foundational histories are quite different from one another, Boston, New York, and Philadelphia were all founded looking toward the ocean. Thanks to their overlapping hinterlands, all three essentially functioned as one major maritime region in the Atlantic Ocean. If one zooms in on the map, each city maintained its own port complex with differences between one another. If one zooms out and examines the greater global economy, one will then see that the port complexes of Boston, New York, and Philadelphia blur into one large node that was connected to many of the same regions around the world (see Figure 1). As a result, the many merchants in all three cities had good reason to work together.

As all three cities were still relatively young by 1700, merchants lacked capital and credit to compete with England-based merchants in Atlantic trade. Available sources show that up to the early eighteenth century, there was a general reliance on credit, capital, and goods from merchants in England. By the 1720s, however, merchants in all three cities had developed their own fleets and accumulated capital sufficient to fund their commercial enterprise.[35]

Throughout the period, the three cities maintained their preeminence in the region as major ports on the North Atlantic coast of British America. Boston remained the top exporter until the mid-1760s, when Philadelphia finally surpassed it in total volume (see Table 3). New York consistently remained third in total tonnage leaving its wharves, but it continued to expand its trade in a similar trajectory with the others. In just twenty years between 1750 and 1772, the entire region nearly doubled its total export tonnage from a little over sixty-five thousand tons to about 117,000, and New York more than doubled its average annual export volume.

---

34 Thomas M. Doerflinger, *A Vigorous Spirit of Enterprise: Merchants and Economic Development in Revolutionary Philadelphia* (Chapel Hill: University of North Carolina Press, 1986), 102–3.

35 Matson, *Merchants & Empire*, 142–43; Bailyn and Bailyn, *Massachusetts Shipping*, 125; John J. McCusker, "Source of Investment Capital in the Colonial Philadelphia Shipping Industry," in John J. McCusker, *Essays in the Economic History of the Atlantic World* (London: Routledge, 1997), 251–53.

TABLE 3   Tonnage clearing Boston, New York, and Philadelphia annually for selected years, 1750–72

Port of Origin	Years	Total
Boston	1753–54	27,200
	1765–66	28,000
	1772	42,500
New York	1754	12,700
	1765–66	19,800
	1772	28,600
Philadelphia	1750–54	25,200
	1765–66	39,500
	1772	45,800
Regional Total	*1750s*	*65,100*
	1765–66	*87,300*
	1772	*116,900*

SOURCE: JOHN J. MCCUSKER AND RUSSELL R. MENARD, *THE ECONOMY OF BRITISH AMERICA: 1607–1789* (CHAPEL HILL: UNIVERSITY OF NORTH CAROLINA PRESS, 1985), 195–97.

Merchants of each of these port cities collaborated with and complemented those of the others in a variety of ways. Their account books, in which they maintained meticulous records tracking the movement of goods, currency, and credit between business partners, show that many of them had trading partners or agents in the other cities to carry out commercial transactions on their behalf. In one such account book of an anonymous Boston shipping firm, there are hundreds of entries showing grain and flour trade between Boston and Philadelphia and import of iron ware from New York, which most likely arrived from England.[36] Merchants' account books, such as those of Daniel Clark, are particularly loaded with accounts and invoices to and from New York merchants.[37] Often, merchants in one city would send goods to another to be sold on consignment, as was generally the case with Philadelphia's provisions trade with the North American coast. Philadelphia merchants made a profit

---

36   Boston Shipping Firm Account Book, 1763–65, MHS.
37   Daniel Clark Letter and Invoice Book, 1760–62, HSP.

through commissions for selling the product, but this arrangement worked both ways.[38]

Merchants of these cities also provided supplementary commercial services such as insurance, with which they could divide the risk and minimize losses arising from any costs or damage to ships and merchandise during the voyage. By the middle of the eighteenth century, some merchants had established insurance companies. For example, Ezekiel Price in Boston insured merchant goods not only for Boston merchants but consistently sold policies to merchants in New York and Philadelphia as well, not to mention the various smaller ports in between.[39] Frequently, ships sailed in groups to reduce the risk of capture by pirates, privateers, and, in times of war, imperial navies. In many cases, a merchant's goods were spread throughout the ships in any given convoy.

Merchants of these cities in the eighteenth century shared some of the same concerns and challenges as well. British imperial policies, such as the Navigation Acts, affected Boston merchants in the same way as those of New York and Philadelphia. Their responses and reactions to those policies were, therefore, also similar and, at times, collective. For example, during the political crises that gripped the British American colonies in the 1760s and 1770s, merchants of these cities signed multiple non-importation agreements in response to imperial trade and tax policies, such as the Revenue Acts and the Townshend Acts.[40] Their responses to the anticipated repeal of these acts too were remarkably similar. When the merchants of New York found out that their counterparts in Boston and Philadelphia had placed orders for English goods to their contacts in London in anticipation of the repeal of some of the Townshend Acts, they quickly followed suit and instructed their partners and agents to procure English goods for them.[41] Incidents like these also show that merchants were in close communication with each other and benefited from an efficient network, which bound these cities together through the circulation of goods and information.

Notwithstanding this cooperation and complementarity, merchants of these cities were watchful of their commercial interests, and that sometimes

---

38 Michelle L. Craig, "Grounds for Debate? The Place of the Caribbean Provisions Trade in Philadelphia's Prerevolutionary Economy," *Pennsylvania Magazine of History and Biography* 128, no. 2 (April 2004): 149–77, at 154.
39 Ezekiel Price Papers, 1754–85, MHS.
40 See Chapter 6 for more details on these acts and merchants' responses to them.
41 Jane T. Merritt, *The Trouble with Tea: The Politics of Consumption in the Eighteenth-Century Global Economy* (Baltimore, MD: Johns Hopkins University Press, 2017), 74–75.

put them in a competitive relationship. This was particularly the case between New York and Philadelphia, which competed to access grain for export and consumers for imported merchandise. Merchants frequently complained about other merchants buying grain from their common suppliers, making it difficult for them to procure any.[42]

During the non-importation movements in the 1760s and 1770s, merchants who subscribed to those agreements jealously guarded their hinterlands from those who would import English goods in violation of the agreements. They were often quick to condemn, both publicly and privately, merchants from other cities who encroached on their territory. For example, merchants of Maryland, who were opposed to the non-importation agreements, brought goods overland and by ship into the rural areas around Philadelphia. An anonymous author of a pamphlet protested this and wrote that Maryland merchants had "imported … three times the quantity of Goods which were necessary for their own consumption, and by those means supplied our back countries, and this city."[43] The same thing happened in New York, where merchants were concerned about the adverse effects of New Jersey merchants bringing British goods into New York markets. The fear resulted in many merchants seeking to dissolve the non-importation agreements, and some ignored the agreement altogether.[44]

3 Imperial Constraints and Limits

As a colony, North America's production and trade were meant to enrich Britain and British merchants. Between 1660 and 1673, several laws and acts were passed by the British Parliament to create a mercantilist empire wherein the colonies were only to trade with or through Britain. The Navigation Act of 1660 stipulated that "no goods or commodities whatsoever shall be imported into or exported out of any lands, islands, plantations, or territories [that belong to the king of Britain] … but in such ships or vessels as do truly and without fraud belong only to the people of England or Ireland."[45] In short, trade can only be conducted outside of the British Empire as long as the ships or cargoes be majority owned or operated by British merchants and mariners.

---

42   Allen and Turner Letterbook, 1755–74, HSP.
43   *To the Freeholders, Merchants, Tradesman, and Farmers, of the City and County of Philadelphia* (Philadelphia, September 26, 1770), LCP.
44   Merritt, *The Trouble with Tea*, 75–76.
45   "The Navigation Act of (Sept. 13) 1660," as printed in Greene, *Settlements to Society*, 134–36.

The Staple Act of 1663 and the Plantation Duties Acts of 1673 levied taxes, duties, and penalties on commodities entering or leaving British colonies.[46] Responsibility to enforce these laws was given to the governors of the colonies, under the supervision of the Privy Council's Committee on Plantation Affairs (or "Lords of Trade"), which was also tasked with overseeing trade throughout the entire British Empire.[47] Because colonial merchants frequently violated the laws, Britain issued new acts renewing the original ones and increasing the penalties. The Navigation Act of 1696, the Wool Act of 1699, and the Naval Stores Act in 1705 increased the number of commodities that were to be taxed, which further restricted the scale and scope of trade carried out by colonial merchants.[48]

To enforce these laws, the British Parliament created a supervisory agency that formally brought the previously decentralized customs houses and officers into alignment. The Commission of the Board of Trade, passed on May 15, 1696, formally created a "Board of Trade" tasked with centralizing and improving the enforcement of trade restrictions and collection of duties in the British colonies, which replaced the old Lords of Trade with commissioners of trade.[49] At the same time, the Commissioners of the Customs, based in London, was revamped to approve basic salaries for customs officers and collectors to be paid out of the government's accounts. Under the reforms of 1696, twenty-nine positions for customs collectors were formalized, but many of these positions remained unfilled until 1764. It seems that the customs department never received the full resources it required to enforce the acts, which then enabled the colonial governments and merchants to circumvent and even disregard the laws, a subject discussed in more detail in Chapters 5 and 6.[50] Britain's desire and attempt to control and dictate how and where British Americans could conduct trade certainly created friction between the empire and its colonies.

Another difficulty that British American merchants faced was a chronic shortage of hard specie and inefficiencies of colonial currencies. Sitting on the edge of an expanding British Empire, the currency needs of merchants in Boston, New York, and Philadelphia rarely, if ever, received any attention

---

46 "The Staple Act of (July 27) 1663" and "The Plantation Duties Act of (Mar. 29) 1673," as printed in Greene, *Settlements to Society*, 136–39.
47 Thomas C. Barrow, *Trade and Empire: The British Customs Service in Colonial America, 1660–1775* (Cambridge, MA: Harvard University Press, 1967), 7.
48 "The Navigation Act of (Apr. 10) 1696," "The Woolen Act (May 4, 1699)," and "The Naval Stores Act (Mar. 14, 1705)," as printed in Greene, *Settlements to Society*, 210–17.
49 "The Commission of the Board of Trade (May 15, 1696)," as printed in Greene, *Settlements to Society*, 218–21.
50 Barrow, *Trade and Empire*, 64–66.

from the British Treasury and government. This was not a condition unique to Britain's North American colonies. In fact, all European colonies, even gold-rich Brazil, faced a chronic shortage of money, which was crucial to fuel the local economy and to sustain long-distance maritime trade.[51] As a result, colonial governments and merchants were forced to find alternatives to help fund their economic endeavors.

In British America, colonial governments created their own currencies, modeled after the British pound, to help foster and sustain the local economies. In most cases, colonial governments only created and distributed new currency when substantial public outlays were required during times of crises, such as war or drought. The first to create their own unit of currency was Massachusetts in 1690 to pay the militia members that had participated in a failed effort to capture Quebec. The rest of the colonies followed suit, with Virginia being the last in 1755 at the beginning of the Seven Years' War.[52] These currencies rarely kept their value at printing, though they were used so frequently that colonial governments occasionally reissued currency to replace worn out or destroyed paper bills.[53] Farley Grubb provides estimates of total currency in circulation for colonial Pennsylvania. As Table 4 shows, the total amount of currency remains quite low until the 1760s, and much of the new Pennsylvania currency is due to military spending during the Seven Years' War. We also see an influx of metallic currency—mostly Spanish silver coins—around the same time, the volume of which had increased substantially by 1775. Still, imports from England into Pennsylvania alone totaled more than £144,000 (British pound) in 1755 (worth more than £240,000 in Pennsylvania currency)—imports that could not be paid with colonial currency.[54]

These limits to imperial capacity directly influenced not only where American merchants conducted business but their business practices as well.

51　John J. McCusker, *Money and Exchange in Europe and America, 1600–1775: A Handbook* (Chapel Hill: University of North Carolina Press, 1978), 117.

52　Ron Michener, "Money in the American Colonies," *EH.Net Encyclopedia*, ed. Robert Whaples, June 8, 2003, revised January 13, 2011, http://eh.net/encyclopedia/money-in-the-american-colonies (accessed October 26, 2022).

53　Farley W. Grubb, "The Circulating Medium of Exchange in Colonial Pennsylvania, 1729–1775: New Estimates of Monetary Composition, Performance, and Economic Growth," *Explorations in Economic History* 41, no. 4 (2004): 333–36.

54　Import total from Chapter Eg, S. B. Carter et al., *Historical Statistics of the United States: Millennial Edition* (Cambridge: Cambridge University Press, 2006), 5:710–13. This influx of silver may also be related to an increase in the number of ships coming from and going to Spanish colonies in the Caribbean, Central America, and South America around the same time. See Chapter 5 for some data on the increase in ships coming from non-British destinations.

TABLE 4 Estimates of currency in circulation in Pennsylvania 1735–75 (in Pennsylvania £)

Year	Pennsylvania Currency	Metal Specie	Total Estimated Currency
1735	68,890	0	68,890
1745	80,000	3,810	83,810
1755	96,000	7,724	103,724
1765	305,095	40,927	346,022
1775	318,613	314,528	633,141

SOURCE: FARLEY W. GRUBB, "THE CIRCULATING MEDIUM OF EXCHANGE IN COLONIAL PENNSYLVANIA, 1729–1775: NEW ESTIMATES OF MONETARY COMPOSITION, PERFORMANCE, AND ECONOMIC GROWTH," *EXPLORATIONS IN ECONOMIC HISTORY* 41, NO. 4 (2004): 329–60, AT 334–35

Faced with this constant shortage of currency, merchants resorted to an amalgamation of credit, accounting, and mixed currencies to finance and facilitate commercial exchange.[55] Further, the British Isles had little interest in many of the commodities that Boston, New York, and Philadelphia produced, leaving little that colonial merchants could directly exchange for British manufactures and reexports.

4 Conclusion

Boston, New York, and Philadelphia developed as the main ports in their respective port complex. Each was bound to the other through trade and communication networks, and a mix of complementarity and competition characterized their relationship. Together, they functioned as a regional port complex and a nodal center within the Atlantic and global maritime economies. They shared hinterlands and reached out to many of the same forelands, which is a compelling reason to treat these ports as parts of a single port complex in British North America. While their commodities and volumes varied here and there, all three experienced a similar rate of growth throughout colonial period. The cities prospered and continued to extend their mercantile reach to ports on

---

55 Much more on this in the following chapter.

both shores of the Atlantic Ocean and indirectly provided a growing consumer base for East Asian goods. Facing the same challenges and impediments, such as the British mercantilist policies and a chronic shortage of currency, colonial merchants in the region adapted and overcame these obstacles to develop into an economic power. At the same time, they developed, maintained, and strengthened merchant networks within their own cities and between cities that facilitated a growing sense of unity and shared vision, leading to the creation of political ties that later defined the end of the eighteenth century.

CHAPTER 2

Merchants and Mercantile Networks

Essential to the success of the port complexes of Boston, New York, and Philadelphia, merchants created strong and complex networks of exchange, communication, and investment. These networks were not merely peripheral or auxiliary links built on the backs of English merchants from London, as some studies have shown.[1] While resembling their English compatriots, they created and sustained networks of exchange of ideas, goods, and capital, which spanned the four continents surrounding the Atlantic Ocean. Throughout the eighteenth century, merchants in all three cities consistently and tirelessly sought products and customers to buy and sell for profit, caring little for the mercantilist policies and wishes of the British Empire. They sought access to markets beyond the borders of the empire, in pursuit of which they circumvented and even disregarded the British mercantilist policies.

Merchants in colonial America were a stratified group of people engaged in trade and commerce, specializing in one or more activities such as overseas, coastal, and overland shipping, banking, brokering, wholesaling, retailing, and peddling. Due to the interdependent and complementary nature of these professional activities, merchants were inextricably linked to one another through relationships of trust and cooperation.[2] Trust is key in developing a relationship of mutual commercial benefits. Family, kinship, religion, language, and many other factors played a vital role in building and sustaining this relationship. Xabier Lamikiz highlights this in his study of Spanish merchants in the Atlantic World. In the Spanish case, culture supplied the integrative tissue that created trust among merchants.[3] Cultural connections were important for most, if not all, merchant groups that operated in the early modern world. Merchant networks in the Indian Ocean World, in particular,

---

1 Some scholars imply that metropolitan merchants were at the center of the British Atlantic's mercantile networks, providing both capital and credit to merchants throughout the empire. One of the most recent and influential books to take this tack is Nuala Zahedieh, *The Capital and the Colonies: London and the Atlantic Economy, 1660–1700* (Cambridge: Cambridge University Press, 2010). Zahedieh suggests that the eighteenth-century Atlantic economy was built on the foundations created by merchants based in London.
2 Doerflinger, *Vigorous Spirit of Enterprise*, 17; Jensen, *Maritime Commerce of Colonial Philadelphia*, 11–12.
3 Xabier Lamikiz, *Trade and Trust in the Eighteenth-Century Atlantic World: Spanish Merchants and Their Overseas Networks* (Woodbridge: Boydell Press, 2010).

often consisted of diasporic communities of ethnic and linguistic groups. Armenian merchants were one example of how culture facilitated global networks of ethnically aligned individuals throughout the Mediterranean and the Indian Ocean.[4] The Armenians, even though culturally closely knit, certainly established commercial contacts and provided credit and banking services to Indian and other Asian merchants.[5]

British American merchants, in general, shared linguistic and Protestant backgrounds, facilitating communication. Combined with the spread of the English language throughout the Atlantic Ocean, American merchants tapped into and helped develop a culture of business practices in the Atlantic World. Sheryllynne Haggerty shows how British merchants depended upon their personal reputations to maintain and expand commercial ties. A merchant's social responsibility to maintain honor and character restrained the worst intentions of most British merchants, and when a merchant abandoned moral reasoning, the merchant communities corrected or expelled the deviant merchant. Additionally, the state provided safety nets to prevent abuses, creating laws to punish fraudulent commercial behavior. The state also provided naval and military power to reduce risk and protect trade from external (non-British) threats.[6] This assistance was more helpful to merchants in the Caribbean but not offered to the same extent to merchants in North America, and imperial and state participation in the economy was not always beneficial. In both the Atlantic and Indian Oceans, state-chartered monopolies were given priority over non-company merchants, regardless of the negative effects on the economies in colonial possessions. American merchants resisted laws and policies that prevented access to desirable markets, and this is also true of British merchants in the Caribbean and elsewhere.[7] American merchants capitalized on

---

4   Sebouh D. Aslanian, *From the Indian Ocean to the Mediterranean: The Global Trade Networks of Armenian Merchants from New Julfa* (Berkeley: University of California Press, 2011).
5   Aslanian, *From the Indian Ocean to the Mediterranean*; Ghulam A. Nadri, *Eighteenth-Century Gujarat: The Dynamics of Its Political Economy, 1750–1800* (Leiden: Brill, 2009), 52.
6   Sheryllynne Haggerty, *"Merely for Money?" Business Culture in the British Atlantic, 1750–1815* (Liverpool: Liverpool University Press, 2012). See also John Haggerty and Sheryllynne Haggerty, "Visual Analytics of an Eighteenth-Century Business Network," *Enterprise and Society* 11, no. 1 (2010): 1–25; Haggerty and Haggerty, "The Life Cycle of a Metropolitan Business Network, 1750–1810," *Explorations in Economic History* 48, no. 2 (2011): 189–206.
7   Abigail L. Swingen, *Competing Visions of Empire: Labor, Slavery, and the Origins of the British Atlantic Empire* (New Haven: Yale University Press, 2015). Swingen describes imperial efforts to enforce the monopoly of the Royal African Company, which was detrimental to the plantation owners who needed a consistent supply of labor and to merchants, who supplied labor to them. In view of an impending resistance, imperial officials sent the British Navy to blockade and threaten military occupation if the colonies failed to

the robust and open mercantile culture of the British Empire, despite limited state assistance and laws restricting their access to global markets.

While they capitalized on the shared language and culture of the British mercantile community, American merchants also established multilingual networks with merchants outside of the British Empire. Merchants conducted trade with Dutch, Spanish, Portuguese, and French merchants on a regular basis. While communication was generally in English, merchants frequently received letters in a variety of languages. Nicholas Oursel, a Boston merchant, established trade with merchants based in Brazil, and his accounts and letters are written in Portuguese.[8] The letter books of Thomas Greg and Waddell Cunningham, of New York, contain multiple letters, many in Dutch, between the partners and merchants in Amsterdam and Rotterdam.[9] David Jeffries, also a Boston merchant, traded frequently with French and Spanish merchants throughout the Atlantic, answering letters received in both French and Spanish.[10] Though not all merchants were capable of conversing in multiple languages, many managed to communicate outside both the British Empire and the English language.

These networks and relationships were all the more important to colonial American merchants, as the British imperial system failed to provide enough specie or consumer markets to adequately support direct transfers of cash and goods. Rather, American merchants created intricate mechanisms of barter, credit, and accounting to counter the nearly constant shortage of currency and specie. This meant that trust and good behavior was integral to the maintenance of trade and credit networks. This chapter explores the dynamics of the merchant communities of Boston, New York, and Philadelphia and the complexities and challenges of carrying out maritime trade in the age of empires and colonial/imperial rivalries. It also examines the extent to which these merchants were able to overcome the challenges and constraints of colonial policies and control. It also explains many of the mechanisms that helped to facilitate the creation of mercantile and commodity networks and overcome

---

obey laws prohibiting non-Royal African Company slave shipments. In short, even the most loyal of subjects resisted imperial prohibitions on free trade, especially if those regulations hurt local merchants and landowners.

8   Nicholas Oursel Account Book, Amory Family Papers, MHS.
9   Greg and Cunningham to Isaac and Zachary Hope, Rotterdam, June 14, 1756; Greg and Cunningham to Thomas and Adrian Hope, Amsterdam, November 29, 1756, *LGC*, 139, 258. These are just a couple of examples, but many more exist. The number of those letters indicates a working knowledge of Dutch as they are clearly responding to letters from Dutch merchants in many of the letters.
10 Papers of David Jeffries II, 1668–1719, vol. 18, Jeffries Family Papers, MHS.

the relative absence of imperial state capacity manifesting itself in inadequate currency and financial support.

1 Merchants and Communities

In British America, merchant communities were remarkably diverse, and new members joined the community in myriad ways. At the outset, colonial settlers came to British America with the intention of making a profit in the commercial basin of the Atlantic. According to Phyllis Whitman Hunter, Massachusetts merchants particularly were focused on distinguishing themselves from the perceived excess and luxury of British merchants. As Puritans, they desired to support the entire community rather than just a small number of wealthy merchants. While their goals were admirable, Massachusetts merchants found the lure of wealth too strong to resist. Eventually, they became social elites in their own right.[11] However, Boston merchants did not give up their Puritan ideals; instead, they capitalized on shared beliefs and institutions to increase the size and efficacy of their mercantile networks. Puritan ideology helped but was not essential to the creation of merchant networks, and similar cultural connections in Philadelphia and New York provided the foundations for expanding communities of merchants.[12] Merchants in all three cities benefited from this shared culture and imperial system, and a prosperous merchant community had emerged in the region by 1700, whose members communicated, collaborated, and competed with one another.

Many of the region's earliest merchants leaned on ties with European merchants for capital and connections to begin transatlantic trade, but by the end of the seventeenth century, an entirely new and locally developed group of merchants constituted the mercantile community of these cities.[13] Some of them began as artisans and, through a mix of capital accumulation, marriage, and local networks, became a part of the ever-expanding transatlantic trade networks.[14] Other merchants entered maritime trade through shopkeeping,

---

11 Hunter, *Purchasing Identity in the Atlantic World*.
12 Christine Leigh Heyrman, *Commerce and Culture: The Maritime Communities of Colonial Massachusetts, 1690–1750* (New York: W. W. Norton and Co., 1984); Stephen Innes, *Creating the Commonwealth: The Economic Culture of Puritan New England* (New York: W. W. Norton and Co., 1995).
13 Hunter, *Purchasing Identity in the Atlantic World*, 20–22; Doerflinger, *Vigorous Spirit of Enterprise*, 14–16; Matson, *Merchants & Empire*, 17.
14 Hunter, *Purchasing Identity in the Atlantic World*, 22–24.

serving as mariners, or apprenticing with established merchants or merchant companies. Still others found their way into the community by virtue of being members of religious institutions, such as Boston's Puritan churches and Philadelphia's Quaker meeting houses. In all three cities, merchants developed strong ties with one another and used a common commercial language.

In eighteenth-century Boston, commercial ties were just as important as the religious ties that sparked the settlement of the region. Some of the earliest merchants in Boston were skilled artisans, who invested their incomes and savings in commercial ventures. John Hull, for example, was a silversmith who became well known in the community for excellent craftmanship and assessing the value of non-British coins—an important service that ensured the functioning of the monetary system in the colonial economy. Hull gradually developed his network with merchants in Boston, the surrounding regions, and other transatlantic ports including many in England, Southern Europe, and the West Indies. He married the daughter of an important Massachusetts family—Judith Quincy—instantly becoming respectable and, therefore, creditworthy.[15]

By the middle of the eighteenth century, Boston's merchant community had established itself as a pillar of the society and economy. Though not all merchants could be considered members of Boston's elite, many were part of upper society and played major roles in the city's political economy. Peter Faneuil and his descendants were so important to Boston that Faneuil Hall, a public marketplace built by Faneuil at his own expense in the 1740s, remains central to Boston's economy—now more important for its tourism industry.[16] Ward Nicholas Boylston also left his name behind on streets, buildings, and even a town. The town of Boylston, Massachusetts, received its charter thanks to a large grant from Boylston; hence the town's leaders named it Boylston in his honor.[17] Some elite merchants became key participants in the protests and resistance against imperial policies. Leading merchants, such as John Hancock, Caleb Davis, and John Rowe, were all deeply involved in political dissent before, during, and after the American Revolution. Davis served as an important organizer in non-importation discussions and agreements, and Hancock is well

---

15   Hunter, *Purchasing Identity in the Atlantic World*, 23–25.
16   Boston Records Commissioners, *A Report of the Record Commissioners of the City of Boston, Containing the Selectmen's Minutes from 1736 through 1742* (Boston: Rockwell and Churchill, City Printers, 1889), 8–10.
17   William Bentick-Smith, "Nicholas Boylston and His Harvard Chair," *Proceedings of the Massachusetts Historical Society*, 3rd series, 93 (1981): 17–39.

known for his unusually large signature on the Declaration of Independence.[18] Other merchants were also involved in political resistance, as the numerous non-importation acts of the 1760s and 1770s highlight. Dozens of agreements in these port cities were signed by hundreds of merchants, which indicates their commitment to stop importing English goods until certain imperial policies were repealed.[19]

New York merchants, similarly, contributed to the city's economy and society. Situated at the mouth of a major inland river, New York's merchant community, initially part of the Dutch Empire, earned much profit from the fur trade. Once the English gained ownership of New York in 1664, most of the Dutch settlers and merchants continued their trade with the Dutch Empire and established trade with England and its growing empire. By the early 1700s, New York's merchant community was quite diverse, with Dutch, English, German, and Spanish heritage.[20] Most of the important and wealthiest families in New York were involved in maritime trade. Landowning families such as the Crugers, Waltons, and Cuylers had at least one member of their families capitalizing on the produce of their estates by exporting agricultural products in exchange for manufactures, tea, sugar, and other commodities.[21] Some families set up second or third sons in ports throughout the Atlantic. John and Henry Cruger established a major trading firm in New York and sent their sons abroad to various ports in the Atlantic. John Harris Cruger conducted trade in Jamaica. Telemon Cruger settled in Curaçao, and Henry Cruger Jr. connected his family to Bristol.[22]

Entry into the New York merchant community was comparatively easy when contrasted with entry into British mercantile circles. As in Boston, many newcomers found their way into wholesaling through marriage, especially recent arrivals with connections to overseas markets. One such migrant, Henry White, arrived in New York from Wales in 1756. Leaning on his connections with the family back in Wales, he married a daughter of the prominent Van Cortlandt-Philipse, a prominent family in the city. This marriage gave him access to capital and credit, which he turned into a fortune, becoming a

---

18 Hancock Family Accounts and Receipts, Caleb Davis Papers, John Rowe Papers, MHS; Anne Rowe Cunningham, ed. *Letters and Diary of John Rowe: Boston Merchant, 1759–1762, 1764–1779* (Boston: W. B. Clarke Company, 1969 [1903]).
19 Matson, *Merchants & Empire*, 298–300. An example of these documents can be found in Chapter 6, along with a more in-depth discussion of non-importation agreements.
20 Matson, *Merchants & Empire*, 139; Virginia D. Harrington, "The New York Merchant on the Eve of the Revolution" (PhD diss., Columbia University, 1935), 13–18.
21 Harrington, "New York Merchant on the Eve of the Revolution," 13.
22 Harrington, "New York Merchant on the Eve of the Revolution," 12–14.

member of government and president of the Chamber of Commerce in 1772. Hugh Wallace, Irish by birth, emigrated to New York, married into a wealthy circle of friends, and also became president of the Chamber of Commerce in 1770. By the 1750s, most descendants of the original Dutch, French, and English settlers claimed heritage from multiple empires after nearly a century of intermarriage. The only group that remained distinct was a small number of Jewish merchants, descendants of Portuguese Jews, or emigres from German states and principalities.[23]

Philadelphia's merchants, like those of Boston and New York, followed a variety of paths to become traders. Thomas Doerflinger, in his seminal work on Philadelphia's merchants, argues that individuals could become successful merchants in four distinct ways. The first and easiest entry into commerce was being a young, white male of significant wealth. Merchants such as Tench Coxe, Joshua and William Fisher, and Thomas Willing were all worth at least twenty thousand pounds, and their sons generally succeeded their fathers with few difficulties in maintaining successful commerce. A second path into Philadelphia's merchant community was being a son or member of a well-respected family. These men, in general, had a little capital and relied on existing merchants within the community. Often, second or third sons of large landowners would apprentice or work for an established merchant. Eventually, many would strike out on their own, either traveling as a supercargo (agent responsible for selling the merchandise at the destination) or borrowing money from a mentor. The famous Robert Morris, often called the financier of the American Revolution, followed the apprentice route to the top echelons of the Philadelphia (and ultimately American) merchant community.[24]

A third method to become a merchant in Philadelphia was to accumulate capital earned from occupations, such as retailing, running a grocery, working as an artisan, or as a mariner, and use it to begin wholesale trading. For example, in the 1750s and 1760s, Captain Samuel Bunting, while shipping and freighting goods for Philadelphia merchants, acquired business skills and made contacts with other merchants in the Atlantic. In 1763, he got into the British dry goods trade through his contacts and started his career as a merchant. Lastly, individuals who had traveled throughout the Atlantic and had foreign contacts were in a great position to join Philadelphia's mercantile community. Many merchants had commercial experience in other parts of the world and had served as agents for other merchants. One such merchant was Isaac Norris, who came

23   Harrington, "New York Merchant on the Eve of the Revolution," 16–17.
24   Doerflinger, *Vigorous Spirit of Enterprise*, 47–49.

to Philadelphia for what he assumed would be a short trip to conduct business, but an earthquake in Jamaica literally wiped out his home and family. Instead of returning to Jamaica, he decided to settle down in Philadelphia as a maritime merchant.[25] Many traders in Philadelphia tapped into an ever-expanding network of Quaker merchants, leaning on shared religious ideology. European Quakers established footholds in Amsterdam and several major German and French ports, and Quaker merchants in Philadelphia developed commercial networks with European Quakers. The willingness of Quaker merchants on both sides of the Atlantic to challenge the traditional religious beliefs helped them engage in maritime trade across the Atlantic Ocean.[26]

In each of the three cities, the community of maritime merchants was highly stratified. There were merchants who owned one or at most two ships and carried out their own trade on a small scale. Many of them used all or part of their ship's cargo space to freight other merchants' goods. One such merchant was Thomas Nicholson based in Boston, who regularly shipped goods from Boston to the West Indies. He carried goods for George Watson and Thomas Davis, among a few others, to several destinations in the Caribbean, including Suriname and Saint-Domingue (now known as Haiti).[27] In the maritime trading world, this was a common practice and a strategy to pool capital and resources for commercial voyages and divide the risk. There were other merchants who freighted their goods on ships owned by other merchants. There were others who served as captains and officers on other merchants' ships and carried their own merchandise on board for trade. There were still others who, along with trading, also provided banking and brokering or agency services to merchants. The complementarity and cooperation that characterized the maritime world of these port cities benefited merchants and contributed to their varying degree of success in trade.

Many became rich merchants and were successful in passing their businesses on to their progeny. In Boston, the Boylston, Hancock, Davis, and

---

25   Doerflinger, *Vigorous Spirit of Enterprise*, 49–57.
26   Sünne Juterczenka, "Meeting Friends and Doing Business: Quaker Missionary and Commercial Activities in Europe, 1655–1720," in *Cosmopolitan Networks in Commerce and Society, 1660–1914*, ed. Andreas Gestrich and Margrit Schulte Beerbühl (London: German Historical Institute London, 2011), 187–93. As Quaker ideology was, in general, quite different from Christian beliefs of the time, Quakers were already resisting societal norms. In their view, imperial mercantilist policies were not that different from traditional Christianity. As Quakers had communities in nearly all parts of continental Europe, Quaker ideology already transcended imperial boundaries, why not their goods?
27   Thomas Nicholson Account Book, 1773–74, Thomas Nicholson Navigation and Logbooks, 1766–1813, MHS.

Faneuil families created and maintained commercial empires that spanned several generations, owning or having investments in numerous ships and warehouses.[28] New York's most famous merchant families were the Cuylers, Livingstons, and the Beekmans.[29] The Francises, Dickinsons, and Fishers were Philadelphia's leading merchant families. While members of a family generally worked together as partners or stakeholders in the family business, there are instances when they established their own independent businesses. Tench and Philip Francis, for example, carried out trade independently of the other and maintained separate accounts.[30] Either way, these families were successful in intergenerational transmission of wealth and businesses.

Maritime commerce was an integral part of the communities of all three cities. The number of people *directly* involved in maritime trade, those we can safely call merchants, was small in each of the three cities. According to Cathy Matson, between three hundred and four hundred individuals in New York in 1771 were considered maritime merchants out of a total population of nineteen thousand.[31] Boston had about two hundred merchants out of 5,500 tax-paying males (the total population of the city including women, slaves, and children exceeded fifteen thousand), and Philadelphia with a total population exceeding forty thousand in 1774 had about 320 maritime merchants.[32] There were, however, many others who were engaged in a number of commercial activities and facilitated trade in a variety of ways. In Boston, New York, and Philadelphia, much of the population was geared toward production and manufacturing for

---

28   Hunter, *Purchasing Identity in the Atlantic World*, 52–54; W. T. Baxter, *The House of Hancock: Business in Boston, 1724–1775* (Cambridge, MA: Harvard University Press, 1945), 15; Hancock Family Papers, MHS; Faneuil Family Papers, MHS, Caleb Davis Papers, MHS.
29   Matson, *Merchants & Empire*, 55–56, 81, 146–51; White, *Beekman Mercantile Papers*.
30   Doerflinger, *Vigorous Spirit of Enterprise*, 120–34; Tench Francis Invoice Book and Philip Francis Invoice Book, HSP.
31   Matson, *Merchants & Empire*, 128–29, 171.
32   Bettye Hobbs Pruitt, ed., *The Massachusetts Tax Valuation List of 1771* (Boston: G. K. Hall and Co., 1978). These figures are derived from a list of taxable assets, meaning that women are not generally listed as entries based on provincial law at the time. I counted all individuals who owned or partly owned one or more of the following: warehouses, tonnage, feet of wharf, and merchandise. Some were left off who owned just a warehouse, as some of those owned tanneries or other types of production facilities, and it was inconclusive whether they also participated in maritime commerce, though they would certainly be involved at least indirectly. In short, this is an estimate based on arbitrary conditions, but it lines up with the figures from the other two cities. In appendix B, the number counted is about half that counted in 1770. There are two reasons for this. One, appendix B only accounts for those that Jacob Price could explicitly count, and two, Boston experienced a significant population decline immediately after the Revolutionary War. Philadelphia figures from: Doerflinger, *Vigorous Spirit of Enterprise*, 15–17, 31–32.

local marketplaces as well as trade. In appendix B, each city's tax-paying population has been broken down into various sectors. Unfortunately, New York's data is not well developed, and for both Boston and New York we only have complete data from 1795. That said, the data from Boston is not dissimilar to the 1770 tax evaluation list discussed earlier. If we use only the most conservative definition of one who has a role in the commodity chains of the region, then we can safely assume that in Boston 16.3 percent of the population could be considered merchants and their support staff.[33] In New York, 14 percent were considered merchants, and in Philadelphia 14 percent were directly involved in commerce. However, if we expand our definition to include mariners, then in Boston, New York, and Philadelphia the percentage of each city's population employed by maritime commerce increases to 25.6, 23.3, and 22.7 percent respectively.

Naturally, the proportion of the cities' population involved in producing, selling, and transporting commodities is likely much higher, as the above figures do not include middlemen, retailers, and other types of activities associated with trade. Brokers or agents worked for other merchants or large landowners and helped them with procurement and distribution of commodities. Though not all brokers became merchants, many often found their way into the merchant community, as they were much like apprentices to merchants.[34] Brokers maintained close relationships with farmers and merchants, earning respect and also functioning as minor retailers. Larger shopkeepers were often brokers for larger merchants and suppliers for farmers and consumers in the region, leaning on their connections with merchants for consistent supplies of commodities. The system grew increasingly complicated as the volume of exports continued to grow throughout the eighteenth century. As such, merchants and farmers remained in communication, regardless of the number of middlemen, yet the number of stops a commodity made on its way to a ship increased dramatically.[35] If we include just the retailers of Boston, New York, and Philadelphia, then as much as 35.4, 34.9, and 30.7 percent respectively of the population directly handled products moving through all three ports.

There are several other sectors and types of laborers who could have been involved in the commodity chains, but certainly the group that should be included is the shipbuilding sector. In both Boston and Philadelphia,

---

33   Support staff includes secretaries, apprentices, agents, and others who assisted the daily operations of merchants.
34   Doerflinger, *Vigorous Spirit of Enterprise*, 54–56.
35   Jacob M. Price, "Economic Function and the Growth of American Port Towns in the Eighteenth Century," *Perspectives in American History* 8 (1974): 121–86, at 138–39.

shipbuilding was a major part of the local economy, with ships being commissioned and purchased by local merchants. However, a fairly large percentage of those ships were also exported to merchants in ports throughout the Atlantic, in effect becoming another type of commodity. Boston had the largest shipbuilding industry in the region followed by New York and Philadelphia, both of which had robust shipbuilding and outfitting industries. When we add shipbuilders to the percentage involved in commodity trading, we find that 44 percent in Boston, 39.5 percent in New York, and 35.6 percent in Philadelphia were part of the region's maritime economy.

2 Local Capital Investment in Trade

Often, historians have assumed that colonial merchants, especially in the cities of Boston, New York, and Philadelphia, were dependent on merchants from the metropole for capital investment and credit. While not alone in his assertions, David Hancock argues that the rise of the United States as a commercial power by the end of the eighteenth century was due in large part to a small group of London merchants who had the foresight to invest and establish robust trade with British America. As a result of capital and commodities from London merchants, British America rose to greatness.[36] While American merchants' dependence on English capital investment may have been greater in the seventeenth century, by the mid-eighteenth century—the period Hancock studies in *Citizens of the World*—British American merchants had created local sources of capital investment and relied less on sources from the metropole.

One way to measure the levels and sources of commercial investment is to quantify the amount invested in ships and the residence of the principal investors or owners. In the seventeenth century, much of the tonnage engaged in transoceanic commerce had owners based in Britain, but most of the tonnage employed in coastal trade was owned by merchants based in Boston, New York,

---

36 David Hancock, *Citizens of the World: London Merchants and the Integration of the British Atlantic Community, 1735–1785* (Cambridge: Cambridge University Press, 1995), 2–3. Other scholars, like James Shepherd and Gary Walton, have argued that the British colonies in North America were dependent on British trade, with some using the balance of payments to show how the colonies carried a negative balance with British merchants. See Shepherd and Walton, *Shipping, Maritime Trade and the Economic Development of Colonial North America*. Furthermore, Hancock uses only a small sample size of London merchants for his data and source material, but he generalizes his conclusions to imply a greater level of dependency than may have existed. More on this discussion will come in Chapters 5 and 6.

and Philadelphia. From the beginning of the eighteenth century, however, local merchants' share in the total tonnage in transoceanic trade increased in large part due to the success of the region's maritime economy and growing distance between colony and metropole.

In Massachusetts, 1,725 individuals invested in building or purchasing new vessels between 1699 and 1714, nearly all of which conducted trade in and out of New England. Of those individuals, 976 were investors from British America and 156 were investors based in the West Indies (not surprising considering that much of Boston's trade was with Caribbean ports). Of the 976 from British America, 903 were from Massachusetts, 544 were from Boston, and fifty-five from Salem. Of the total individuals, 492 resided in the British Isles and only 275 in London. More than 57 percent of the total number of investors were based in British America, whereas only 29 percent were from Britain. If one looks at the total number of investments, meaning the total times an investment in a vessel was made, Boston's merchants were dominant in the total number of times they invested in ships. In this case, an investment is an ownership of ships. Investments varied in size, but Boston's share was the largest in terms of both number of investments and percentage of capital invested. Of the total 3,939 investments, Boston accounted for 2,236 or 57 percent and, together with other ports in the complex, it accounted for 72 percent or 2,825 of the total.[37] By 1770, nearly 88 percent of the tonnage that plied the ocean between New England and Britain was owned by merchants residing in British America (see Table 5).[38]

Pennsylvania's merchant marine was largely in the hands of colonial Americans and not of British investors. John McCusker provides even greater detail for Philadelphia's sources of capital. He shows a growing dominance of local capital throughout the eighteenth century. In Table 6 below, the sources and levels in investment are compared for two periods of time, 1726–29 and 1770–75. From 1726 to 1729, roughly 24 percent of total investment in Philadelphia's shipping industry was made by British merchants and investors, which declined to 9 percent by the end of the colonial period. Investments by Philadelphia merchants during this period rose from 47 percent to 77 percent, and total investment by colonial merchants, including those of the West Indies, exceeded 85 percent. By the 1770s, Pennsylvanians (both in Philadelphia and in the greater port complex) held a total of ship tonnage capacity worth roughly £500,000 sterling.[39]

---

37 Bailyn and Bailyn, *Massachusetts Shipping, 1697–1714*, 124–25.
38 McCusker and Menard, *Economy of British America*, 192.
39 John J. McCusker, "Sources of Investment Capital in the Colonial Philadelphia Shipping Industry," in McCusker, *Essays in the Economic History of the Atlantic World*, 254.

TABLE 5   Ownership of vessels trading between British ports and colonial ports on the North American Continent, 1770

Colony that vessels cleared	Residence of vessels' owners (%)	
	Great Britain	Total of continental colonies
New England	12.5	87.5
New York	37.5	62.5
Pennsylvania	25	75
Maryland and Virginia	75	25
North Carolina	62.5	37.5
South Carolina and Georgia	62.5	37.5

SOURCE: MCCUSKER AND MENARD, *ECONOMY OF BRITISH AMERICA*, 192

New York's direct trade with Great Britain was a greater proportion of its total maritime trade, and as a result, New York relied more heavily on British sources of capital investment than Boston and Philadelphia. As shown in Table 5, just over 37 percent of the vessels moving goods between Britain and New York in 1770 had owners based in Britain, considerably more than both Boston and Philadelphia. However, roughly three-quarters of tonnage employed in New York's Caribbean trade was owned by the merchants of New York.[40] Even with a greater reliance on British capital, most vessels were owned by merchants based in the colonies, and British sources of capital continued to fall as a proportion of total investment in all three cities.

Often overlooked in more recent scholarship on the economy of British America is its robust shipbuilding industry, especially in Boston and Philadelphia. North America contained vast forests of lumber in close proximity to major ports like Boston. The number of vessels built in the colonies each year, on average, increased throughout the eighteenth century and indicates a robust demand for more tonnage to import and export an ever-growing volume and variety of goods. Boston and Philadelphia dominated the shipbuilding industry in colonial America. In 1697–1714, Boston shipbuilders built 1,106 ships, whereas Connecticut builders and merchants built twenty-five between

---

40   Matson, *Merchants & Empire*, 184–85.

TABLE 6 The sources of capital invested in the shipping industry of Colonial Philadelphia, 1726–29 and 1770–75

Source	1726–29 Average annual investment			1770–75 Average annual investment		
	Tonnage	Value (£ sterling)	% of total value[a]	Tonnage	Value (£ sterling)	% of total value[a]
Pennsylvania	1,007	5,790	47	8,276	61,653	77
Great Britain	513	2,950	24	926	6,898	9
Ireland	253	1,455	12	442	3,293	4
Europe and Africa	0	0	0	75	561	< 1
British N. America[b]	0	0	0	16	118	< 1
British West Indies	147	845	7	352	2,624	3
New Jersey	43	247	2	92	688	< 1
Delaware	117	673	5	239	1,781	2
Other Cont. Colonies	60	345	3	389	2,901	4
Totals	2,140	12,305	100	10,807	80,517	100

a Percentages have been rounded to the nearest whole number, so the total percentage may not total exactly 100
b This category represents British Canada, whereas the other Continental Colonies includes the original thirteen colonies that eventually declared independence from Britain

SOURCE AND NOTES: JOHN J. MCCUSKER, "SOURCES OF INVESTMENT CAPITAL IN THE COLONIAL PHILADELPHIA SHIPPING INDUSTRY," IN MCCUSKER, *ESSAYS IN THE ECONOMIC HISTORY OF THE ATLANTIC WORLD* (LONDON: ROUTLEDGE, 1997), 252

1678 and 1714.[41] Massachusetts shipbuilders in 1714 built forty-four vessels and in 1770 built 144 ships.[42] Ships were not built for local merchants alone. While most of the shipbuilding activity was due to local investments, by the 1770s Boston was selling between £60,000 and £90,000 sterling worth of vessels to merchants in other Atlantic ports.[43]

---

41 Connecticut had a longer period of time, 1678–1714, in comparison to Boston. Hunter, *Purchasing Identity in the Atlantic World*, 9–10; Bailyn and Bailyn, *Massachusetts Shipping, 1697–1714*, 104–5.
42 Price, "Economic Function and the Growth of American Port Towns in the Eighteenth Century," 185.
43 Jacob M. Price, "A Note on the Value of Colonial Exports of Shipping," *Journal of Economic History* 36, no. 3 (September 1976): 704–24, at 721.

Philadelphia also experienced a substantial improvement in its shipbuilding industry, largely due to local investment. As Table 6 shows, Philadelphia built on average 2,140 tons for the years 1726–29. Contrast that number with the 10,807 on average built in the years 1770–75, and Philadelphia expanded their production by 505 percent, a steeper gain than Boston. Boston remained the top shipbuilder in the region, but Philadelphia doubled New York's output by the 1770s.[44]

Partnerships and joint ownerships were common ways for merchants to raise funds to purchase vessels. Often, vessels were owned by more than one person or firms, but as the eighteenth century wore on, partnerships declined in number of investors because merchants accumulated large capital and could purchase vessels on their own. At the beginning of the century, more than three investors frequently joined forces to buy one or more vessels and shared the tonnage and risks associated with ownership. In New York's West Indies trade, between 1700 and 1709, partnerships between three and twelve merchants accounted for at least 78 percent of the vessels leaving for the Caribbean whereas merely 9 percent of vessels were individually owned. By 1764, however, only 58 percent of ships were jointly owned by three to five merchants, and about 37 percent were solely or dually owned, indicating both a decrease in the number of investors needed and an increase in the capacities of individual merchants to purchase ships.[45] Similarly, in Boston the number of investors who owned a share of a single vessel declined over time, especially in the first decade and a half of the eighteenth century. In the years 1607–98, ships with five or more owners comprised 27.5 percent of total tonnage, but by 1714, the percentage of vessels with five or more owners was only a little more than 10 percent.[46] This decline continued throughout the eighteenth century largely due to merchants earning enough profits to either purchase a ship in partnership with one or two other merchants or entirely by themselves. In both cases, the number of ships that had five or more owners dropped throughout the period.

Many times, a merchant from one city created partnerships or agreements with merchants from one or both other cities to build, own, and operate new ships and fleets to expand their commerce. As shown above in

---

44 Price, "Economic Function and the Growth of American Port Towns in the Eighteenth Century," 185.
45 Matson, *Merchants & Empire*, 184–85. This data is indicative of the overall tonnage employed in New York's trade as at least half of New York's trade was with West Indian ports on both British and non-British islands. See chapter 4 for more information on colonial trade in the Caribbean.
46 Bailyn and Bailyn, *Massachusetts Shipping, 1697–1714*, 127.

Table 6, Philadelphia's tonnage had some investment from other colonies, most of which came from Boston and New York.[47] Boston was also a popular destination for capital from the other two cities. As early as 1714, dozens of investors from New York and Philadelphia had purchased partial ownership of vessels conducting trade in Boston, allowing them to earn profit when those ships carried cargo. Generally, these individuals were cooperating with merchants based in Boston, and they were usually involved in either coastal and/or the Caribbean trade.[48]

More importantly, the port complexes of each city were also vital sources of investment capital. New York's merchant marine garnered investors from New Jersey, Rhode Island, and other regions of its hinterland.[49] In Boston, its feeder ports were dependable sources of capital. One Salem merchant, Timothy Orne, was a major lender to merchants in Boston as well as its feeder ports. He extended loans worth £9,000 to Massachusetts merchants, much of which was surplus profit from his successful wholesale business. Orne's loans were not exclusively for merchants. In 1760, thirty-five individuals owed Orne for loans worth between £15 and £150, many of those to small shopkeepers, farmers, and local artisans. In 1765 alone, Orne lent £2,020, at interest, to thirty-three people.[50] Philadelphia also obtained substantial investments from Delaware, New Jersey, and the Chesapeake.[51] Local ownership was important to the political leaders of the region, as they recognized the benefits to the local economy. In 1734, New York's Assembly decided to raise tonnage duties on foreign-registered vessels to encourage local merchants to purchase and register ships within the colony. Though there was resistance to the law, especially from transatlantic traders, who still depended on foreign-registered vessels, the law remained on the books and largely fulfilled its purpose mainly because most of the vessels were owned and operated by local merchants and captains.[52]

Merchants did not stop at investing in ships and merchandise; they also reinvested a part of their capital in production, banking services, and even in land and housing properties. In all three cities, merchants invested in local production of manufactures or refinement of agricultural products. The growing

---

47 McCusker, "Sources of Investment Capital in the Colonial Philadelphia Shipping Industry," 254.
48 Bailyn and Bailyn, *Massachusetts Shipping, 1697–1714*, 125.
49 Harrington, "New York Merchant on the Eve of the Revolution," 100–12.
50 Hunter, *Purchasing Identity in the Atlantic World*, 124–26.
51 McCusker, "Sources of Investment Capital in the Colonial Philadelphia Shipping Industry," 252–54.
52 Matson, *Merchants & Empire*, 221–22.

number of distilleries, mills, tanneries, insurance agencies, paper mills, and sugar refineries indicates substantial reinvestment and prospects of profit in such ventures due to growth in shipping and trade.[53] Like Timothy Orne, many merchants lent money at interest to startup merchants, farmers, and artisans. Others purchased tanneries, houses, and land to either rent or for other productive purposes.[54] Some merchants even engaged in buying British government bonds, especially in times of war. Merchants, who combined trade with other businesses and financial ventures, operated in many ways like modern portfolio capitalists. For them, this was a strategy to divide risks and avoid a total loss. In 1747, John Watts and William Alexander of New York purchased a few thousand pounds of government securities when Britain issued £4 million in bonds.[55] Alice Hanson Jones described it best when she wrote that "despite the seeming handicaps of absence of banking institutions, shortage of coins, and varying local paper currency, the colonists proved very *enterprising*." Jones meant that the colonists devised novel and effective ways to avoid dependency on British capital and developed a robust system of capital investment.[56] Considering that colonial merchants owned one-third of the British Empire's total merchant marine tonnage by 1775, colonial investment was quite capable of sustaining itself without being dependent on British capital.[57]

3 Networks and the Regional Complex

Boston, New York, and Philadelphia merchant communities were well integrated with one another, as ships frequently and quickly moved between all three. Furthermore, the many smaller ports that were part of the regional

---

53   Jensen, *Maritime Commerce of Colonial Philadelphia*, 294–95.
54   Hunter, *Purchasing Identity in the Atlantic World*, 124–26; Harrington, "New York Merchant on the Eve of the Revolution," 14–15, 126–30; Matson, *Merchants and Empire*, 3–7. See Lester J. Cappon et al, eds., *Atlas of Early American History: The Revolutionary Era, 1760–1790* (Princeton: Princeton University Press, 1976), 26–32 for maps showing the density and number of manufacturing, insurance, and agricultural refinement facilities and firms. In all maps, the cities of Boston, New York, and Philadelphia are centers of production and, when zoomed out, the region looks more like the nodal center it became by the end of the eighteenth century.
55   Harrington, "New York Merchant on the Eve of the Revolution," 126–27.
56   Alice Hanson Jones, *Wealth of a Nation to Be: The American Colonies on the Eve of Revolution* (New York: Columbia University Press, 1980), 153.
57   McCusker, "Sources of Investment Capital in the Colonial Philadelphia Shipping Industry," 246.

complex of ports were a significant portion of the total number of ships coming and going from all three ports. Merchants in all three cities tended to have accounts with merchants in the other two cities, more so than with merchants elsewhere. While the focus for merchants continued to be Atlantic and global trade, many goods imported by a merchant in one city often found their way to the other two cities via reexports or shared cargoes, as smaller ships (often called "packet" boats) maintained nearly weekly connections between all three. Moreover, some merchants from different cities created short- or long-term partnerships to invest in cargoes, some of which were purchased, shipped, and then sold without ever touching one or both ports, but the profits were shared, providing more capital and credit for the local economy regardless. These regional networks are exemplified by the many newspapers printed and distributed between the three cities that often reported on general economic conditions, such as prices.

Ships regularly traveled between all three cities, with dozens entering and clearing each port for the other two ports annually. Furthermore, packet ships or ships that carried small cargoes and mail maintained weekly routes, usually connecting two cities. These connections were so important that often more than one ship would run between cities. For example, in 1757 the *New York Mercury* reported that a second ship would now run between Philadelphia and New York, one leaving on Monday and the other on Thursday.[58] These ships were also not included in the weekly entries and clearances reports from the Customs Office that were printed in the newspapers of each port. Still, considering that packet ships were not normally counted in the number of ships flowing between all three cities, Philadelphia welcomed forty-one ships from Boston and another thirty-seven returned to Boston in 1770. New York, on the other hand, sent twenty-one ships to Philadelphia in 1770, with fifteen coming directly back from Philadelphia.[59] There are also some discrepancies between the numbers reported by the customs offices of all three cities, which also indicates that some smuggling occurred in this tri-city trade.

The number of ships flowing between the three ports is not surprising when examining the account and letterbooks of the merchants who conducted business in the region. While most of the accounts and letters were with their overseas trading partners, the number of accounts and letters that were shared between merchants of Boston, New York, and Philadelphia is not insignificant. In fact, a glance even at the smallest account book of the era shows that credit

---

58   *New York Mercury*, April 11, 1757.
59   The numbers come from the same compilation in table 21 in Chapter 5, Philadelphia: 1770, *Pennsylvania Gazette*; New York: 1770, *New York Gazette*.

was extended and shared throughout the region, no doubt also sharing and spreading the risk out beyond just one city within the regional complex. Even merchants normally engaged in transoceanic trade depended on access to goods and supplies from the region to help complete cargoes or outfit ships for their long voyages. One such example is Peter Faneuil, a major Boston merchant who depended upon New York and Philadelphia merchants for access to flour, which he regularly imported from both cities, invoices for which can be found throughout his invoice book from the late 1720s.[60]

Perhaps as important as the sharing of credit and accounts, merchant letter books are also filled with communication flowing between the three cities. These letters dealt largely with usual business, but occasionally the letters ventured into discussing potential short- or long-term partnerships for longer and riskier voyages.[61] More importantly, the regular communication also facilitated commerce by fostering trust and the sharing of non-public information. Information that would have been shared ranged from the trivial, such as news of a marriage or birth in a family that both merchants knew, to more important news, such as a ship that sank or a cargo that spoiled. No matter the importance of the communication, these networks of letters and accounts facilitated coherence between the three cities and were later instrumental in political developments in the 1760s and 1770s, when merchants became the core of revolutionary communication networks.

The numerous newspapers printed and distributed between the three cities that often reported on general economic conditions, such as the prices, ship arrivals and departures, and weather conditions (e.g., ice in rivers or harbors) found in the other cities, exemplify the importance and extensive regional mercantile network that brought these three cities closer together. It was not uncommon for newspapers to list wholesale prices of goods in various parts of the Atlantic, especially Britain. Papers also announced prices and ship arrivals in the other major ports of the region. The *Boston Gazette*, for example, listed prices in Salem, Newburyport, New York, and Philadelphia, and newspapers in New York and Philadelphia would do the same for the minor and major ports in the region.[62] Regularly, ship captains or owners advertised that they had tonnage available and listed the dates they expected to leave and their

---

60 Peter Faneuil Invoice Book, 1725–29, Peter Faneuil Papers, 1716–39, Hancock Family Papers, 1664–1854, Baker Library Historical Collections, Harvard Business School.
61 For such an example, see: Articles of Agreement between Joseph Brandon and Benjamin Dolbeare, April 14, 1739, Dolbeare Family Papers, Box 4, Folder 8, MHS.
62 *Boston Gazette*, 1719–98. This was a common practice throughout the major cities and towns in the colonies. See also *Pennsylvania Gazette* and the *New York Mercury*.

destinations.[63] Advertisements were carefully worded, especially when goods were received from non-British sources, such as tea from the Netherlands. Therefore, merchants would enter Dutch goods into their accounts as "Holland goods" but rarely listed them as such in ads.[64]

Merchants and shopkeepers reached out to prospective buyers or consumers through weekly newspapers, which reported the arrival of ships, their ports of origin, commodities they brought to the port, and prices. Merchants could purchase ads to offer goods at wholesale, and retailers frequently placed ads describing the goods they carried, usually indicating the quality and source of the said goods. As newspapers also printed recent wholesale prices and ship arrivals, merchants were in a constant search for information to find the location and the person with whom one could make a profitable transaction. Merchants also used newspapers to post ads soliciting locally produced goods to ship overseas. In fact, much of the printed space of newspapers was occupied by commercial content of one kind or another. Without doubt, the success of colonial newspapers owed much to the patronage of merchants and retailers.[65]

Along with the cargoes and letters that the above-mentioned ships carried, newspapers from all three cities were also distributed to the other ports. In fact, merchants regularly subscribed to the newspapers of all three cities, and newspapers found their way deep into the interior of their hinterlands. Prices of subscriptions were based on distance, and newspapers were available to most ports within reach. For example, the *American Weekly Mercury*, published in Philadelphia, began its life in December 1719 with a price of ten shillings for those in Philadelphia, fifteen shillings for those in New York, New Jersey, and Maryland, and twenty shillings for those in Virginia, Rhode Island, and Boston.[66] Newspapers, like merchant letters and accounts, also strengthened the unity of the regional port complex.

4   Mechanisms of Trade

These accomplishments were possible because of extensive networks of people who communicated with each other and carried out commercial transactions

---

63   Doerflinger, *Vigorous Spirit of Enterprise*, 90–92.
64   Harrington, "New York Merchant on the Eve of the Revolution," 62–63.
65   Doerflinger, *Vigorous Spirit of Enterprise*, 93–95. Several collections of newspapers from colonial Boston are held by the Massachusetts Historical Society, the most complete being the *Boston Gazette*, which ran nearly continuously from 1719 throughout the period discussed in this book.
66   *American Weekly Mercury*, December 22, 1719.

at their respective locations. The networks included principal merchants and shipowners, members of the household, and agents or representatives. In the study of early American merchants, the fundamental processes and institutions that facilitated the expansion and complexity of colonial trade are often subsumed in the discussion of great merchants or merchant houses, limiting our understanding of the complex functions within a given network or group of networks. While communication is a key aspect of network creation and maintenance, the actual mechanisms by which goods moved from the hinterland into the foreland and vice versa are more complex than merely writing letters. Moreover, these mechanisms were developed largely in the absence of the British imperial state, wherein very little hard specie and imperially backed currency found its way into the colonial economy. Rather, colonial merchants were constantly short of hard specie, and both colonial governments and merchants were forced to find ways to conduct trade in the nearly constant absence of adequate specie.

Frequently, merchants would partner with other merchants or shopkeepers in the desired destination. They wrote letters to their partners or correspondents exchanging information about goods, prices, and demand as well as placing orders for merchandise. Once an order was placed, the goods were shipped to corresponding merchants or agents who would then sell the merchandise and, after deducting the mutually agreed commission, remit the proceeds either in money or in merchandise to the sender as per their wishes. If the principal and corresponding merchants were partners in trade, they shared the proceeds and remitted the sender's share in cash or merchandise. Peter Faneuil of Boston utilized a few different merchants in French Canada to establish a consistent trade with French merchants in Louisbourg and the surrounding region. He leaned on his connections with French merchants in both the North Atlantic and in the West Indies, where he could get access to goods such as sugar, rum, cocoa, wine, and silks (likely sourced from India and reexported from France). In the case of the West Indies trade, Faneuil would often instruct his partners in Louisbourg to purchase goods, send them to islands in the Caribbean, and then return to Louisbourg with sugar, molasses, and rum. It was not uncommon for merchants like Faneuil to make a profit from goods traded between distant ports that never once touched land in New England.[67]

---

67 Donald F. Chard, "Massachusetts–Louisbourg Trade, 1713–1744," in Colonial Society of Massachusetts, *Seafaring in Colonial Massachusetts: A Conference Held by the Colonial Society of Massachusetts, 21–22 November 1975* (Boston: Colonial Society of Massachusetts, 1980), 146–47; Peter Faneuil Invoice Book, 1725–37, Peter Faneuil Ledger, etc. MHS.

Like the partnerships in purchasing and building ships, partnerships were also useful in creating networks, purchasing commodities, and sharing or reducing financial risks. In general, there were three types of partnerships: familial, non-familial, and temporary. Merchants would legally formalize their partnerships, especially in the case of non-familial arrangements. For example, Benjamin Dolbeare and Joseph Brandon, both merchants of Boston, entered into a partnership, signing "Articles of Agreement" to formalize their relationship in April of 1739. In the document, they agree that they "shall and will be ... partners together and joint dealers in all goods that shall be consigned to them from any person or persons in Great Britain or elsewhere." This agreement was to continue for at least seven years, and if either party were to break the contract, an arbiter could impose a "penal sum of two thousand pounds lawful money of New England."[68]

Common in colonial commerce, family firms and partnerships were the easiest method to ensure a successful partnership. Usually, merchants could readily trust family members to properly conduct trade, as the success of the family's business meant profit and success for the entire family. Partnerships between brothers, cousins, and sons and fathers were the most common. Often partnerships between family members were a form of vertical integration. Philadelphia merchant Daniel Clark's brother, John, owned a retail shop and depended upon Daniel's imports to provide the merchandise his customers requested.[69] Often sons followed their fathers into maritime commerce. Thomas Hancock of Boston built a hugely successful maritime business between 1724 and 1764. Even before his death in 1764, Thomas Hancock raised his son John as a maritime trader. By the 1770s, John Hancock was a successful merchant and well known for trading with non-British ports. He was a constant defender of free trade for colonial merchants.[70]

Some of the most successful trading firms were partnerships between two or more people. In Philadelphia, companies such as Orr, Dunlop, and Glenhope, and Allen and Turner combined the networks, capital, and credit of multiple individuals into permanent partnerships or firms.[71] Often marriages between two merchant families, such as the Slade and Rogers families in Boston, resulted

---

68   Articles of Agreement between Joseph Brandon and Benjamin Dolbeare, April 14, 1739, Dolbeare Family Papers, Box 4, Folder 8, MHS.
69   Daniel Clark Letter and Invoice Book, 1760–62, HSP, 54–55.
70   Hancock Family Accounts and Papers, MHS. For a more complete discussion of the Hancock Family Business, see Baxter, *House of Hancock*.
71   Orr, Dunlop, and Glenhope Letterbook, 1767–69; Allen and Turner Letterbook, 1755–74, HSP.

in joint enterprises that expanded both families' access to Atlantic markets.[72] Sometimes partnerships spanned oceans and imperial boundaries. The mercantile business of Thomas Greg and Waddell Cunningham (occasional clients of Orr, Dunlop, and Glenhope) opened business in 1761. By the end of the 1760s, Greg, based in Belfast, and Cunningham, based in New York, operated a small import/export empire that bridged the British Isles, New York, the West Indies, and the Netherlands.[73]

Occasionally, merchants would engage in temporary partnerships, especially in transatlantic commerce, as the size of ships and the quantities and values of cargoes moving between Europe and the Americas were on average larger and more difficult to obtain. In Philadelphia, Israel Pemberton entered into a short-term agreement with two London merchants, John Hunt and Elias Bland, to purchase and ship merchandise between London, Philadelphia, and the West Indies. Abel James and Henry Drinker, also in Philadelphia, owned a ship jointly with William Neate, who was based in London. Temporary partnerships were common especially in the provisions trade in the West Indies. Samuel Bean in Jamaica worked with John Reynell in Philadelphia, each procuring goods the other needed to cater to the consumer demand in their respective ports.[74] These temporary arrangements were useful in gaining access to highly sought-after commodities. In such cases, generally, both partners made quick profits and were free to reinvest their capital in another short-term enterprise.

Many merchants established agents in ports around the Atlantic. Merchants would often pay housing (at least for a short while), provisioning, and then give a percentage of the profits to agents who sold and procured goods for them. In the Atlantic during the eighteenth century, a growing class of professional agents moved throughout the ocean working for merchants. Trust and recommendations were important in choosing one's agents and developing a professional relationship with them. Boston merchant Hugh Hall regularly updated his account books with wages, reimbursements, and other expenses due to his employees in Barbados. In one entry, he listed eleven individuals who worked for Hall to procure and sell commodities while stationed in Barbados, making payments to five of them in advance. In total, he owed over £600 in commissions and wages. It appears from other parts of these records that this trade

---

72 Slade–Rogers Family Papers, MHS.
73 Thomas M. Truxes, ed., *Letterbook of Greg and Cunningham, 1756–57: Merchants of New York and Belfast* (Oxford: Oxford University Press on behalf of the British Academy, 2001).
74 Jensen, *Maritime Commerce of Colonial Philadelphia*, 12–13.

was mainly an exchange of dried cod for West Indian sugar and molasses.[75] Merchants rarely personally viewed the goods they purchased, especially goods that were imported. Thus, it was essential to have faith that a merchant's representatives would find the highest quality goods at the best prices.[76]

Naturally, one's family was often the quickest solution to find agents or partners. Caleb Davis, in Boston, sent his brother to Saint-Domingue to procure sugar, molasses, and rum. In this particular case, it was a dangerous mission, as Saint-Domingue was technically off-limits to American-based merchants as it was a part of the French Empire, and in the 1770s Britain was increasing its enforcement of the Navigation Acts. To avoid the prying eyes of the British Navy, Davis's brother, Nathaniel, settled in Môle-Saint-Nicolas, on the edge of the northern peninsula of Saint-Domingue away from its main port, Cap-François.[77] In New York, Philip Cuyler served as his father's agent in England, procuring English manufactures for resale in New York.[78]

In Philadelphia, the Norris family contained multiple generations of merchants and businessmen. The elder Isaac Norris (1671–1735) established a career as a merchant and had two sons, Isaac and Charles, who followed a similar path. The younger Isaac Norris (1701–66) continued his father's mercantile business. Charles Norris (1705–61) dabbled in commercial operations, but he focused more on the financial side of mercantile pursuits.[79] He served as a trustee of the General Loan Office of Pennsylvania, which supplied loans primarily for home and land purchases. The capital for these loans came largely from merchants in the Philadelphia area, acting in many ways like a small-town bank or credit union.[80] However, Isaac maintained a substantial account with his brother Charles, wherein Charles was acting as an investor or owner of cargoes that were coming and going from Philadelphia. More intriguing,

---

75 Hugh Hall Account Book, 1728–33, MHS.
76 Harrington, "New York Merchant on the Eve of the Revolution," 76–77; Jensen, *Maritime Commerce of Colonial Philadelphia*, 18–19.
77 Caleb Davis Papers, Box 7, January 1774 Folder, MHS. This situation is routinely discussed between the brothers in several letters, invoices, and other papers. The aforementioned citation is the folder that best summarizes the difficulties faced by Nathaniel and Caleb Davis.
78 Harrington, "New York Merchant on the Eve of the Revolution," 99.
79 Isaac Norris Account Books, LCP. See also Norris Family Papers, HSP.
80 Charles Norris Papers, Norris Family Papers, HSP. Many of his papers include lists of mortgages and other types of business, including payments and discharges of debt. Though the papers are not entirely clear, the loan office appears to have been partly funded or supported by the colonial government of Pennsylvania, indicating some public interest in supporting economic growth.

however, is the "petty cash" account Isaac kept with Charles. In it, several bills of exchanges are cashed. In one instance, a £100 bill of exchange was bought by Isaac for £168. Though it is not noted in the account entry, the £168 was likely in Pennsylvania currency, which was worth less than a British pound sterling. In that same account, Isaac supplied £500 and £600 respectively in two different loan orders from the General Loan Office.[81] In the case of the brothers Isaac and Charles Norris, Isaac's profits were used as capital to either provide or back mortgages for local land and building purchases. Isaac benefited by using the General Loan Office to draw and cash bills of exchange, providing easier access to capital and credit.

Some merchants began their career as agents or supercargoes (individuals that accompanied ship cargoes on their voyage) for a merchant or merchant company. Robert Morris, for example, served as supercargo and agent for the firm Charles Willing and Son, traveling between Philadelphia and Jamaica before he eventually became a partner with Thomas Willing.[82] Other merchants found their way into maritime trade by means of experience, such as Ezekiel Edwards and John Reynell, who developed networks throughout the Atlantic wherever they traveled and conducted business.[83]

Ship captains and masters served as intermediaries for merchants, who consigned merchandise to their agents/representatives at the port of destination. Ships were often laden with cargoes from multiple merchants, and captains and the occasional supercargoes were responsible for properly handling the merchandise. In New York's West Indies trade, many ships contained cargoes from more than a dozen merchants.[84] Transoceanic vessels were notorious for holding unique cargoes for dozens of merchants. The cargo of a New York ship arriving in London included goods belonging to thirty-two merchants and merchant companies.[85] Frequently, merchants were forced to wait on ship captains to send and receive more goods. Philadelphia merchant John Stamper wrote to his colleagues in a port who were waiting for Stamper to send new goods. Stamper wrote that he was waiting on a Captain Harrison to conclude selling his current cargo, "as fast as he can," adding that "he will be ready in a few days."[86]

---

81   Isaac Norris Account Books, LCP.
82   Doerflinger, *Vigorous Spirit of Enterprise*, 133.
83   Jensen, *Maritime Commerce of Colonial Philadelphia*, 19–20.
84   Matson, *Merchants & Empire*, 184.
85   Matson, *Merchants & Empire*, 139.
86   John Stamper Letterbook, 1751–72, HSP, 3.

In the early eighteenth century, merchants used cash or credit to purchase export merchandise directly from suppliers like farmers and fishermen in the main port cities. This meant that merchants had to deal with several producers to obtain enough merchandise to trade either locally or overseas. In 1736, a Boston merchant made twenty transactions in a day to acquire wheat for export.[87] As the volume of trade grew rapidly in the middle decades of the eighteenth century, merchants could no longer depend on small-scale supplies of grain or fish from primary producers. By the 1750s, therefore, a number of intermediary merchants and brokers or agents joined the network and helped the merchants of Boston, New York, and Philadelphia with the procurement of exports and sale and distribution of imports. These middlemen also helped to fulfill the growing demand and further expand commodity production and trade. Brokers were individuals who handled transactions between merchants and producers and usually charged a commission. Intermediary merchants, on the other hand, were a more varied lot. Some were shopkeepers and retailers and supplied goods to principal merchants of the main ports. They purchased merchandise from farmers and fishermen and then sold it to merchants in the port cities. Others were mill owners who procured raw grains, processed them, then sold flour and other products to merchants, acting like middlemen. They made it easier for smaller farmers to sell surplus products while earning credit or currency that could be exchanged for non-essential goods such as porcelain, tea, and manufactures. Large landowners also employed brokers and agents to help sell their agricultural products. While they were likely already well connected with merchants, many large landowners leaned on brokers and traders to find buyers long before expected harvest time. The large landowners sometimes employed a single full-time broker, and merchants trading on a large scale usually had their own agents or representatives, often family members or close friends.[88]

Merchants of these port cities and their partners or representatives at overseas destinations (the foreland) similarly depended on brokers and intermediaries for the sale of exported merchandise and procurement of the return cargo. Upon receiving orders, the recipient merchant procured goods through his network of brokers and intermediaries, prepared invoices, and consigned them to the principal merchant. The invoices often accompanied replies to

---

87   December 22, 1736, Account Book by Boston Merchant, 1736–41, MHS. The archive has not yet determined to whom the account book belonged.

88   Much of this information comes from a variety of account books, collections of papers, and letterbooks from various merchants, companies, and individuals from Boston, New York, and Philadelphia.

letters that contained orders specifying quantity and quality of goods. Goods were then listed as being consigned or to be delivered to a specific merchant. Ship captains were commonly promised commissions, especially when they acted as brokers at the destination. One such captain was Captain John Nutt, who operated his ship on behalf of other merchants who trusted him to act on their behalf. His ship's invoices frequently contained a list of goods and to whom they were consigned.[89] Key to organizing the various cargoes and destinations of cargoes, bills of lading were essential documents that listed the amount, type, and destinations of goods. Usually, three bills were prepared—one going with the cargo, one staying with the merchant, and one to be given to customs officials or receiving merchant. This practice was followed throughout the British Atlantic. Information contained in a bill of lading generally included the name of the ship, the origin of the voyage, the master or captain of the ship, and many of the copies that merchants kept for themselves included notes on the prices, values, and quantities of the goods shipped.[90] Merchants would also include a more detailed invoice either packed with the cargo or sent by mail as part of a letter (sometimes both).[91]

Maritime trade was a risky enterprise. Nautical hazards, pirates, and political conflicts could cause a loss of merchandise and ships. Merchants reduced the risk of financial catastrophe by obtaining insurance for their cargoes. Early in the eighteenth century, many merchants purchased insurance from another merchant who did not have a stake in the voyage. Letters from this period frequently contained discussions and negotiations between merchants about the value of a cargo, how much insurance would cost, and the terms of an insurance agreement. But, by the middle of the century, several insurance firms existed to insure ships and their cargoes in each of the three cities.[92] One insurance provider, Ezekiel Price, was a common provider of maritime insurance in Boston

---

89   Captain John Nutt Invoice Book, 1772–84, MHS. One of those merchants, Edward Ireland, was based in Barbados but regularly conducted trade between Marblehead, a feeder port of Boston, and the West Indies. Nutt sold several shipments of rum on behalf of Ireland in both Barbados and Marblehead.
90   Bills of lading can be found in a variety of archival records. Some merchants compiled their bills of lading into volumes for easier recordkeeping. Some examples of these are John Erving Bills of Lading, MHS, and Uriah Woolsman Bills of Lading, HSP.
91   A more detailed discussion of invoices can be found in the next chapter on commodities.
92   In 1763, there were fourteen insurance firms in British North America. Of those fourteen, twelve were based in Boston, New York, and Philadelphia and their feeding ports. The remaining two firms were in Providence, conveniently situated between Boston and New York. Boston dominated the insurance business, with major players, like Ezekiel Price, insuring merchants in all three cities.

and the surrounding ports. He maintained detailed records and receipts for insured cargoes, their values, and the premiums paid. The value of cargo was assessed, and a premium was applied to it by the insurer. In Price's records, premiums varied between 6 and 11 percent of the value of merchandise, most likely due to the track record of the individual requesting insurance, the type of good, and the destination of the ship. Rates tended to be higher as the length of the voyage increased, but insurance agents provided some exceptions to repeat customers or friends.[93]

Communication was key to the success of merchants in the early modern world, and this was no less true in colonial British America. Merchants relied on their widespread networks of partners and agents for information on prices, consumer demand, arrival and departure of ships, and their cargoes, in addition to political developments and government policies. Merchant ships crisscrossing the Atlantic Ocean carried letters and commercial papers transmitting vital information, which enabled merchants to respond to market conditions and make informed business decisions. Packet ships running between Boston, New York, and Philadelphia and their dependent ports facilitated a constant flow of information and provided opportunities for merchants to transact business throughout the region much more quickly and efficiently. These ships contained small cargoes or packages meant for specific individuals or merchants in the three ports. They also functioned as mail ships, carrying letters and information between merchants in different cities. An agent in Baltimore regularly updated his patron/client in Boston, Caleb Davis, on the prices of commodities that could be acquired there, such as grain, and informed him what goods were in high demand there.[94] In addition to local news, merchants would often share prices, which they received from friends or agents in European, Caribbean, or local North American ports, with their partners or close friends.[95] Gerard Beekman, unable to procure wheat in New York for a profitable price, arranged through his agent in Philadelphia for a cargo of grain to be shipped from there to Madeira.[96] Information received and shared among merchants could be used to negotiate prices with other merchants. When the firm of Greg and Cunningham in New York discovered that a merchant company in Manchester had sold goods of the same quality to another firm at a cheaper price than that given to Greg and Cunningham, it demanded

---

93   Ezekiel Price Receipt and Invoice Book, 1764–74, Ezekiel Price Papers, MHS.
94   Caleb Davis Papers, Box 5, April 1771, MHS.
95   Caleb Davis Papers, Box 5, MHS; OS Box 1, Folder 1774, MHS.
96   Harrington, "New York Merchant on the Eve of the Revolution," 77; *BMP*, 1:300.

a price match, writing to the Manchester company that they "expected an abatement only to put us on a footing with other people."[97]

Businessmen shared news from colonial governments, weather updates, notices of new ship arrivals, and other information necessary to make good commercial decisions. Generally, merchants cooperated in sharing as much as information as could be gathered, especially since news traveled slowly across the ocean, but the amount of information merchants provided to the community tended to be more general, such as wars, pirate activity, and weather conditions.

Once commodities landed in a port, merchants usually delivered a large percentage of their goods to waiting shopkeepers and retailers. Generally, merchants made sure that the goods they purchased from overseas had a buyer waiting in the city. They communicated specific requests to their partners, agents, and captains waiting in ports throughout the Atlantic. One merchant in 1740 wrote to a captain acting as his agent asking him to purchase wine in Lisbon on his return from Britain to Boston.[98] Responsiveness to demand was an essential function of the merchant, and packet ships plied the waters between major ports of call to accelerate the process.

As cooperative as the ports were, the merchants in each of the cities were also competitive. Throughout the eighteenth century, merchants within cities battled for a growing number of consumers. In newspapers, merchants advertised their goods, often remarking on the quality of the tea, porcelain, sugar, or salt they were peddling. Almost daily, ads highlighted recent shipments that arrived on newly arrived ships. For example, a single column in an issue of the *Boston Gazette* in 1735 highlighted three different advertisements. One from Samuel Otis described a list of sundry goods that included linens, gun powder, Jamaican sugar, New England and West Indian rum, and several more items. The second listed whale oil in both barrels and candles for sale most likely to other merchants who would ship some overseas or along the coast. The third advertised pepper, bohea tea, and nutmeg, all of which initially came from East Asia.[99]

Shipowners, often merchants in their own right, would regularly advertise when and to where they would sail in order to fill their hulls with as much product as possible. In Philadelphia in 1773, a half-dozen ships were waiting to leave the port for Europe. Some were heading to Dublin; others were heading

---

97   Greg and Cunningham to Hyde and Hamilton, Manchester, June 20, 1756, LGC, 157–58.
98   Henderson and Hewes to Captain James Dalton, June 27, 1740, Dalton Family Papers, vol. 3, MHS.
99   *Boston Gazette*, 1735, MHS.

to Belfast. Most were waiting to sail together as soon as the flaxseed harvest was complete, with which most were well laden. Though the advertisement was in a Philadelphia paper, one ship was waiting to leave from Baltimore, further evidence that smaller ports were often tied directly to Philadelphia's economy.[100]

From the beginning of the British colonial settlements in North America, the colonists had to conduct business under severe limitations, specifically a constant shortage of currency. Colonial governments attempted to create their own currencies with varying degrees of success. In Massachusetts, the colonial currency mirrored the structure of the British pound, but it never fully matched its value. In times of crisis and as political conflict became inevitable, colonial currencies lost their value relative to imperial specie.[101] Thus, currencies from all over the Atlantic World found their way into merchant coffers, and even colonial governments were forced to accept non-colonial and non-British currency for tax payments, often in direct opposition to laws otherwise. Thomas Hancock, for example, once received a collection of currencies that included Spanish dollars, French guineas, Portuguese moidores, and a variety of small silver and copper pieces from around the world.[102] Non-British currencies were so important to the economy that a New York paper published a list of coins and their value in comparison to the British pound sterling, listing coins from all over the world including but not limited to Dutch, Spanish, French, German, Portuguese, and Old English coins.[103] This list would surely have been useful for all merchants in the city to help mitigate uncertainty regarding the value of the many varieties of coins circulating.

Merchants overcame this problem of inadequate currency by taking advantage of the credit facility at the ports through bills of exchange. Eventually, the receipts and promises of payment often served as currency between merchants; credit, therefore, became a primary method of exchange between individuals. Merchants received or delivered goods on credit, anticipating a later payment in either currency or return goods. Accounting provided the opportunity to move goods throughout the Atlantic without a constant stream

---

100 November 19, 1773, *Pennsylvania Gazette*. This is just one of thousands of similar advertisements that can be found in nearly any major newspaper in colonial America. Even smaller papers farther inland would advertise for merchants or shipowners who had ships coming into or leaving Boston, New York, or Philadelphia. Generally, most ships would either leave from one of the three major ports or stop by to pick up more goods on the way out to ocean.
101 McCusker and Menard, *Economy of British America*, 337–38.
102 Baxter, *House of Hancock*, 15.
103 December 29, *New York Weekly Journal*.

of currency flowing throughout the region. So instead of bilateral exchange of commodities, most merchants engaged in multilateral trade, utilizing and extending credit where necessary. While most merchants sold goods on credit to their customers and partners, the debts were sometimes not paid, which then had to be litigated in the colonial court of law. Throughout the colonial period, court dockets were full of cases related to bad debts, including suits among partners and friends.[104] In one case in 1755, a captain from North Carolina, John Devereaux, attempted to cash a bill of exchange off Philadelphia merchant Charles Stewart for a cargo of goods. According to Stewart, another captain from North Carolina had failed to make delivery on another cargo that Stewart had ordered from his colleagues in the southern colony. Instead, the delinquent captain paid Devereaux for another cargo of goods with the credit he expected to receive from Stewart.[105] While in this particular example the system failed to properly function, it still shows the complexity of a system wherein merchants, captains, and consumers throughout the Atlantic could obtain, ship, and consume goods without the use of currency or specie.

The most common method of payment was the bill of exchange. Similar to a modern check, bills of exchange were used in place of currency when a merchant could not procure enough specie to pay the total balance. According to Arthur Jensen: "A bill of exchange was simply an order by a first person to his correspondent (i.e., banker) to pay a specified sum of money to the order of a third person named in the bill."[106] Other merchants might endorse another merchant's bills, or a signatory would guarantee payment with his own credit. Merchants could choose to accept or reject a bill, but in general practice, merchants used bills in much the same way as currency, especially as merchants kept careful accounting records as described above. Bills of exchange were essentially money orders that functioned like short-term loans. If one wished to pay for goods in London from Philadelphia, a person would approach someone who maintained regular commerce with merchants in London. They would buy a set amount of the credit or account that they held with their colleagues in London. Bills would be drawn for a certain period after "sight" or notification of a bill being drawn. The length of time varied depending on destination, size of bill, and so on. In New York, most bills were drawn for thirty or forty days. The drawee would then be able to use the buyer's money for a few months or more, and the buyer could safely expect his account in London paid, without

---

104 Amory Family Paper, Dalton Family Papers, Caleb Davis Papers, Jeffries Family Papers, MHS.
105 Charles Stewart to Mr. W. Jackson, January 6, 1755, Charles Stewart Letterbook, 1751–58, HSP.
106 Jensen, *Maritime Commerce of Colonial Philadelphia*, 14.

paying the extra costs of shipping and insuring a cargo or sending specie to pay the original bill.[107] Bills of exchange were only successful replacements for currency because of the robustness and complexity of the mercantile networks of colonial America. Without the development and maintenance of trust between merchants, bills would not have been as widely accepted. Bills of exchange also replaced local currency between non-merchants, all of which depended on the credit and reputation of one or more merchants.[108]

More often than not, merchants cobbled together a mix of these methods to conduct business, accepting specie when possible and extending credit when hard currency was in short supply. Commonly found among colonial merchant papers are receipts for transfers of goods where goods were purchased, and only a small portion was paid for with currency. Sometimes, merchants used or accepted multiple currencies. For example, several receipts in Caleb Davis's Papers from 1761 show partial payments in English sterling and "old tenor," a particularly undesirable form of colonial currency that rarely kept its value compared with the English pound.[109] Frequently, merchants exchanged colonial notes or specie for British pound sterling in order to pay for goods coming from outside the colonies. As Boston consumers developed stronger demand for goods from outside the British Empire, hard currencies, including Spanish pieces of eight, became essential for merchants to procure those goods. As an alternative, merchants acquired commodities from local producers, especially fish and wheat, to be exchanged in non-British ports, specifically Lisbon and Cádiz.[110]

5 Merchants and the Political Economy

Merchants often served as key political leaders in their respective cities. A number of them served on local city councils or assemblies. In the 1704 minutes of Philadelphia's Common Council, several merchants appear on the council list. In addition, large landowners served as aldermen or council members, and they were often aligned politically with merchants, at least in their efforts to

---

107 McCusker, *Money and Exchange in Europe and America*, 20–22.
108 McCusker, *Money and Exchange in Europe and America*, 14–16; Harrington, "New York Merchant on the Eve of the Revolution," 112–14.
109 While there are hundreds of receipts and documents that show this, this citation is one of the easiest to read and understand, with multiple examples within a single folder: Box 1, 1761 Folder, Caleb Davis Papers, MHS.
110 Box 1, 1761 Folder, Caleb Davis Papers, MHS; Dalton Family Papers, vol. 3, MHS.

use public funds to improve maritime and transportation infrastructure.[111] A similar prevalence of merchants in city leadership existed in both New York and Boston. In all three, local governments undertook major infrastructure projects, including warehouses, public markets, wharves, and interior roads.[112]

Sometimes, merchants invested directly in the infrastructure of their respective cities. In the 1670s, groups of Boston merchants joined forces and finances to help build sea walls, wharves, and warehouses that could be used by the merchants of the city. In the early eighteenth century, city councils again leaned on merchants to repair, build, and extend both public and private wharves to accommodate more ships and cargoes. Merchant investment in public infrastructure did not end at the shoreline. A small group of transoceanic traders, Oliver Noyes, Elisha Cook, William Payne, and David Jefferies, pooled money to substantially improve the main road that connected Boston to its hinterland farms in 1708. It was commonly washed out by seasonal flooding, and merchants had to rebuild it to continue receiving goods from the hinterland.[113] Merchants were also important financiers for churches, town halls, and other public buildings, earning both political and social capital in the process. Port cities relied heavily on merchants for assistance in times of crises, such as fires, not only for rebuilding efforts but to help supply emergency funds for operations.[114]

Merchants, therefore, were active participants in local policymaking, in both city and provincial governments. Already by the 1700s, merchants were quick to resist any efforts to regulate commerce within and among the colonies. In 1685, New York's governor attempted to impose export and import duties to protect the profits of wealthier merchants in New York by preventing New York vessels from landing or loading goods in any of the feeder ports. This protected the wealthier merchants as they controlled much of the available docks and wharves, forcing both hinterland producers and merchants to go through the elite and influential merchants of New York. Merchants successfully lobbied the city and provincial governments to end many of these sorts of

---

111   *Minutes of the Common Council of the City of Philadelphia, 1704 to 1776*.
112   Matson, *Merchants & Empire*, 165; Boston Records Commissioners, *A Report of the Record Commissioners of the City of Boston, Containing the Selectmen's Minutes from 1764 through 1768* (Boston: Rockwell and Churchill, City Printers, 1889). The Boston Records Commissioners published several volumes of colonial records, and this is just one example of many that provide names and functions of various city leaders. See bibliography for a more complete listing of records available.
113   Hunter, *Purchasing Identity in the Atlantic World*, 84–87.
114   *Minutes of the Common Council of the City of Philadelphia, 1704 to 1776*, 491–92; Hunter, *Purchasing Identity in the Atlantic World*, 84–87.

localized policies that resembled the mercantilist and monopolist policies of the metropolis, policies that tended to restrict rather than support open access to both local and global markets.[115]

Throughout the colonial period, merchants promoted policies that encouraged free, or at least easier, access to markets and resisted policies that placed undue burden on the profitability of merchants. Often, many of their positions resembled some of the ideas that Adam Smith would later put to paper in his famous treatise *The Wealth of Nations*. In Boston, profit and wealth became an identifying mark of God's blessings, leading many to consider governmental restrictions on the ability to make a profit, especially from commerce, not only bad for business but also an affront to the creator.[116] In New York in the 1720s, the provincial government sought to impose duties on imports into the colony. Merchants opposed those measures, even though provincial officials suggested they could just pass along the costs to consumers. Merchants replied that eventually only the wealthiest could afford the products they imported, limiting economic growth and profitability.[117]

By the 1760s, city governments were overwhelmed with issues related to maritime commerce. As imperial policies gradually eroded the de facto free access to markets and commercial opportunities of British American merchants, political leaders were inundated with protests from angry traders seeking recompense or relief from increasingly oppressive policies from the imperial administration of Britain, but they also continued to argue against local policies that inhibited free trade. Between 1768 and 1770, the first two years of British military occupation in Boston, the city council of selectmen installed price controls on grain and bread in an effort to limit the impact of rising grain prices on the consumers in Boston. Importers of grain were understandably upset. They viewed the restrictions as limiting the profitability and viability of the grain import business. While they vocally opposed and sometimes ignored the price controls, Boston's grain importers were only successful in adjusting upwards the price-limits on occasion, especially in 1770 when wholesale prices were the most severe.[118] In the eighteenth century, merchants

---

115   Matson, *Merchants & Empire*, 101–2.
116   Hunter, *Purchasing Identity in the Atlantic World*, 20–25.
117   Matson, *Merchants and Empire*, 165–66.
118   Boston Records Commissioners, *A Report of the Records Commissioners of the City of Boston, Containing the Selectmen's Minutes from 1769 through April, 1775* (Boston: Rockwell and Churchill, City Printers, 1893), 3; Gary B. Nash, *The Urban Crucible: Social Change, Political Consciousness, and the Origins of the American Revolution* (Cambridge, MA: Harvard University Press, 1979), 414; Commons Debate, April 19, 1774, printed in

played a significant role in the political economies of Boston, New York, and Philadelphia and exerted their influence in shaping the colonial government's policies on trade and economy.

6 Conclusion

One word can adequately describe the mercantile networks of Boston, New York, and Philadelphia: complex. Between 1700 and 1775, merchants gradually diversified both their commerce and the ways in which they conducted business, including financial and industrial ventures by providing capital and credit for local economic development. The region's merchants found a variety of ways to overcome the disadvantages of being on the edge of the empire. They used clever accounting methods and a mixture of payment methods to import and export goods and services, overcoming the constant shortages of currency and lack of financial support from the metropole. Communication, both private and public, was the glue that held the region's merchants together and the web that connected it with the larger Atlantic and global mercantile community. Later, merchants throughout the region used their commercial networks for more political topics of discussion. Merchant cooperation was key in the growing movements of non-importation in the late 1760s and early 1770s. Merchants were acutely aware of the adverse consequences of stricter enforcement of British mercantilist policies for their trade and other economic activities. Therefore, they used their favored status within colonial society to help lead the efforts to resist what they viewed as oppressive imperial policies.

Proceedings and Debates of the British Parliament Respecting North America, 1754–1783, ed. R. C. Simmons and P. D. G. Thomas (Millwood, NY: Kraus International Publications, 1984), 3:180–81. The price control debate is not limited to the above-cited source from the Boston Selectmen Minutes. Rather, it is indicative of the ways in which price controls were implemented. Protests were filed regularly, and occasional entries deal with violations to price limitations.

CHAPTER 3

Trade and Commodities

Merchants and their extensive commercial networks facilitated exchange of commodities on a large scale between Boston, New York, and Philadelphia and the ports and hinterlands on both European and American shores of the Atlantic Ocean. In the eighteenth century, these port cities imported, exported, consumed, and produced myriad commodities, many of which traversed the oceans of the world to find consumers. These commodities bound Boston, New York, and Philadelphia to one another and with other ports of the Atlantic Ocean and the global maritime economy. This chapter seeks to understand the importance of this trade for the region's economy, the reasons why certain goods were exported and imported to and from various parts of the world, and how merchants navigated the challenges of restrictive imperial policies. First, it details the primary imports and exports of each city in comparison with one another while keeping an eye on the region's influence in the Atlantic economy. Sugar and East Indian goods take center stage as Boston, New York, and Philadelphia maintained a special relationship with those goods. Finally, the chapter closes with a study of the ways in which demand for certain goods imported into the region were communicated and how those goods found their way into the hands of consumers. The volume and variety of goods flowing through Boston, New York, and Philadelphia establishes the importance of the region as a nodal center within the Atlantic and global economies.

Much of the older historiography provides little agency to commodities or the consumers who purchased those goods. Older histories tend to assume that the monopolies of the East India Company and merchants of England dominated trade in British America, forcing consumers to purchase the products they provided, yet the East India Company was only involved in the importation of tea and East Asian goods. It had little or nothing to do with exports leaving British America and even less to do with non-Asian imports.[1] More recently, historians and economists have used various approaches to investigate these networks that do not give preeminence to the efforts of governments. Some focus on specific commodities, such as David Hancock and his study of Madeira wine. According to Hancock, consumer demand, individuals,

---

1 Merritt, *Trouble with Tea*, 3–5.

and market forces were far more influential in the creation and maintenance of trade networks for Madeira than imperial policies or state-chartered monopolies. It was the interplay between individuals and the market that established Madeira as a commercial product, not mercantilism or any specific imperial policy. The state was influential, but it was not the primary force in the wine market in the Atlantic.[2]

In her seminal work on tobacco and chocolate, Marcy Norton explains that many commodities fail to find consumers quickly. Some are even condemned by religious elites or considered disgusting by experimental consumers. Norton writes, "The initial revulsion that so often characterized European first encounters with tobacco and chocolate is part of the reason Europeans did not use these goods on a wide scale until the seventeenth century."[3] Often, commodities only found consumers thanks to the exotic nature attributed to them by European elites fascinated with other cultures and their products. In addition to the difficulties in finding consumers, some commodities require extensive manipulation from raw form to produce a good ready for consumption. In the case of chocolate, it requires the cacao pod to be broken down into its seeds, fermented, ground, and then brewed like a beverage. Only then was it consumed by Europeans, and even after all the processing, consumers usually mixed it with flavoring and sweeteners.[4]

In British America, the state had little direct influence on the composition of the goods that traveled into and out of the three ports. However, it did have an influence on the conditions of trade in that it attempted to enforce a mercantilist system with the colonies serving as the consumer base for Britain's exports while at the same time producing raw materials and foodstuffs for the metropole. Unfortunately for Britain, its limited capacity to either enforce or provide a large enough market for the products of Boston, New York, and Philadelphia effectively forced colonial merchants to look elsewhere for the profit and specie to afford their imports from Europe and Britain. As discussed in the following pages, the imbalance of trade with far more goods flowing from Britain and into the three ports than vice versa placed American merchants and consumers in a difficult spot. While the next two chapters explore the consequences of such imbalances, the composition of the three cities' maritime trade provides a foundation that will help explain why trade flowed in certain directions.

---

2   Hancock, *Oceans of Wine*.
3   Marcy Norton, *Sacred Gifts, Profane Pleasures: A History of Tobacco and Chocolate in the Atlantic World* (Ithaca, NY: Cornell University Press, 2008), 8.
4   Norton, *Sacred Gifts, Profane Pleasures*, 7–10.

1   **Imports**

Boston, New York, and Philadelphia imported many of the same commodities, with the only difference being the volumes of goods. As much of the food, fuel, and other goods necessary for sustenance were already in abundance in the three cities, the region primarily required luxury items, clothing, and raw materials, such as sugar and molasses for making rum. In comparison with their European counterparts, white colonial Americans had higher purchasing power and cheaper and easier access to food and necessities.[5] As such, the region primarily imported European manufactures, sugar products, salt, and wine—all luxury products, with the exception of clothing and metal products.

In all three ports, English and European manufactures, salt, and sugar products (including rum, molasses, and muscovado) were the primary types received by merchants and consumers in the region.[6] By the middle of the eighteenth century, however, East Asian goods became more important to the overall economy of the region, with tea, Asian textiles, and spices appearing more frequently in retail shops and ship invoices. Nevertheless, the buying power of the three ports increased dramatically by the 1760s. In Philadelphia, for example, Isaac Norris, a prominent merchant in the region, estimated that Philadelphians imported at least £15,000 worth of English manufactures in 1707, but by the 1770s, more than £600,000 of British goods were offloaded on the docks of Philadelphia.[7] All three cities experienced substantial increases in the quantities and values of imports in the eighteenth century, and the numbers and types of European manufactures and reexports made invoices and customs documents more complex. The main imports into these three cities can be grouped into four categories: manufactures, East Asian goods, sugar products, and salt.

---

5   Lindert and Williamson, *Unequal Gains*, 39–42, 60–64, see especially tables labeled in the source as 3-4, 3-5, 3-6, and figure 3-3 The purchasing power of New Englanders was more closely aligned with Europeans, but the Middle Colonies (which according to Lindert and Williamson includes New York and Philadelphia) had a much higher purchasing power relative to Europeans, bringing up the region's average purchasing power.
6   A primary good in this discussion is one that is imported and consumed by most of the entire region's merchants and consumers.
7   Isaac Norris to William Penn, April 2–3, 1707, in *Correspondence between William Penn and James Logan, Secretary of the Province of Pennsylvania, and Others, 1700–1750*, ed. Edward Armstrong (Philadelphia: J. B. Lippincott and Co., for the Historical Society of Pennsylvania, 1872), 2:203; David MacPherson, *Annals of Commerce, Manufactures, Fisheries, and Navigation with Brief Notices of the Arts and Sciences Connected with Them* (London: n.p., 1805), 3:564.

Manufactures were items that were processed into finished products, such as clothing, metal wares, and furniture. These items can largely be considered luxury goods, except for metal products. Clothing and furniture were marketed largely at middle-class consumers in quality and price, as basic clothing and furniture could be made in most colonial homes. Pots, pans, and tools came in every level of quality and price imaginable. For the most part, the colonies depended upon Europe to provide the metal products they required, as the colonies were limited in their ability to produce finished metal wares.[8] They did develop a larger capacity to manufacture metal products over time, but it did not replace the need to import European metal goods.[9]

East Asian goods included tea, spices, silks, and porcelain. Again, these goods could largely be considered luxury items, especially spices and porcelain. Tea, on the other hand, did not find a ready and willing market in British America until the 1740s, and when it finally became a desirable commodity, its use quickly became ubiquitous. Its large-scale consumption was in no small part due to the availability of sugar to help sweeten the drink. The stimulation provided by the caffeine in the tea, initially treated with much skepticism by colonists, offered elites, artisans, and laborers a relatively cheap energy boost. While elites still preferred more expensive varieties such as green and oolong, most other consumers in the cities of Boston, New York, and Philadelphia could buy bohea tea.[10]

Sugar products and salt, the last two categories, were important not only for local consumption but also to produce commodities for export. While refined sugar was in high demand in all three port cities and their hinterlands, molasses was also important for the large distilling industries in the region. While Boston dominated the production of rum, New York and Philadelphia also imported molasses and exported rum in large quantities.[11] Salt was an important import from Southern Europe as it was used to produce dried fish, which was then exported to Portugal, Spain, and the West Indies. It was also used to preserve beef and pork, which were also important exports for the region. Sugar products and salt also helped add calories and variety to the colonial dinner table, adding flavor to other commodities and products.[12] While these

---

8   McCusker and Menard, *Economy of British America*, 309–12.
9   See chapter 2 for more on the development of local iron production.
10 Merritt, *Trouble with Tea*, 45–50.
11 John J. McCusker, "The Rum Trade and the Balance of Payments of the Thirteen Continental Colonies, 1650–1775," *Journal of Economic History* 30, no. 1 (March 1970): 244–47.
12 McCusker and Menard, *Economy of British America*, 108–10.

TABLE 7   Value of colonial imports in 1744–48 and 1754–58 (£ sterling)

Year	£
1744	640,115
1745	534,316
1746	754,945
1747	726,648
1748	830,244
Total	3,486,268
1754	1,246,615
1755	1,177,848
1756	1,428,721
1757	1,727,924
1758	1,832,949
Total	7,414,057

SOURCE: TIMOTHY PITKIN, *A STATISTICAL VIEW OF THE COMMERCE OF THE UNITED STATES OF AMERICA* (NEW YORK: JAMES EASTBURN AND COMPANY, 1816), 12–13. THE TABLE INCLUDES FIGURES FROM THE THIRTEEN COLONIES THAT BECAME THE UNITED STATES

four categories of goods are not inclusive of all the imports that arrived in the region's ports, they contain the most important commodities to the region's economy.

Imports into these three cities continuously grew throughout the eighteenth century, mirroring or exceeding the level of growth throughout colonial America. The value of colonial imports increased substantially from the 1740s to the 1750s (Table 7). Combined with the data from Tables 8 and 9, which highlight the import levels in each region by commodity and category, it is clear that imports and consumption of goods in colonial America were substantial, easily accommodating the growing populations of the three ports. For example, the total value of English imports in 1768–72 was more than £14.1 million, and total imports, not just English, for the 1754–58 period were a little more than £7.4 million, indicating a substantial increase in import levels for the thirteen colonies that became the United States.

TABLE 8   Yearly average commodity imports by New England and the Middle Colonies, 1768–72 (£ sterling)

Commodity (unit)	Yearly average 1768–1772					
	Southern Europe		West Indies		Total	
	Quantity	Value	Quantity	Value	Quantity	Value
New England						
Coffee (cwt)	-	-	764	3,143	764	3,143
Cotton (lb)	-	-	303,031	13,645	303,031	13,645
Molasses (gal)	-	-	2,808,496	141,361	2,808,496	141,361
Rum (gal)	-	-	734,058	74,834	734,058	74,834
Salt (bu)	210,895	11,033	402,136	20,949	613,031	31,982
Sugar (cwt)	-	-	25,186	40,426	25,186	40,426
Wine (tn)	113	6,952	2	105	115	7,057
Middle Colonies						
Coffee (cwt)	-	-	1,824	7,787	1,824	7,787
Cotton (lb)	-	-	102,246	4,417	102,246	4,417
Molasses (gal)	-	-	750,178	42,051	750,178	42,051
Rum (gal)	-	-	1,001,334	102,423	1,001,384	102,423
Salt (bu)	186,681	9,719	59,380	3,141	246,060	12,860
Sugar (cwt)	-	-	38,413	61,035	38,413	61,035
Wine (tn)	362	22,489	1	87	364	22,576
Regional Total						
Coffee (cwt)	-	-	2,588	10,930	2,588	10,930
Cotton (lb)	-	-	405,276	18,061	405,276	18,061
Molasses (gal)	-	-	3,558,674	183,413	3,558,674	183,413
Rum (gal)	-	-	1,735,442	177,257	1,735,442	177,257
Salt (bu)	397,576	20,752	461,516	24,091	859,091	44,842
Sugar (cwt)	-	-	63,599	101,461	63,599	101,461
Wine (tn)	476	29,442	3	192	479	29,634
Total Value		*50,193*		*515,405*		*565,598*

SOURCE: JAMES F. SHEPHERD AND GARY M. WALTON, SHIPPING, MARITIME TRADE AND THE ECONOMIC DEVELOPMENT OF COLONIAL NORTH AMERICA (CAMBRIDGE: CAMBRIDGE UNIVERSITY PRESS, 1972), 228–29

Boston, New York, and Philadelphia traded with both Southern Europe and the West Indies on a large scale. Sugar, molasses, and rum from the West Indies and salt and wine from Southern Europe comprised the main imports. The region maintained an immense appetite for sugar, and other commodities such as tea, coffee, and cocoa, and relied on sugar to make them more appetizing to consumers. McCusker has rightly noted that local consumption, especially of rum and sugar, outpaced other parts of the world with nearly twenty gallons of rum consumed per year for each adult male.[13]

For Boston, salt was an essential part of the economy. Without it, the fisheries would have been largely useless as salt made cod more profitable and practical. Salted cod was sold to Spanish and Portuguese consumers in exchange for wine and salt.[14] Boston also traded its salted cod for the sugar, molasses, and rum it received from the Caribbean. In Philadelphia and New York, salt and wine were in high demand in both diets and local production. Instead of salted cod, Philadelphia and New York exchanged grains, flour, and bread for sugar, salt, and wine.

English imports, while a large portion of total imports into the three ports, were as varied as they were numerous. Much of the historiography tends to equate the apparent negative balance of trade that the colonies maintained with Britain with dependency.[15] Though there is a kernel of truth to that argument, especially when one only examines the relationship between Britain and its colonies, imports from Britain were so diverse that the invoices that accompanied shipments from London to Boston, New York, or Philadelphia often listed hundreds of different types and quantities of goods. Furthermore, the historical compilations frequently grouped many different commodities and goods together into a small number of categories, limiting historians' understanding of what "manufactures" were being imported into the colonies. As a result, we must look closer at the archives to discover how and why colonists

---

13   John J. McCusker, *Rum and the American Revolution: The Rum Trade and the Balance of Payments of the Thirteen Colonies* (New York: Garland Publishing, 1989); for a shorter overview of the importance of the rum trade, see also McCusker, "Rum Trade and the Balance of Payments of the Thirteen Continental Colonies," 244–47.

14   Vickers, *Farmers and Fishermen*, 98–100.

15   Shepherd and Walton, *Shipping, Maritime Trade and the Economic Development of Colonial North America*, 137–38. Other examples include Hancock, *Citizens of the World*; Robert Paul Thomas, "A Quantitative Approach to the Study of the Effects of British Imperial Policy upon Colonial Welfare: Some Preliminary Findings," *Journal of Economic History* 25, no. 4 (December 1965): 615–38; and T. H. Breen, *The Marketplace of Revolution: How Consumer Politics Shaped American Independence* (Oxford: Oxford University Press, 2004).

TABLE 9   Official values of colonial imports from Britain, 1768–72 (£ sterling)

Destination	Class of Imports	1768–72	Yearly Avg.	% of Total
Northern Colonies	British	1,215,992	243,198	82%
	Reexport	261,579	52,316	18%
	Total	1,477,571	295,514	100%
New England	British	2,289,383	457,877	68%
	Reexport	1,162,275	232,455	35%
	Total	3,351,457	670,291	100%
Middle Colonies	British	3,370,560	674,112	82%
	Reexport	740,738	148,148	18%
	Total	4,111,298	822,260	100%
Upper South	British	3,659,912	731,982	79%
	Reexport	960,923	192,185	21%
	Total	4,620,835	924,167	100%
Lower South	British	1,847,371	369,474	90%
	Reexport	213,467	42,693	10%
	Total	2,060,838	412,168	100%
Florida, Bahamas and Bermuda	British	256,888	51,378	90%
	Reexport	27,101	5,420	10%
	Total	283,989	56,798	100%
Total	British	12,539,905	2,507,981	79%
	Reexport	3,365,083	673,217	21%
	Total	15,905,988	3,181,198	100%

SOURCE: JAMES F. SHEPHERD AND GARY M. WALTON, *SHIPPING, MARITIME TRADE AND THE ECONOMIC DEVELOPMENT OF COLONIAL NORTH AMERICA* (CAMBRIDGE: CAMBRIDGE UNIVERSITY PRESS, 1972), 235–36

imported British goods. This negative balance of trade required a substantial positive balance of trade with other parts of the world. As chapters 4 and 5 make clear, the colonies looked beyond the British Empire to find the profits necessary to continue importing an ever-increasing amount of British goods.

The figures in Tables 8 and 9 show that average annual values of imports from Great Britain were quite substantial, about three-fifths of the total imports into the region. These figures do not include coastal trade, as data for coastal trade is not as easy to track. According to James Shepherd and Samuel Williamson, during 1768–72, at least another £467,000 worth of goods was imported from coastal North America into the region.[16] There is evidence to suggest that these figures are likely underestimated due to the inaccuracies of the customs offices in the colonies—a fact that Shepherd and Williamson noted.[17] Considering that merchants consistently sought to avoid customs agents for a variety of commodity imports, including coastal trade and trans-imperial trade, the numerous small ports, coves, bays, and rivers provided ample opportunities to land and trade goods without being counted.[18]

For Britain, the American colonies were essential to the export trade of British manufactures and reexports from other parts of the world. In Table 10 below, selected commodities imported by British and American merchants into British America are shown alongside the percentage of total British exports that the quantities represent. English exports to British America accounted for more than 50 percent of many of the listed commodities. Iron, copper, printed cotton, and silk are some examples of the importance of British America to English merchants and manufacturing. Iron nails and linen were extremely dependent on colonial consumers and importers, as British American imports accounted for more than three-quarters of total British exports for those goods.[19] As New England and the Middle Colonies accounted for roughly half of all British imports into America (see Table 9), it is likely that Boston, New York, and Philadelphia were the main recipients of British exports to the colonies.

British imports into Boston, New York, and Philadelphia were an important part of the region's overall economy, not just the import economy. Looking more closely at the invoices of American merchants provides a detailed view of goods arriving in these cities. Below is a transcription of an invoice

---

16   James F. Shepherd and Samuel H. Williamson, "The Coastal Trade of the British North American Colonies, 1768–1772," *Journal of Economic History* 32, no. 4 (December 1972): 798.
17   Shepherd and Williamson, "Coastal Trade of the British North American Colonies," 785.
18   There are multiple examples of letters between merchants attempting to land goods without being inspected by customs agents. One example is Waddell Cunningham to Isaac and Zachary Hope, Rotterdam, May 10, 1756, LGC, 99. In this particular case, Cunningham wrote to his partner in Rotterdam that there were delays in getting the ship offloaded, but that it would happen as soon as they could find a suitable place to land the goods without the prying eyes of customs agents. In terms of coastal trade that circumvented normal entry and exit procedures, see Chard, "Massachusetts–Louisbourg Trade, 1713–1744."
19   Elizabeth Boody Schumpeter, *English Overseas Trade Statistics, 1697–1808* (Oxford: Oxford University Press, 1960), 63–69.

TABLE 10 Selected english exports to British America, 1770

Commodity	Quantities Exported to British America	% of Total Exported from England
Coal	6,085 chaldrons	2.8
Pilchards	160 hogsheads	0.8
White salt	11,024 pounds	23
Refined sugar	12,062 hundredweight	31.7
Wrought brass	8,073 hundredweight	25.2
Wrought copper	13,778 hundredweight	55.3
Wrought iron	130,687 hundredweight	59.8
Lead & shot	1,652 fodders	9.3
Tin	216 hundredweight	31.7
Beaver hats	10,790 dozen	69.4
Cordage	11,837 hundredweight	65.6
Glassware & earthenware	2,742,253 pieces	47.9
Iron nails	24,147 hundredweight	76.5
Tanned leather	408 hundredweight	5.2
Fustians	5,116 pieces	15.7
Linen	88,072 pieces	79.2
Wrought silk	30,978 pounds	57.2
Printed cotton & linen	155,789 yards	58.9
Double bays	17,812 pieces	19.9
Single bays	8,702 pieces	12.3
Long cloths	5,176 pieces	15.8
Short cloths	18,249 pieces	36.8
Spanish cloths	1,985 pieces	70.4
Flannel	346,740 yards	42.6
Perpets & surges	76,396 pounds	2.2
Men's worsted stockings	28,806 dozen pairs	34.9
Stuffs	1,225,750 pounds	14.8

SOURCE: ELIZABETH BOODY SCHUMPETER, *ENGLISH OVERSEAS TRADE STATISTICS, 1697–1808* (OXFORD: OXFORD UNIVERSITY PRESS, 1960), 63–69

received by Joseph Ogden in Philadelphia from an English firm named Neate and Neave:

> Invoice of Sundrys Ship'd by Neate and Neave on Board the Troton Cap'tn James Shirley to Philadelphia on the proper Account and Risque of Joseph Ogden there and to him Consigned
>
> London, August 31, 1750[20]

			£	d	p
O*	Ground Red Wood qt. £4 d1 p14				
	R------------------------d2 p25 *Custom*		-	3	-
	Neate £3 d2 p17 at 28/		5	2	3
32	Cask			2	6
	Fine Umbr's Madder qt 4"1"14 Custom		9	3	6
	R-------------------------2"14			7	
	Neate 3"3"- at 50/				
33	Cask			2	6
	4 Gro. Best small aul blades at 2/6			10	
	1 Gro. Best Pegging Do Sorted			9	6
	4 Gro. Small steel Tacks sorted at 6.5			2	2
	1 Gro. Farthing ditto			2	2
	2 Doz Small Sharp 3 Sqr files at 20			3	4
	2 Doz fine flatt rasps at 4/			8	
	2 Doz fine ½ round Do at 4/			8	
	56 Best Blue Alepo Galls at 75/		1	17	6
	2 Large 4to Bibles		2		
	1 Elwoods Sacred History 2 vols.		1	1	
34	Cask			1	10
	2 pr Double Crown Lin'n qt 18q Ells on Boat 8		6	6	
	2 pr Double Sprigg Do 164 Do 8 3/8		5	19	7
	Inside Wrapper ----- 21 ------ 6 ½			11	4
35	Bale 14 Ells Hessen 7 ¼			8	5
	1 pr ½ White Watered Tabby 28 ½ 6/6		9	5	3
	1 pr Ditto ------- 29 -------- 7/9		11	4	9
	Paper Parcel in a Trunk PG 120				

---

20 Joseph Ogden Invoice Records, 1749–55, HSP. This is one of the shortest invoices available. Many within this source go on for several pages and total in the hundreds and thousands of pounds sterling. This invoice was chosen specifically for its relative brevity. *This is the mark of the merchant company, but it does not translate well in a transcription. In effect, it should be a circle within a diamond.

To Entry Shiping and Debent'r Charges		18	6
Freight prim'a & Bills Lading	2	8	7
Insurance on £60 at 2 ½ pct per policy 1/	1	11	
Comm:o 2 ½ pct on £60	1	10	
	62	7	8
By Bounty on 7 ½ wrought silk at 3/	1	2	6
	£ 61	5	2

Errors Excepted
Neate & Neave

In this invoice, Ogden has imported a variety of goods, most of which appear to be small items, such as tacks, books, and linens. There is a reason to believe, based on Ogden's records, that most of the items he imported were specifically requested by consumers in Philadelphia. He appears to be responding to consumer demand, and many of the other invoices contain very specific quantities of goods, generally packed into casks, chests, or bales. The containers were then branded with a merchant's mark (or several) identifying the containers from others.

2   East Asian Goods

A significant portion of colonial imports into New England and the Middle Colonies consisted of commodities that Britain received from Asia and other parts of Europe. In 1768–72, this comprised 35 and 18 percent of the total imports from Britain to these colonies respectively. Most of these goods were likely Asian goods, such as tea, pepper, and textiles. British mercantilist policies limited the importation of Asian goods into British America to British merchants and British ships alone. Britain, therefore, was certainly supposed to be the main supplier of Asian goods to its American colonies. Importing Asian commodities into Boston, New York, and Philadelphia by other channels was considered illegal, but as chapter 5 shows, this may not have deterred many from conducting illicit trade.

By far the most ubiquitous and famous East Asian commodity in colonial America, tea became a staple of colonial American diets and retail shops. Initially, in the 1720s and 1730s, tea was met with disgust and skepticism from American colonists. Many ministers and political leaders in Boston, New York, and Philadelphia considered the good a luxury item that symbolized excess and the exotic. It was not uncommon to find treatises and pamphlets warning of the evils the "wicked" leaf could have on families and one's soul. Women especially were targeted by the campaign against tea, suggesting that women who partook in the stimulant were more susceptible to gossip and evil suggestions.[21] Nevertheless, tea along with the sweetness that sugar provided eventually found a ready and willing consumer base in British America.

By the 1760s, hundreds of thousands of pounds of tea found its way to British American shores. England alone exported nearly five million pounds (weight) of tea to the American colonies between 1761 and 1775 (Table 11). It is not entirely certain exactly how much tea found its way to the tables of American colonists, as smuggling was a concern for English officials especially regarding the import of tea. Tea was a popular and, apparently, easy commodity to smuggle. Wim Klooster suggests that as much as 75 percent of all tea consumed in the colonies was smuggled from non-English sources.[22] If that is true, then as much as twenty million pounds of tea were imported into British America between 1761 and 1775.

Boston, New York, and Philadelphia were the most important ports for English imports of tea. During 1761–75, imports into these three ports comprised 82 percent of all English tea brought into British America (Table 11). This is not surprising, especially when one considers the primary locations of resistance to British efforts to enforce the East India Company's monopoly of tea. The infamous tea party of Boston in 1773 was accompanied by similar protests and "parties" throughout the colonies.[23] Moreover, the population of the region was far more dense around the ports of Boston, New York, and Philadelphia than the populations of Virginia, the Carolinas, and the rest of British America. However, a more practical reason for the discrepancy is that Boston, New York, and Philadelphia exported and imported a significant proportion of other commodities to and from all parts of the Atlantic. In effect, the region was the largest importer in British America regardless of the origin or type of good imported.

Textiles and spices were imported frequently. Unfortunately, spices are hard to track in the customs records, as they were used as ballast or filler for packaging other items such as wine and rum. More often, they appear as "dry goods" in invoices or in advertisements for products. Pepper was a popular item in the region, and a newspaper advertisement by Greg and Cunningham, a New York firm, offered "many other articles of DRY goods; also pepper, gunpowder, lead, shot ..." and more.[24] Sometimes, merchants in the three cities imported East

---

21 Merritt, *Trouble with Tea*, 44–49.
22 Klooster, "Inter-imperial Smuggling in the Americas," 179.
23 Merritt, *Trouble with Tea*, 106–7.
24 November 22, 1756, *New York Mercury*.

TRADE AND COMMODITIES 83

TABLE 11 Tea imported from England by American Colonies, 1761–75 (in pounds)

Year	New England	New York	Pennsylvania	Virginia & Maryland	Carolinas	Georgia	Florida	Total
1761	6,992	3,837	144	22,244	22,893	-	-	56,110
1762	51,618	70,460	7,884	12,773	17,850	1,003	-	161,588
1763	37,525	83,870	18,281	23,481	22,860	2,768	-	188,785
1764	143,284	265,385	41,949	18,249	18,374	1,989	72	489,252
1765	175,389	226,232	54,538	23,280	36,067	2,918	-	518,424
1766	118,982	124,464	60,796	29,177	20,112	6,798	672	361,001
1767	152,435	177,111	87,741	36,088	24,261	2,325	415	480,276
1768	291,899	320,214	174,883	41,944	34,639	5,212	4,953	873,744
1769	86,004	4,282	81,729	37,355	12,982	4,426	2,661	229,439
1770	85,935	269	-	18,270	1,175	2,980	1,757	110,386
1771	282,857	1,035	495	32,961	36,385	5,420	3,104	362,257
1772	151,184	530	128	78,117	22,916	10,265	1,742	264,882
1773	206,312	208,385	208,191	26,491	83,959	5,070	813	739,221
1774	30,161	1,304	-	31,273	4,332	3,661	2,543	73,274
1775	8,005	-	-	8,825	-	-	5,368	22,198
Total	1,828,582	1,487,378	736,759	440,528	358,805	54,835	24,100	4,930,837

SOURCE: CHAPTER Z, UNITED STATES DEPARTMENT OF COMMERCE, *HISTORICAL STATISTICS OF THE UNITED STATES FROM COLONIAL TIMES TO 1970: BICENTENNIAL EDITION* (U.S. GOVERNMENT PRINTING OFFICE, WASHINGTON, D.C.: 1975), 1192

Asian goods to reexport to other parts of North America as part of smaller collections of "sundry" goods. In one example, Daniel Clark shipped nutmeg and green tea as part of a larger shipment of goods in 1761 to a customer in the newly conquered port of Quebec.[25]

Many of the textiles exported from Britain were either reexported or manufactured from East Asian imports. As we can see in Table 10, silk was a substantial part of the British exports to British America. The colonies, as a whole, comprised 57 percent of total British exports of silk, most of which was imported from East Asia, but the British East India Company also imported silks from Persia and Italy.[26] All sorts of silk found a way into Boston, New York, and Philadelphia. One invoice contained fifty bags of basic silk, a small amount of fine silk twist, silk thread, and other smaller silk-made items.[27] Though it is not always clear in the invoices which type of cloth was made in Britain and which was made in Asia, two distinct indicators can be used to determine the origin of the cloth. Detailing the origins of cloth was important for pricing the good, but it also determined how the good was treated by customs agents. Some merchants delineated between broad cloth and fine cloth, with fine cloth carrying a higher cost.[28] Another way is to compare the price of listed items. In general, cloth from Asia carried a higher price than European-manufactured cloth, but occasionally English cloth would be dyed with East Asian indigo, greatly adding value to English cloth.[29]

3   Exports

Whereas British American colonies south of Pennsylvania largely exported staple crops such as tobacco and rice, Boston, New York, and Philadelphia exported wheat and fish products, much of which had already been processed, to Southern colonies, the West Indies, French and, later, British Canada, and Europe.[30] All three ports had a similar composition of commodity exports, with one exception. Wheat and flour constituted their major overseas exports (which includes Britain, Europe, and the West Indies) for New York and Philadelphia (see Table 12). Boston mainly exported dried fish and salted cod.

---

25   Daniel Clark Letter and Invoice Book, 1760–62, p. 54, HSP.
26   Schumpeter, *English Overseas Trade Statistics*, 63–69.
27   Benjamin Dolbeare Invoice Book, vol. 2, Invoice no. 16, May 10, 1740, MHS.
28   Tench Francis Invoice Book, 1759–61, 12, HSP.
29   Tench Francis Invoice Book, 1759–61, 20, HSP.
30   Shepherd and Williamson, "Coastal Trade of the British North America Colonies," 788–93.

In large part due to the growing distance between merchants and producers, Boston, New York, and Philadelphia experienced a substantial increase in the number of refineries, mills, and distilleries. The profitability of more refined products was much higher than raw forms of commodities. For example, the large part of grain exports from Philadelphia was raw grains in the first three to four decades of the eighteenth century, but by the 1760s the largest proportion of its trade, in terms of value, was bread and flour. In Boston, distilleries capitalized on the growing consumption of rum, turning imported sugar and molasses into valuable exports.[31] Often, middlemen and brokers functioned as refiners as well, paying farmers in either currency or products in exchange for raw grain. For example, Caleb Davis paid Andrew Black for eighteen barrels of flour and a half barrel of super fine flour in 1769, indicating Black was a miller who could produce different qualities of flour. It appears, also, that Davis provided merchandise at a later date to pay for the flour.[32] The discrepancy in value between the raw form of a good can be seen in Table 12 with flour being worth nearly twice as much as its raw form.

First on the list of Boston's exports is cod. Boston and its port complex dominated the cod fisheries off the coast of Newfoundland. Large fishing fleets plied the North Atlantic waters and filled the docks of growing feeder ports like Marblehead and Salem. The smell of salted fish permeated the wharves and small coves surrounding Boston and its auxiliary ports.[33] During 1768–72, dried salted fish accounted for more than 55 percent of Boston's exports. Most of the dried fish was exported to Southern Europe and the West Indies, but much of the local economic development followed the success or failure of the cod industry, with shipbuilding being an important auxiliary industry. Cod was so important to the local economy that it occasionally served as payment, especially in the seventeenth century and the early decades of the eighteenth century. Timothy Orne, a major merchant based in Salem, accepted fish instead of currency for other commodities or naval supplies. This was beneficial to both fishermen and Orne, as Orne required massive quantities of dried fish to maintain his trade relationship with Spain and the West Indies.[34]

---

31   Peter C. Mancall, Joshua L. Rosenbloom, and Thomas Weiss, "Exports from the Colonies and States of the Middle Atlantic Region 1720–1800," *Research in Economic History* 29 (2013): 257–305, at 262; James F. Shepherd, "Commodity Exports from the British North American Colonies to Overseas Areas, 1768–1772: Magnitudes and Patterns of Trade," *Explorations in Economic History* 8, no. 1 (June 1970): 5–76.

32   Andrew Black to Caleb Davis, May 16, 1769, Folder May 1–19, 1769, Box 5, Caleb Davis Papers, MHS.

33   Vickers, *Farmers and Fishermen*, 175.

34   Hunter, *Purchasing Identity in the Atlantic World*, 126.

TABLE 12   Average annual quantities and values of overseas exports of specified commodities by Boston, New York, and Philadelphia, 1768–72

Commodity	Units	Quantity	Value (£)	% of Total
Boston				
Bread and Flour	tons	328	3,431	1.4
Beef and Pork	bbl	1,868	3,856	1.6
Flaxseed	bu	7,867	1,410	1.0
Candles, Spermaceti	lb	71,905	4,858	2.0
Fish, dried	quintal	263,062	131,279	55.7
Oil, whale	tons	2,967	35,601	14.8
Potash	tons	719	18,041	7.5
Wood products, pine boards	1,000 ft.	12,624	19,299	8.0
Wood Products, Staves and Headings	1,000 ft.	1,537	4,513	1.9
Rum, American	gal	108,218	6,735	2.8
Value of Itemized Commodities			229,023	95.4
Value of All Commodity Exports			240,057	100.0
New York				
Bread and Flour	tons	6,647	71,923	41.4
Beef and Pork	bbl	2,913	6,112	3.5
Flaxseed	bu	118,550	21,373	12.3
Grain - Indian Corn	bu	67,704	7,018	4.0
Grain - Wheat	bu	65,210	12,669	7.3
Iron, bar	tons	767	11,538	6.6
Iron, pig	tons	922	4,591	2.6
Potash	tons	446	11,415	6.6
Wood Products, Staves and Headings	1,000 ft.	2,420	7,252	4.2
Rum, American	gal	11,151	762	0.4
Value of Itemized Commodities			154,652	89.1
Value of All Commodity Exports			173,620	100.0
Philadelphia				
Bread and Flour	tons	22,065	233,450	69.8
Beef and Pork	bbl	4,124	8,553	2.6

TABLE 12 Average annual quantities and values of overseas exports (*cont.*)

Commodity	Units	Quantity	Value (£)	% of Total
Flaxseed	bu	79,348	14,583	4.4
Grain - Indian Corn	bu	103,860	10,199	3.1
Grain - Wheat	bu	124,360	24,003	7.2
Iron, bar	tons	324	4,759	1.4
Iron, pig	tons	1,019	5,058	1.5
Potash	tons	34	845	0.3
Wood Products, Staves and Headings	1,000 ft.	5,051	14,997	4.5
Rum, American	gal	4,396	1,472	0.4
Value of Itemized Commodities			317,919	94.7
Value of All Commodity Exports			334,304	100.0

All Three Ports Combined

Commodity	Units	Quantity	Value (£)	% of Total
Bread and Flour	tons	29,040	308,804	41.3
Beef and Pork	bbl	8,905	18,521	2.5
Flaxseed	bu	205,765	37,366	5.0
Grain - Indian Corn	bu	171,564	17,217	2.3
Grain - Wheat	bu	189,570	36,672	4.9
Iron, bar	tons	1,091	16,297	2.2
Iron, pig	tons	1,941	9,649	1.3
Potash	tons	1,199	30,301	4.1
Wood products, pine boards	1,000 ft.	12,624	12,624	1.7
Wood Products, Staves and Headings	1000s	9,008	26,762	3.6
Rum, American	gal	123,765	8,969	1.2
Candles, Spermaceti	lb	71,905	4,858	0.6
Fish, dried	quintal	263,062	131,279	17.6
Oil, whale	tons	2,967	35,601	4.8
Value of Itemized Commodities			694,919	92.9
Value of All Commodity Exports			747,981	100.0

SOURCE: PETER C. MANCALL, JOSHUA L. ROSENBLOOM AND THOMAS WEISS, "EXPORTS FROM THE COLONIES AND STATES OF THE MIDDLE ATLANTIC REGION 1720–1800," *RESEARCH IN ECONOMIC HISTORY*, VOL. 29: PP. 257–305 (PAGE 262); JAMES F. SHEPHERD, "COMMODITY EXPORTS FROM THE BRITISH NORTH AMERICAN COLONIES TO OVERSEAS AREAS, 1768–1772: MAGNITUDES AND PATTERNS OF TRADE," *EXPLORATIONS IN ECONOMIC HISTORY*, VOL. 8 NO. 1 (JUN 1970), PP. 5–76

Boston also exported a substantial amount of whale oil, nearly three thousand tons yearly by the 1770s. Whale oil was one of the only products that found a large demand in Britain, helping to offset the trade deficit the colony had with Britain. It was valuable enough to garner substantial quantities of British manufactures to sell in Boston.[35] It comprised about 15 percent of Boston's total trade, but combined with dried fish, the Massachusetts fishing industry comprised more than 70 percent of total overseas exports. Other whaling products, such as candles, added more value to the whaling industry, with much of that production being consumed locally for lighting and heating. Whale oil was also important for the local and regional trade of Boston, as it was an integral part of coastal North American trade. For example, New England exported more than 129,000 pounds of candles per year to the Middle Colonies (most of which went to New York and Philadelphia), far more than the amount Boston sent overseas.[36]

Wood products is another primary category of overseas exports from Boston. Pine boards were the largest of the wood product category with 8 percent of total exports, followed closely by Potash at 7.5 percent. The smallest group, staves and headings, accounted for under 2 percent of total overseas exports. In the case of pine boards, most of the local production most likely went to the shipyards in Boston, New York, and Philadelphia. Of the total amount of boards shipped overseas, more than 90 percent were sent to the West Indies (see appendix A, Table A.2). Staves were primarily used for the creation of barrels, and again, most of these exports went to the West Indies, though a substantial portion were sent to Southern Europe, likely to the wine-producing regions such as Madeira and Málaga. New York and Philadelphia also exported substantial quantities of staves and heading, comprising more than 4 percent of total overseas exports for both ports. Again, like Boston, most of the wood products from New York and Philadelphia found their way into the West Indies (see appendix A, Tables A.3 and A.4). The importance of potash to the region's economy is often looked over by scholars.[37] As a wood product that required processing, Boston and New York exported much more than

---

35 Richard C. Kugler, "The Whale Oil Trade, 1750–1775," in Colonial Society of Massachusetts, *Seafaring in Colonial Massachusetts*, 153.

36 British North American Customs Papers, 1765–74, MHS. A more complete discussion of coastal trade can be found in the following chapter, but also see Shepherd and Williamson, "Coastal Trade of the British North American Colonies."

37 Potash is produced by taking wood ash, submerging and leaching the ash in water, and evaporating the water off to leave behind a potassium-heavy product. The finished product can be used for fertilizer or manufacturing glass, soap, and other products.

Philadelphia, because of their larger shipbuilding industries.[38] Between 1768 and 1772, Boston exported a little more than £18,000 worth of potash on average per year, New York £11,400, and Philadelphia £845 (see appendix A, Tables A.2–A.4).[39] Much of the potash leaving the region went to England, as it was one of the few goods that found a steady demand, but Philadelphia's ships that carried flour and grain to Portugal also carried potash, which could fill empty holds in a ship and be sold or traded for other goods.

Grains were by far the most important export from the region as a whole. In the first two decades of the eighteenth century, Philadelphia exported a substantial amount of tobacco grown in and around the Chesapeake, and New York was still exporting more furs than anything else. By the 1720s and 1730s, however, both New York and Philadelphia primarily exported grains to other parts of the Atlantic.[40] However, exports of raw grain were gradually superseded as flour production became more common in the region. In Philadelphia alone, the production and export of flour substantially increased decade to decade. In 1730, Philadelphia exported 38,570 barrels of flour.[41] By 1750, that number had increased to 82,095, and 284,872 barrels by 1773.[42] In fact, by the 1760s, Philadelphia imported the same amount of raw wheat from other North American colonies as the port sent overseas, likely meaning that Philadelphia's milling industry had developed into a production center for North America.[43] During 1768–72, the overall value of Philadelphia's raw wheat exports fell from over £56,000 to under £33,000. In the same period, Philadelphia's total exports of flour and bread increased from about £330,000 to over £615,000.[44] Clearly, flour was far more valuable than raw wheat, with a growing number of mills popping up throughout the region that contributed to local economic development.

---

38 Lisbon Municipal Archive, Historical Archive, Collection "Taxes," Tonnage Tax Fund, Tonnage Tax Book of Entries, refs. AML-AH-MN.
39 Shepherd, "Commodity Exports from the British North American Colonies to Overseas Areas," 5–76.
40 Port of Philadelphia Customs House Papers, 1704–89, vol. 1, HSP; Matson, *Merchants & Empire*, 108–10.
41 Each barrel's weight varied, and each invoice accounted for the weight of flour in each barrel. However, on average, each barrel contained about two hundred pounds of flour. See Invoice no. 2, Thomas Chalkley Account Book, 1718–27, HSP.
42 Jensen, *Maritime Commerce of Colonial Philadelphia*, 292.
43 Jensen, *Maritime Commerce of Colonial Philadelphia*, 8.
44 Jensen, *Maritime Commerce of Colonial Philadelphia*, 293. These figures include coastal exports, whereas the figures in table 4.6 only include overseas exports.

Acknowledging the large quantities of refined products that were exported, substantial manufacturing and processing industries, such as sugar refineries, flour mills, and iron foundries, developed in this region, which may be characterized as proto-industrialization. In Philadelphia alone, the transition to bread/flour in the grain trade was an indication of growing industrial capacity and local reinvestment. As discussed in the previous chapter, the proportion of individuals engaged in the commodity chains that traveled throughout the three ports and the Atlantic Ocean was large, and mills employed plenty of people, especially in New York and Philadelphia. Unfortunately, many of these mills were located just outside of the cities, shielding our ability to track how many mills were in operation in the region.[45]

Somewhat surprisingly, however, the region exported a substantial amount of iron, both in bar form and its less refined cousin, pig iron. The eighteenth century was a period of economic growth, especially in the hinterlands of Philadelphia, for the region's iron industry centered in Pennsylvania, which had abundant deposits of iron ore.[46] Though iron exports only comprised about 3.5 percent of the region's total overseas exports, the growth in the iron industry greatly reduced the reliance on iron imports from Europe. In fact, metal products, such as nails and hoops (used for barrels), were also exported overseas by the three ports (see appendix A, Tables A.2–A.4). Much of the capital investment for the growth in local iron production came from merchants who used their capital to invest in local production such as ironmaking and mining.[47] By 1770, 132 ironworks were operating in the thirteen continental colonies. Of those, 87 percent were in and around the three ports. New England had the fewest of the region with just eleven. Philadelphia and New York had sixty-three and forty-one respectively.[48] Philadelphia alone accounted for nearly half of the total ironworks in operation. Ultimately, the region controlled most of the fledgling industrial capacity of British America, signifying growing capital investment.

Imports were not only meant for local consumption. Many merchants imported specific commodities that were used to manufacture or produce other commodities that were later exported. For example, salt from Portugal was imported into Boston, and fishermen then used that salt to preserve the cod that they then sold to merchants to ship to Portugal and the West Indies. Some merchants were invested in local production. Caleb Davis was one merchant

---

45 Doerflinger, *Vigorous Spirit of Enterprise*, 122–23.
46 Cappon et al., *Atlas of Early American History*, 105.
47 Doerflinger, *Vigorous Spirit of Enterprise*, 67.
48 Cappon et al., *Atlas of Early American History*, 26–32.

who directly supported local manufacturing. Davis provided both materials and capital to Dorothy Forbes, who was married to or widowed by (the source is not clear) a close friend of Davis. Davis maintained detailed accounts with her and bought thread, needles, and fabric at wholesale. Forbes then produced hats and mantillas, a traditional Spanish veil for Catholic women. Though mantillas may have found a few local buyers, it appears that much of what Forbes produced was shipped along with other commodities to Cádiz and Málaga in Spain. As Davis frequently traded with Spanish merchants, it is not unreasonable to assume that the hats and mantillas Forbes made were useful in trading for salt, wine, and other Spanish goods.[49] In effect, merchants developed close relationships with local producers to find goods that allowed greater possibilities for exchange throughout the Atlantic.

4   Sugar

Sugar was a key commodity for all three cities not just in terms of imports and consumption but also with respect to their exports. Sugar products composed the vast majority of imports into the three ports, and most of those imports came from the West Indies. In Table 10 above, a little over twelve thousand hundredweight of refined sugar was reexported from Britain to all of British America, representing slightly more than 31 percent of all British sugar exports, most of which came from British West Indian sugar plantations. By comparison, New England (primarily Boston) imported more than twenty-five thousand hundredweight, and the Middle Colonies (primarily New York and Pennsylvania) imported more than thirty-eight thousand (see Table 8), from the West Indies. Boston, New York, and Philadelphia were oriented toward the Caribbean for their refined sugar needs in exchange for the wheat and fish that these ports exported to the West Indies. Large quantities of molasses (a byproduct of the refining process) imported into the three cities helped to create a local distilling and refining industry.

By the middle of the eighteenth century, proto-industrial production developed in each city. Sometimes the industries that developed were unique to each city, such as milling in Philadelphia and cod and whale processing in Boston. But in the case of sugar, sugar refineries appeared in all three port complexes. In New York, wealthy families such as the Bayards and Roosevelts

---

49   Caleb Davis Papers, Box 19, Folder 1771–82, and though there were many bills of lading and invoices that listed goods sent to Cádiz, some of the examples can be found in Box 7, Folder January 1774, MHS.

made their fortunes in refining sugar.[50] By 1770, New England had thirteen refineries, New York maintained four, and Philadelphia had seven. The rest of the continental colonies only had two refineries, both of which were in Charleston. More than 92 percent of all sugar refineries in North America were in or around the three ports.[51] The refineries helped process the excess cane sugar from the West Indies, producing both refined sugar and molasses. The molasses was likely purchased by local rum distilleries, creating a cooperative relationship between sugar refiners and distillers.

Though sugar refining was an important part of the local economy, rum distilling was far more profitable for both local producers and merchants. Refined sugar, while resilient, was still susceptible to spoilage and damage from water. Rum, on the other hand, had a much longer shelf life and provided high calories, fortified by alcohol. It became an essential ship provision and an important part of the diet of colonial Americans.[52] Thanks to the higher value of rum compared to molasses and refined sugar, rum distilleries proliferated throughout the region. By 1770, at least 143 distilleries were in operation throughout the continental colonies. In the vicinity of Boston, thirty-six distilleries developed. New England (most of which was within Boston's realm of influence) owned ninety-six establishments. New York owned twenty, and Philadelphia had at least fifteen distilleries. Like sugar refineries, the region controlled 92 percent of rum production, with New England controlling well more than half.[53]

Sugar and rum were also essential components of the region's coastal trade. Ship invoices and bills of lading moving between the three cities contain references to rum and sugar. Boston exported a substantial amount of rum to other parts of the colonies. In one instance, a firm sent five hogsheads of rum, as part of a larger shipment to Georgia, three of which were consigned to Jeremiah Green and the other two to be sold as part of another collection of merchandise.[54] In March of 1761, Daniel Clark, of Philadelphia, sent sixteen hogsheads of reexported West Indian rum to New York, which earned him more than £430.[55]

Boston, New York, and Philadelphia also shipped rum and sugar to the West Indies and Africa, even if in smaller quantities than they exported along the

---

50   Harrington, "New York Merchant on the Eve of the Revolution," 12–13.
51   Cappon et al., *Atlas of Early American History*, 26.
52   McCusker, "Rum Trade and the Balance of Payments of the Thirteen Continental Colonies," 247. As noted earlier in the chapter, some twenty gallons per year was consumed by each male colonist.
53   Cappon et al., *Atlas of Early American History*, 26.
54   Boston Shipping Firm Account Book, 1763–65, June 20, 1763, MHS.
55   Invoice from Daniel Clark to William Howard, March 7, 1761, Daniel Clark Letter and Invoice Book, 1760–62, HSP.

coast of North America. Some merchants made a decent living by selling North American rum in the West Indies. The merchant firm Murdock and White, of Philadelphia, frequently sold rum to customers in St. Christopher's (St. Kitts). In one instance, they accepted payment of £99 in June 1765 for an overdue account that belonged to John Phipps.[56] Thomas Gordon, a merchant of Philadelphia, sent five barrels of sugar to the Virgin Islands along with flour and fish in June 1753.[57] In 1769, Massachusetts alone sent over 130,000 gallons of rum to Africa (see appendix A, Table A.2). Between 1768 and 1772, the region exported a little more than £31,000 worth of American rum to Africa.

Rum meant for ship use rarely appears in the official customs records as exports or imports, primarily because it is considered a ship provision. Nevertheless, the number of ships entering and leaving Boston, New York, and Philadelphia would have needed large quantities of rum on a regular basis. Mariners had a notorious appetite for rum. It is hard to track rum purchases that were meant for ship provisions, but in one account book by an unknown shipping firm, ten hogsheads of New England rum were sold that were meant "for Snow Diamond" in 1763. A snow is a common type of ship, so it is highly likely, though not certain, that this entry of rum worth a little more than £89 was destined for the ship's crew.[58] Given that hundreds of ships arrived, unloaded, resupplied, and reloaded as many as three or four times a year, the provisioning industry for the constant flow of maritime trade must have been extremely large.

Both the iron and lumber industries were intertwined with sugar and rum production. Iron hoops were created to fit wooden staves to create barrels of various sizes to carry sugar products to and from the refineries and distilleries. As much of the exports of wood products went to the West Indies, it is safe to assume that many of the staves and hoops sent to the West Indies arrived back in Boston, New York, and Philadelphia filled with molasses, sugar, and rum. Furthermore, a substantial portion of the copper and metalcrafts imported from Britain was likely used by local distilleries and refineries (see Table 10). Considering the concentration of sugar refineries and distilleries in Boston, New York, and Philadelphia, it is likely that the three ports served as an extension of the major sugar production center of the West Indies.

Beyond the production and consumption of sugar and sugar-based products, the three cities were heavily dependent on Caribbean sugar plantations

---

56   Murdock Receipt Book, 1765–71, June 1, 1765, HSP.
57   Bill of Lading for Thomas Gordon on the Ship *Neptune*, June 1753, Port of Philadelphia Bills of Lading, 1716–72, HSP.
58   Boston Shipping Firm Account Book, 1763–65, May 1763, MHS.

and, more precisely, the slaves who worked those plantations for a significant portion of their export trade. The Caribbean trade served two interrelated purposes. First, it provided direct access to the sugar and molasses local consumers and distilleries demanded. Second, it provided a steady and consistent market for the exports that merchants in Boston, New York, and Philadelphia provided. The relationship was interdependent, as the ever-growing slave plantations of the West Indies required a constant stream of foodstuffs and wood products (i.e., barrel staves) to feed slaves and package their products. Though plantation owners were encouraged to plant their own sources of food, profits became more important than local sources of food, and North American merchants were more than happy to fill the gap.[59] As discussed in more detail in the following chapters, the West Indies accounted for 36 percent of the total tonnage that all three cities exported, more than any other segment of colonial American trade.[60]

Sugar production and trade also provided opportunities for merchants and ship captains to conduct island-to-island trade within the Caribbean, with many ships stopping at several islands and ports. Some stopped at multiple islands to find enough cargo to make the return trip worthwhile. Samuel Murdock, a ship captain and merchant based in Philadelphia, made many stops to find enough West Indian rum at several islands in the late 1760s.[61] Other ships bought rum, sugar, and molasses from one island but would sell it at other stops in the West Indies to local merchants and other ship captains looking to outfit their own ship, whether for provisions or to complete their cargo. Thomas Nicholson, from Boston, was one such merchant who stopped at Suriname, Saint-Domingue, and St. Kitts, each belonging to a different empire.[62] These are just some examples among many that can be listed, but clearly, sugar provided the core of a robust and profitable economic relationship between the islands in the Caribbean and Boston, New York, and Philadelphia.

5   Mechanisms of Consumption and Demand

Merchants assessed the demand for the goods they imported. Consumers expressed their wants and needs in a variety of ways. Most colonists, of any

---

59   Richard Pares, *Yankees and Creoles: The Trade between North America and the West Indies before the American Revolution* (Cambridge, MA: Harvard University Press, 1956), 86–88.
60   See chapter 4 for a complete discussion.
61   Murdock Receipt Book, 1765–71, HSP.
62   Thomas Nicholson Accounts, 1773–74, MHS.

means, maintained accounts with merchants. Merchants usually maintained account books that would keep records annually, biannually, or, for high-volume merchants, monthly. These books record the various goods and items that consumers purchased. As a result, one can see which goods were in high demand. Each book's page normally contained one or two individuals who conducted business with each merchant. While this is not unusual even when specie was easy to find, colonial merchants often accepted goods as payment, especially from other merchants and farmers. Still, each line was valued in currency, in the event that currency was used to make payment. In most cases, merchants imported and exported goods, allowing individuals in more rural parts of Massachusetts to send wheat, pork, or other agricultural goods to merchants in exchange for tea, sugar, or salt. Barter was often supplemented by labor or promises of future deliveries. For example, Caleb Davis in Boston in 1760 promised to deliver thirty-four quintals and forty pounds of fish in exchange for freight charges that he owed to Captain Nathanial Law.[63]

In Boston, New York, and Philadelphia, merchants and consumers communicated their desire for certain goods in a variety of ways. Often, customers, especially wealthier consumers, sent notes or letters to merchants requesting certain quantities or types of products. Boston merchant Caleb Davis's papers are filled with direct requests for goods from merchants and consumers. One example reads as follows:

> Littleton, 11 June 1764
> Mr. Caleb Davis,
> Sir, please to send me by the bearer Mr. Peter Poaster one Hogshead of good Rock Salt and as many pales as he can bring and charge them to Your friend
> ROBERT HARRIS[64]

In this particular case, Harris wished to have the deliverer of the message take the goods back with him. Similarly, in invoices from England to Boston, New York, and Philadelphia, English merchants responded to specific requests from colonial merchants, who had collected requests from local producers of goods. These requests were separate from the invoices, in that they communicated the desired quantities, goods, and dates of delivery long before the

---

63 Caleb Davis to Nathanial Law, August 13, 1760, Folder August 1760, Box 1, Caleb Davis Papers, MHS.
64 Robert Harris to Caleb Davis, June 11, 1764, Caleb Davis Papers, Box 3, MHS.

goods were purchased or packed on ships. Considering the numerous entries in many of the invoices, British imports tended to have consumers or buyers already waiting for the goods once they arrived in the colonies. This was mainly because a part of the goods imported by colonial merchants from Britain was used to create higher-value products, some of which were then reexported to other parts of North America, the West Indies, and in a few cases, Southern Europe.[65]

In the invoice book of a Boston merchant, Benjamin Dolbeare, there are many invoices that go on for pages, detailing the various types of threads, pins, ribbons, and buttons.[66] It appears that many of these shipments were imported specifically for tailors and other artisans in Boston. In another invoice, a variety of brushes and fans were imported, likely for a shoemaker and a shopkeeper respectively.[67]

Shopkeepers played an important role in keeping up with demand, not to mention how they contributed via their own needs. Merchants communicated with them, both in person and by letters, and knew their needs and wants. In June 1763, Jonathan Orne requested that a shipping company send him two hogsheads of molasses, which he in turn intended to sell to a local distiller.[68] The records of the Amory family of merchants contain several account books that detail standing accounts with shopkeepers throughout the region. One shopkeeper, Luke Bliss, from Springfield, Massachusetts, more than ninety miles into the hinterland, sent for more than £50 of cloth, buttons, clothing, and other materials, likely for a tailor or clothier in the small rural town.[69] Shopkeepers were also attuned to the needs of their customers, as much or more so than merchants, and they became essential nodal points in the communication chains between consumers and merchants.

Merchants relied upon their communication networks for an assessment of demand and market conditions in the areas they wished to trade. In one instance, a Philadelphia merchant sent a letter to his colleagues in Virginia, who appear to be readying a voyage to the West Indies, to request a shipment of West Indian or Jamaican rum. He wrote: "West India Rum is very scarce in

---

65 More examples can be found in Benjamin Dolbeare Invoice Book, vol. 2, MHS; Joseph Ogden Invoice Records, 1749–55, HSP; Daniel Clark Letter and Invoice Book, 1760–62, HSP. For exports of local production to Southern Europe, see the above discussion of Caleb Davis and Dorothy Forbes.
66 Benjamin Dolbeare Invoice Book, vol. 2, Invoice no. 13, May 10, 1740, MHS.
67 Benjamin Dolbeare Invoice Book, vol. 2, Invoice no. 15, May 13, 1740, MHS.
68 Boston Shipping Firm Account Book, 1763–65, June 20, 1763, MHS.
69 May 1, 1769, vol. 4, Account Book, 1769–71, Amory Family Papers, MHS.

town there being a great demand for it."[70] He also included a price list for various types of rum. As Jamaica and West India rum was sold at a price almost twice that of New England rum, merchants in Philadelphia anticipated high profit margins on rum imported from the West Indies. Merchants from the region cooperated to procure the quantities of goods to meet transatlantic requests as well. Thomas Greg, a New York-based merchant, requested flour from a fellow merchant in Philadelphia to ensure that their ship could leave port on time and still fill the order Greg had received from Lisbon.[71]

There were multiple avenues by which prospective customers could obtain one or more goods. They could usually buy goods from wholesale stores of retail shops in the cities and in the hinterlands that maintained small quantities of essentials and dry goods.[72] Merchants generally reached out to consumers and local retailers by advertising new arrivals and available stocks in newspapers and magazines. The merchant firm of Greg and Cunningham was one New York firm that purchased a substantial number of ads. One example reads:

> To be sold reasonable by Gregg [sic] and Cunningham at their store in Queen-street, for cash or short credit: GREEN and bohea TEA, pepper, oil, olives, indigo, lead, shot, musquets, herrings, English beer, beaver, and other furrs. Also a compleat assortment of Manchester goods and Irish linnens [and] women's shoes, with many other articles of dry goods. All persons that they are indebted to may have their money for calling, and they request those who are too long due them to discharge their accounts.[73]

Merchants also advertised wholesale goods they had just received from overseas. In 1735, Samuel Otis, in Boston, purchased an ad detailing his new arrivals, including West Indian sugar, rum, and manufactures from England. He specifically mentioned they would be selling by wholesale, likely targeting shopkeepers and other retailers in the port.[74]

Women, often invisible in the historic record, were essential to the commodity markets in Boston, New York, and Philadelphia. Ellen Hartigan-O'Connor, a

---

70   John Clark to Richard Bentley, March 21, 1761, Daniel Clark Letter and Invoice Book, 1760–62, HSP.
71   To Scott and McMichael, November 29, 1756, LGC, 255.
72   Price, "Economic Function and the Growth of American Port Towns in the Eighteenth Century," 138–39.
73   July 18, 1757, New York Mercury.
74   Boston Gazette, 1735, MHS.

TABLE 13   Estimates of gross income per capita, 1700–74 (in £ sterling)

	Per capita gross income				
Region	1700	1725	1750	1770	1774
New England	7.7	8.3	10.3	11.6	11.3
Middle Colonies	10.1	10.5	11.7	14.7	13.5
Great Britain	11.5	11.9	12.9	15.2	15.7
	Bare-bones consumer bundle for one-person				
Region	1700	1725	1750	1770	1774
New England	5.5	5.9	5.8	6.7	6.1
Middle Colonies	8.2	7.9	8.2	8.2	8.6
Great Britain	6.5	6.4	6.6	6.7	6.2

SOURCE: PETER H. LINDERT AND JEFFREY G. WILLIAMSON, *UNEQUAL GAINS: AMERICAN GROWTH AND INEQUALITY SINCE 1700* (PRINCETON: PRINCETON UNIVERSITY PRESS, 2016), 62–63

scholar who examines the role of women in colonial commerce, suggests that women directly engaged with the economy, whether as buyers or sellers: "Free women combined their own labor, credits from neighbors at local shops, and cash to mobilize spending power in the marketplace."[75] This assertion is borne out in merchant papers. In New York, Christopher Bancker maintained accounts directly with women in the city. In one account entry, Bancker sold Elizabeth Bohea a small amount of sugar, putting a portion of the just over three pounds total on her standing account with Bancker.[76] More frequently, women would send requests by way of their husbands. One husband, Thomas Sparhawke, specifically mentioned his wife who requested that tea and West Indian sugar be sent to their house in the interior of Massachusetts.[77] Whether directly or indirectly, women helped shape commodity markets through their choices in consumption.

At the root of the growing consumption of goods in the region, the purchasing power of the people of Boston, New York, and Philadelphia and the surrounding hinterlands was substantial in comparison with that of the average European. Peter Lindert and Jeffrey Williamson have estimated the purchasing power of colonial residents in the region compared with that of residents

---

75   Ellen Hartigan-O'Connor, *The Ties That Buy: Women and Commerce in Revolutionary America* (Philadelphia: University of Pennsylvania Press, 2009), 4.
76   September 14, 1722, Christopher Bancker Journals, 1718–50, vol. 1: 1718–39, NYHS.
77   Thomas Sparhawke to Caleb Davis, 1761, Box 1, 1761 Folder, Caleb Davis Papers, MHS.

in Great Britain. In Table 13, estimates are shown at selected years during the eighteenth century for New England, the Middle Colonies, and Great Britain. In 1700, New England average gross income per capita was £7.7, and in the Middle Colonies, the average was slightly higher at £10.1. A bare-bones consumer bundle (or basic necessities for survival) cost, on average, £5.5 in New England and £8.2 in the Middle Colonies. By 1774, New England's gross income was £11.3, and basic necessities cost £6.1. A similar disparity existed in the Middle Colonies with £13.5 gross income and a consumer basket that cost £8.6. The difference between the bare necessities and the average per capita income provided a substantial source of capital with which to purchase additional goods. According to Lindert and Williamson, British American consumers held a nearly 50 percent advantage in real purchasing power over consumers living in Great Britain.[78]

6 Conclusion

By producing commodities and consuming locally produced and imported goods on a large scale, Boston, New York, and Philadelphia played a vital role in Atlantic Ocean trade. The import and export figures presented in the tables above show that this region was a nodal point within the greater Atlantic trade network. As the eighteenth century progressed, colonial American purchasing power increased substantially, especially for those in the greater port complex of Boston, New York, and Philadelphia. As American colonists consumed more and more imports and produced commodities for export on a large scale, American merchants sought greater access to global markets, many of which were not freely accessible due to British mercantilist policies. In many ways, their drive to access these forbidden markets was as much due to the inability of the state to adequately support the commerce of the colonies. In addition, the general lack of consumer demand for goods from Boston, New York, and Philadelphia left colonial merchants no choice but to look outside of the empire for the profits necessary to buy British imports. More importantly, merchants within the region capitalized on their growing importance with the various commodity chains that weaved throughout the three cities and beyond to increase their political and economic power, which placed the region on a collision course with its imperial masters. How these processes unfolded over the eighteenth century forms the narrative of the next two chapters.

---

78 Lindert and Williamson, *Unequal Gains*, 60–64, see especially tables labeled in the source as 3–4, 3–5, 3–6, and figure 3–3.

CHAPTER 4

Inter-colonial Trade

To fully understand the impact of imperial constraints on colonial trade, the destinations, origins, and characteristics of the trade flowing through all cities must be delineated. This chapter focuses on the trade that merchants of Boston, New York, and Philadelphia carried out with other ports in the western half of the Atlantic. This inter-colonial trade comprised about half of the region's total value of trade. In the first section, I question the existing literature's assertion that a negative balance of payments indicates economic dependence and orientation. Rather, the lack of both consumer market and fiscal capacity support from England left Americans with little choice other than to look elsewhere for the specie and profits required to import goods from England. In addition, I argue that the historiography relies too heavily on imperial records that are often incomplete and too broad to fully encapsulate the scale and importance of colonial commerce. Following the discussion of sources and past interpretations of the existing data, the chapter explores the importance of coastal North American trade, using both existing datasets and private papers from the region's merchants. In the final section of the chapter, I explain the robust economic relationship between Boston, New York, and Philadelphia with the various islands and colonies in the West Indies (and northeastern South America) using the same methods described above. The chapter closes with a comparison of inter-colonial trade with the region's trade with Great Britain, showing a dramatic discrepancy both in total volume and value.

1   Quantifying and Defining Inter-colonial Trade

Since the 1970s, scholars have assessed and reassessed the role of inter-colonial trade in the Atlantic World. Excellent compilations of data by scholars such as James Shepherd, Gary Walton, Russell Menard, and John McCusker have enabled historians to explore how British American merchants from this region carried out trade in the Atlantic Ocean and gained significant economic and political power.[1] Phyllis Whitman Hunter, Cathy Matson, and Thomas

---

1   Shepherd and Walton, *Shipping, Maritime Trade and the Economic Development of Colonial North America*; McCusker and Menard, *Economy of British America*. See bibliography for a more complete listing of the works by Shepherd, Walton, McCusker, and Menard.

Doerflinger have shown the importance of coastal trade in the development of Boston, New York, and Philadelphia respectively.[2] Others have focused on the scale and importance of coastal and West Indies trade, highlighting the role of the provisions trade of colonial America.[3] Foremost among the works on coastal trade is James Shepherd and Samuel Williamson's article quantifying the size and scope of coastal trade for the British North American colonies.[4] While several historians have highlighted the special relationship between the West Indies and British North America, one of the first was Daniel Vickers. Vickers explains how colonial Massachusetts and the slavery-driven sugar plantations in the Caribbean were economically inseparable—Boston providing dried fish and the West Indies sending molasses and sugar in exchange.[5] Even with the greater interest in quantifying and understanding inter-colonial trade, however, much is still unknown about the scale and mechanisms of Boston, New York, and Philadelphia's trade with other European colonies in the Western Hemisphere.

Datasets on colonial American trade mentioned above, however, are not complete. Even the most-cited and most comprehensive data compiled by James Shepherd and Gary Walton only details the exports and some imports for British North America for the years 1768–72.[6,7] This dataset, however, is based on the inspector-general's records of the British Empire kept in the Public Records Office of the National Archives of Britain.[8] Trade data in these records for the 1768–72 period, which Shepherd and Walton have compiled, is not complete and presents a number of problems. First, the British enforcement of the Navigation Acts and the addition of new policies during this period placed restrictions on colonial American trade. Second, Boston was under occupation

---

2 Hunter, *Purchasing Identity in the Atlantic World*; Matson, *Merchants & Empire*; Doerflinger, *Vigorous Spirit of Enterprise*.
3 Craig, "Grounds for Debate?," 149–77; McCusker, "Rum Trade and the Balance of Payments of the Thirteen Continental Colonies," 244–47.
4 Shepherd and Williamson, "Coastal Trade of the British North American Colonies," 783–810.
5 Vickers, *Farmers and Fishermen*.
6 Shepherd and Walton, *Shipping, Maritime Trade and the Economic Development of Colonial North America*.
7 Few articles and books published on British America's economy since 1972 fail to cite the scholarship of Shepherd and Walton, as the datasets they compiled contain a host of information awaiting analysis. Even other seminal works on the economy of colonial America, such as McCusker and Menard's *Economy of British America*, depend heavily on the compilations of Shepherd and Walton.
8 For a more detailed accounting of the sources Shepherd and Walton used, see Shepherd and Walton, *Shipping, Maritime Trade and the Economic Development of Colonial North America*, 176–78.

by the British Army and Navy from 1768 to 1775, which further inhibited trade and likely obscured the importance of Boston in the Atlantic economy.[9] There is evidence that during that period of occupation ships arrived in and departed from smaller feeder ports in the port complex. There is a strong likelihood that the data on trade contained in the imperial records for Boston is incomplete and distorted.[10] Third, the 1768–72 period also coincides with a greater enforcement of Britain's Navigation Acts, following the cession of French holdings in North America to the British Empire at the end of the Seven Years' War. Much of the animosity between colonists and Britain appeared after 1763, with many merchants bristling at British efforts to extract additional revenue and control what the British considered smuggling.[11] Fourth, those years also coincide with multiple non-importation agreements and movements and increasing tensions between colonists and Britain. As the British government passed a series of revenue acts and monopolistic policies, American merchants grew increasingly frustrated with the growing barriers to free trade, which limited both merchants' profits and consumer choices. As a result, many merchants sought to hide their activities from British officials to avoid taxes and fees.[12]

In addition, British imperial and colonial records lack details on intercolonial trade, especially local trade. Even the best compilers of coastal trade data recognize the shortcomings in the available data. Shepherd and Williamson note that the customs agents did not list the specific origin or destination of commodities denoted as coastal. Furthermore, price data is not complete, nor do the available sources fully detail the various commodities moving in and out of colonial ports.[13] More importantly, customs agents were more interested in tracking transatlantic trade, where both commissions and quantities were greater, than focusing on coastal trade between the colonies of North America. In fact, there were only a few customs officials available up until the 1760s, and many of the smaller packet ships that plied the coasts of North America were rarely examined or counted by agents.[14]

---

9   Richard Archer, *As if an Enemy's Country: The British Occupation of Boston and the Origins of Revolution* (Oxford: Oxford University Press, 2010).
10 Oliver Morton Dickerson, ed., *Boston under Military Rule, 1768–1769 as Revealed in a Journal of the Times* (Boston: Chapman and Grimes, 1936), 77–78.
11 Dickerson, *Boston under Military Rule*, 16, 77–78; Oliver M. Dickerson, *The Navigation Acts and the American Revolution* (Philadelphia: University of Pennsylvania Press, 1951), 190–200.
12 Justin du Rivage, *Revolution against Empire: Taxes, Politics, and the Origins of American Independence* (New Haven: Yale University Press, 2017), 101–5.
13 Shepherd and Williamson, "Coastal Trade of the British North American Colonies," 784–85.
14 Barrow, *Trade and Empire*, 186–87.

Beyond the limited capacity of the imperial structure to fully detail colonial trade, other empires carried on direct trade with the British colonies, in direct violation of the mercantilist policies of Britain. We know this because even British customs accounting shows a substantial trans-imperial trade (see Table 14 below). As a result, the records kept by other empires likely contain data on trade with British America that is missing from the British imperial records. As direct trade with other empires was generally illegal, it was largely hidden from customs agents and undercounted. The case study of Portuguese records discussed in chapter 5 illustrates this very well and reinforces the hypothesis that current estimates of colonial trade are incomplete. Finally, smuggling was a major concern of the customs officials. It is nigh impossible to ascertain the scale of smuggling in British America. The evidence, however, warrants the assumption that smuggling was rampant in British America. Nowhere is this more evident than the career of John Hancock, a notorious but exceptionally talented illicit trader and a key leader of the fledgling American nation.[15]

In their seminal work on the economy of British America, Shepherd and Walton argue that the negative balance of payments—more imports than exports—that the colonies had with Britain likely means that the colonies were economically oriented toward the British Isles. British America did indeed import more goods (measured by value) from Britain than it exported in goods back to its imperial master, on average £1.5 million between 1768 and 1772. This means that specie flowed from the colonies to Britain. However, New England and the Middle Colonies (in effect, Boston, New York, and Philadelphia) had a high negative balance with Britain. The Southern colonies, in contrast, traded more directly with Britain and did not have as large a negative balance of payments.[16]

This reliance on balance of payments to draw conclusions of colonial dependence on Britain is misplaced. Historians tend to assume that a negative balance of trade indicates that the region with the negative balance is dependent on the one holding the positive balance. In the case of colonial America, this implies that American merchants were both oriented toward and dependent upon British merchants. However, one would not say that the modern United States is dependent upon China because it has a negative balance of trade with China. Instead, many argue that China is the dependent one as it exports more to the United States than it imports. Instead of examining the volumes and values of trade between colonies and Britain alone, we should consider the colonies' trade in totality (i.e., trade with all parts of the Atlantic World) and then

---

15 Baxter, *House of Hancock*, 259–61.
16 Shepherd and Walton, *Shipping, Maritime Trade and the Economic Development of Colonial North America*, 137–40.

examine the proportion of colony–metropole trade to the total. Once one digs deeper into the archives and records, one finds that the total tonnage that was shipped between the region of Boston, New York, and Philadelphia and the rest of the world was far more than the tonnage going to and from Britain (see Table 14 and appendix A, Tables A.5–A.7). While the secondary compilations of data are flawed, they are still useful for any study that examines the economy of British North America, including this one. However, the issues related to the accuracy and completeness of the data discussed above should be kept in mind. As such, this book adds further compilations of data from years both before and after the more commonly used 1768–72 period. But as we will see in this chapter and the next, colonial merchants preferred to conduct trade largely outside of the bilateral networks between Britain and North America. Instead, most exports found their way to places not in the British Isles.

Colonial merchants were at a disadvantage throughout most of the eighteenth century. In most cases, American merchants had to pay for English merchandise with hard specie or currency or use short-term credit that came with less friendly terms than those given to merchants based in England. Moreover, the region's primary products, grain and dried fish, were not in high demand in Britain, thus making it more difficult to pay for imports.[17] In contrast to the unfavorable terms of London merchants, colonial merchants could more easily conduct trade with fellow colonists in both North America and the West Indies through the use of credit, colonial currency, and bills of exchange. Colonial currency was easier to obtain than sterling, though it was not the preferred option. Instead, colonial merchants kept account of commercial transactions with one another, utilizing bookkeeping to maintain accounts, rather than always exchanging goods for cash. Shipping cash and specie required extra insurance and shipping charges, and as cash was in short supply, keeping clear records allowed for goods and services to replace specie. Additionally, the terms of credit were much longer and friendlier than the terms offered by English merchants. Especially in coastal North American trade, colonial merchants found it easier to function without exchanging currency relative to their ability to access metal specie.[18]

Colonial merchants could also provide credit to farmers and laborers instead of currency, especially for those who produced goods that the merchant could

---

17   Doerflinger, *Vigorous Spirit of Enterprise*, 49, 54; Matson, *Merchants & Empire*, 143–45. Letterbooks and invoices are filled with letters and notes about limited funds available to send for goods in London. Some examples can be found in Benjamin Dolbeare Letterbook and Invoice Book, MHS and John Stamper Letterbook, HSP.

18   One of the best examples of this type of accounting is Thomas Chalkley Account Book, HSP.

then export or sell locally. Using their capacities as both wholesalers and brokers, merchants in Boston, New York, and Philadelphia frequently provided merchandise credit to farmers for wheat, flour, or livestock rather than pay in hard specie. This was beneficial for both parties. Farmers could buy commodities they were unable to produce on their own, and merchants could export goods without significant outlays of capital. This system also provided ways to pay laborers for both merchants and farmers. Merchants could give lines of credit to dock workers or sailors, and farmers would give small, handwritten notes to farmhands who could take them to a local merchant. The note would instruct the merchant to give a certain amount of credit, usually less than £5, taken from the farmer's or landowner's account.[19] The ease of doing business in North America and the West Indies in comparison with trading with Britain and dealing with British merchants was a major incentive for the merchants of Boston, New York, and Philadelphia to trade with North American and West Indian ports.

2   Coastal and North American Trade

While transoceanic shipping was significant, it was the coastal North American trade that contributed most to the wealth and prosperity of the three port cities. These port cities moved goods up and down the North American coast to its numerous port cities and their hinterlands. Coastal trade, especially of provisions (grain, fish, rum, etc.), provided the necessary foundations to build larger and more complex trade networks farther afield.[20]

Throughout the eighteenth century, coastal trade comprised between 20 and 50 percent of total exports (see Table 14). West Indian goods were directly related to the coastal trade, as many of the goods imported from the Caribbean were reexported by all three cities to the rest of British North America.[21] Together, Boston, New York, and Philadelphia imported and exported about half of the total value of goods that moved throughout British North America. In Table 15, we can see that the region of Massachusetts, New York, and Pennsylvania was far more important to the continent of North America than

---

19   Examples of the small notes are infrequent, but account books frequently note "credit given to" as an entry in certain accounts. For an example of each of the described mechanisms, see Box 5 of Caleb Davis Papers, MHS. This is one of the few collections that contains many of the smaller notes and letters shared between local producers, consumers, and merchants.
20   Craig, "Grounds for Debate?," 153.
21   McCusker and Menard, *Economy of British America*, 196.

TABLE 14   Shares of tonnage clearing for various destinations from Boston, New York, and Philadelphia by selected time periods

Dates	Great Britain	Ireland	Southern Europe[a]	West Indies	Africa	Coastal
Boston						
1710s	19%	0%	6%	53%	0%	22%
1750s	11%	1%	9%	39%	0%	40%
1763–67	19%	0%	3%	26%	0%	52%
1768–72	16%	0%	3%	25%	1%	55%
1720–72	16%	0%	4%	29%	1%	50%
New York						
1720s	15%	0%	7%	50%	0%	27%
1730s	10%	4%	9%	47%	0%	30%
1750s	16%	12%	6%	49%	1%	16%
1763–67	24%	4%	13%	44%	0%	16%
1768–72	20%	10%	11%	31%	1%	28%
1720–72	19%	7%	11%	40%	0%	23%
Philadelphia						
1720s	16%	0%	14%	51%	0%	19%
1730s	10%	11%	20%	40%	0%	19%
1750s	4%	10%	7%	50%	0%	29%
1763–67	13%	4%	12%	35%	0%	35%
1768–72	9%	9%	22%	33%	0%	27%
1720–72	11%	7%	18%	37%	0%	27%
All Three Ports Combined						
1720s	15%	0%	12%	51%	0%	22%
1730s	10%	9%	17%	42%	0%	21%
1750s	10%	5%	8%	44%	0%	33%
1763–67	18%	3%	10%	36%	0%	33%
1768–72	14%	6%	12%	30%	0%	38%
1720–72	14%	5%	12%	36%	0%	33%

TABLE 14 Shares of tonnage clearing for various destinations (*cont.*)

a Includes the Wine Islands. However, it is not entirely certain that no trade occurred. The reason for breaking the 1760s after 1768 is because Boston was occupied by the British Army and Navy beginning in 1768

SOURCE: MANCALL, ROSENBLOOM, AND WEISS, "EXPORTS FROM THE COLONIES AND STATES OF THE MIDDLE ATLANTIC REGION 1720–1800," 269; CHAPTER Z, "COLONIAL STATISTICS," IN *HISTORICAL STATISTICS OF THE UNITED STATES: EARLIEST TIMES TO THE PRESENT, MILLENNIAL EDITION*, ED. S. B. CARTER ET AL. (CAMBRIDGE: CAMBRIDGE UNIVERSITY PRESS, 2006), 5:719

TABLE 15 Average annual values of selected commodities in the coastal trade, 1768–72 (£ sterling)

Commodity	Massachusetts, New York, and Pennsylvania		Rest of British North America		Total	
	Exports	Imports	Exports	Imports	Exports	Imports
Corn	2,900	25,600	42,500	17,600	45,400	43,200
Wheat	300	26,100	31,600	2,900	31,900	29,000
Rice	2,000	15,500	22,200	10,300	24,200	25,800
Molasses	30,200	25,600	21,810	22,600	52,010	48,200
Brown Sugar	11,300	7,000	8,520	12,200	19,820	19,200
Bread and Flour	109,900	45,300	26,600	54,300	136,500	99,600
Dried Fish	5,000	23,700	21,500	15,800	26,500	39,500
New England Rum	60,200	18,000	23,700	60,300	83,900	78,300
West Indian Rum	16,700	24,700	34,000	21,000	50,700	45,700
Pitch	400	1,600	2,500	600	2,900	2,200
Tar	500	8,900	11,500	3,100	12,000	12,000
Turpentine	300	3,100	4,600	1,200	4,900	4,300
Potash	200	4,800	5,200	100	5,400	4,900
Pine Boards	3,700	600	3,000	7,800	6,700	8,400
Train Oil	17,000	12,300	6,100	12,600	23,100	24,900
Total	260,600	242,800	265,330	242,400	525,930	485,200
% of Total	50%	50%	50%	50%	100%	100%

Notes: For a full accounting of all the North American colonies and their coastal trade, see Table A.8, in Appendix A. British America includes the thirteen colonies, British Canada, and Bermuda.

SOURCE: SHEPHERD AND WILLIAMSON, "THE COASTAL TRADE OF THE BRITISH NORTH AMERICAN COLONIES," 784–85. REEXPORTS ARE NOT INCLUDED AS THEY WERE NOT DISTINGUISHED BY THE LOCAL CUSTOMS AGENTS. THIS DOES NOT INCLUDE WEST INDIES TRADE AS IT WAS TREATED AS A SEPARATE CATEGORY

any other region by the 1770s. More than half of the grain and sugar products that moved throughout British America came from the region, indicating not only a general reliance on the region's exports of flour and bread but also a strong reexport trade of sugar products.

Of the three cities, Boston had the largest share in the exports and imports comprising the coastal trade. Annually exporting more than £100,000 of commodities to British North America by 1768, Boston merchants were heavily invested in the business of coastal trading (see appendix A, Tables A.5 and A.8). The proportion of Boston's export tonnage engaged in coastal commerce increased from just over 20 percent in the 1710s to more than 50 percent by the 1770s. This increase in proportion came as Boston developed into an entrepôt for all of North America, but it was also a result of a greater imperial focus on Boston beginning with the occupation of Boston in 1768. Trade to the West Indies and Southern Europe continued to grow but fell as a percentage of Boston's total trade because some of that trade shifted to feeder ports such as Salem, which these figures do not include. The implementation of the Sugar Act of 1764, which imposed higher duties on sugar imported from the West Indies, also caused this decline.[22] Boston's production of rum (distinguished from West Indian rum by both price and name in the customs records) was no doubt responsible for much of that increase, as New England rum was exported from Boston to other parts of North America. Philadelphia and New York too received supplies of New England rum, some of which was then reexported to the rest of British America.

Boston merchants maintained a close relationship with consumers and merchants in more northerly colonies, such as Nova Scotia, Newfoundland, and French Canada. New England's economic connection with its northerly neighbors is not surprising for two reasons. One, they shared a close geographic relationship, and two, New England fishermen depended upon access to fisheries in the waters off the coast of Newfoundland and Nova Scotia.[23] It was only natural that merchants would use empty ships to carry goods that fishing villages and towns needed as they had limited agricultural capacities (in both climatological and chronological respects). By the 1720s, Boston merchants were already trading regularly with French port towns, especially Louisbourg. To the disapproval of British officials, major merchants and merchant families, such as Peter Faneuil, the Hancocks, and the Pepperrells, engaged with

---

22 A more in-depth discussion of the implications of the Sugar Act of 1764 can be found in chapter 6.
23 Vickers, *Farmers and Fishermen*, 88–89.

French merchants to trade French goods, sugar, molasses, and rum in exchange for wood products and ships. In Île Royale (the major port of French Acadia), more than forty New England vessels arrived each year by the 1740s. Though the eighteenth century was fraught with constant warfare, especially between French and British naval forces in the North Atlantic, Boston merchants continued to expand their trade to the north, earning substantial profits in the process.[24]

Most Boston merchants engaged in coastal trade, even if they were focused on transatlantic or West Indian trade. For example, John Dolbeare shipped goods on seventeen different voyages between 1718 and 1724. Of those seventeen shipments, ten were to coastal North America, including New York and Philadelphia. The remaining seven were divided between London, the West Indies, and Amsterdam.[25] Account books of merchants frequently note small shipments from other North American ports. In an anonymous account book of a shipping firm in Boston, several entries note the arrival of flour from Philadelphia, much of which was then resold to other merchants and captains for provisioning. These entries appear between several examples of transatlantic commerce, indicating a robust reexport trade.[26]

Compared to Boston, New York shipped less as a percentage of its overall exports to other parts of North America. At no point during the eighteenth century did the proportion of New York's exports to British America exceed 30 percent. This does not mean that New York's coastal trade was inconsequential. Even at 23 percent of total tonnage, coastal trade was extremely important to the overall economy of New York. Between the 1710s and 1770s, New York shipments and imports to and from North America doubled. During 1715–18, an average of 33 percent (sixty-eight of 215) of vessels that cleared New York annually left for coastal destinations, but in 1772, 42 percent of the (592 of 1,140) total vessels cleared traveled to North American ports.[27] Nevertheless, coastal trade remained an important segment of the commercial economy.[28]

New York's coastal trade also provided opportunities to reexport European goods to other cities. For example, Gerard Beekman conducted regular trade with consumers and merchants in Rhode Island. He shipped not only locally produced flour but also several trunks and chests of other merchandise to

---

24 Chard, "Massachusetts–Louisbourg Trade," 132–33; Folder 1728–47, Hancock Family Accounts and Receipts, 1728–1829, MHS.
25 Business Records, Folder 8, Box 4, Dolbeare Family Papers, 1665–1830, MHS.
26 Boston Shipping Firm Account Book, 1763–65, MHS, 18, 22–23.
27 Matson, *Merchants & Empire*, 395n58.
28 Matson, *Merchants & Empire*, 196–97; see table 5.1 for the proportion of exports tonnage.

fellow merchants in Rhode Island. Beekman sent several chests and boxes worth £268 to Peleg Thurston and expected him to sell the merchandise quickly at good prices. Similarly, he sent a letter with cloth samples to James Holmes to choose linens and clothing that Beekman expected to import from Europe.[29] By reexporting European imports to other parts of British America, merchants like Beekman expanded the consumer base and established complementary relationships with local merchants in order to sell their goods and make a profit as well as to gain access to goods they wished to export to other destinations.

Unlike New York, the proportion of Philadelphia's overall exports devoted to coastal trade increased over the eighteenth century, though it never reached the proportion of its overall exports that Boston's coastal trade reached. Nevertheless, more than a quarter of Philadelphia's export tonnage traveled to North American destinations. Provisions were the primary exports from Philadelphia to places like Charleston, South Carolina, and Rhode Island. Philadelphia merchants found the coastal trade filled with opportunities for profit and growth, some earning enough capital to begin trade in riskier transatlantic markets.[30]

While merchants in all three cities regularly reexported merchandise they received from Europe, Philadelphia merchants were better placed to reexport European wine, salt, and manufactures than the other two cities thanks to their extensive grain and flour trade with Portugal and Spain. Daniel Clark, for example, consistently sent Madeira and Lisbon salt on to other destinations in North America. In March 1761, Clark shipped two quarter casks of Madeira and five hogsheads of Claret wine to Quebec.[31] In October 1760, Tench Francis received several dozen casks of wine from Lisbon and Amsterdam, and a few months later, in early 1761, Francis shipped several of those casks to other ports in North America, including Providence and New York.[32] Many Philadelphia merchants took advantage of their special connection with Southern Europe to advance their economic position in the region and the rest of North America.

Philadelphia's and New York's main exports to the rest of North America were primarily grain products, but merchants in both cities also reexported a substantial amount of sugar, New England rum, and British manufactures (see appendix A, Table A.8). Most shipping invoices that left New York for

---

29   Gerard G. Beekman to Peleg Thurston, November 2, 1750, Beekman to James Holmes, November 3, 1750, *BMP*, 1:128.
30   Doerflinger, *Vigorous Spirit of Enterprise*, 115–16.
31   Invoice of Sundry Goods Shipped by Daniel Clark to Quebec, March 24, 1761, HSP.
32   Tench Francis Invoice Book, 1759–61, HSP.

other parts of North America included flour or bread and British manufactures, among other commodities. An invoice in the records of Joseph Ogden, a Philadelphia merchant, contains several barrels of flour, a barrel of beer, snuff, inkpots, knives, scissors, thimbles, combs, pins, silverware, buttons, lace, thread, and several other items.[33]

Coastal trade also provided opportunities for merchants in the three cities to cooperate in one another's exports to other parts of North America. In New York, Gerard Beekman sent flour to Henry Lloyd in Boston in 1757, along with a letter that reads:

> Please to try our flour and if it is sweet don't be in a hurry to sell it nor ship any to Halifax at all if not already done as it rises here and at Philadelphia but if you find it on the turn do with it as if it was your own and we shall be content.[34]

In short, Beekman shipped a load of flour that might not have been ready for sale. He suggested that Lloyd hold on to it as prices were rising in Philadelphia, meaning that more profit could be had by waiting to ship that flour even farther north. In short, coastal trade increased as a proportion of the region's overall trade from 22 percent in the 1720s to 38 percent in the 1770s, indicating the region's growing importance for the economy of North America more broadly. Throughout the eighteenth century and for all three major ports of the region, coastal trade provided the means for merchants to find ready and willing producers and consumers, earn profits, and accumulate capital.

3 West Indies Trade

Beyond the North American coastline, the West Indies was a significant regional destination of Boston, New York, and Philadelphia. Packet ships and convoys regularly sailed between these ports and islands in the Caribbean. The West Indies became an extension of the North American coastline, and Boston, New York, and Philadelphia played the role of a distribution center for goods imported from the West Indies.[35] Yet West Indian trade was riskier

---

33   Invoice of Sundry Goods Shipped by Joseph Ogden to Cape Fear, North Carolina, December 16, 1754, HSP.
34   Gerard G. Beekman to Henry Lloyd, September 5, 1757, *BMP*, 1:302.
35   Thomas Chalkley Account Book, 1718–27, Murdock Receipt Book, 1765–71, Allen and Turner Letterbook, 1755–74, HSP; *Boston Gazette*; *Pennsylvania Gazette*; Caleb Davis

and came with different regulations, as the islands in the Caribbean were colonies of many European empires. As such, British customs agents regularly demarcated West Indies trade as a category entirely separate from coastal and transatlantic. We should also treat the West Indies trade of the region as distinct from coastal trade, even though much of this trade remained within the British Empire's borders.

For all three cities, trade with the West Indies was essential not only for their commercial sectors but also for the local production sectors. For New England's dried fish trade, the West Indies was an outlet for lesser qualities of fish that were unlikely to find consumers in Europe or coastal North America. For New York and Philadelphia, the West Indies was a major market for flour and bread.[36] Slave-based plantations in the Caribbean created a huge demand for high calorie and cheap foods that could withstand tropical climates. Salted cod and flour were ideal as they have a longer shelf life. Importing foodstuffs provided plantation owners cheap alternatives to parceling out subsistence lots from valuable acreage. Instead of providing space for slaves to grow their own subsistence crops, plantation owners maximized their sugar and other cash crop production by purchasing foodstuffs from Boston, New York, and Philadelphia.[37] More than a third of the total exports from Boston, New York, and Philadelphia ended up in the West Indies (see Table 14).

Boston, in particular, relied on West Indian trade for its local economy. The large fishing fleets that called Massachusetts home were successful because of dried fish exports to the Caribbean sugar islands. Merchants sent barrels of dried fish to exchange for sugar, molasses, and rum. Much of the West Indian molasses and sugar was then used to produce New England rum, which served as a major export to coastal North America. The account books of Boston merchants are filled with invoices, bills of lading, and accounts with West Indian merchants. Captain John Nutt was one such captain/merchant who regularly traveled to Barbados, where he would sell dried fish and buy rum and other commodities.[38] Some merchants traveled from one island to another trading dried fish and European manufactures for sugar and molasses.[39] Others, like Thomas Nicholson, a captain and merchant, ferried goods on behalf of

---

Papers, 1684–1831, Account Book by Boston Merchant, 1736–41, Captain Nutt Invoice Book, 1772–84, MHS.

36 Vickers, *Farmers and Fishermen*, 99; Matson, *Merchants & Empires*, 90; Doerflinger, *Vigorous Spirit of Enterprise*, 104–5; Craig, "Grounds for Debate?," 153.

37 Craig, "Grounds for Debate?," 155–59.

38 Captain John Nutt Invoice Book, 1772–84, MHS.

39 Lot Stetson Logbook, 1772, MHS.

other merchants to various islands in the West Indies and also benefited from intra-Caribbean trade by purchasing goods on one island and selling them on another. More than once, he purchased rum from Suriname but then sold some of it to other captains and merchants at stops in Saint-Domingue and other smaller islands.[40] Others picked up as much rum as they could find at various islands to fill their ships' holds. Samuel Murdock and his partner traveled throughout the West Indies, purchasing rum at St. Christopher's (St. Kitts), Bermuda, and other small islands before heading back to Philadelphia.[41]

By 1700, regular trade existed between New York and Caribbean ports. Merchants pooled their capital and jointly purchased ships or freighted their merchandise on ships owned by other merchants.[42] Christopher Bancker, a New York merchant, conducted dozens of small transactions for West Indian goods. His trade journals contain numerous references to sales of West Indian rum, sugar, molasses, and occasionally chocolate. According to one entry in the journal, he sold £34 worth of rum to Sarah Van Vechten, and another entry shows that he sold one hogshead of molasses for £8 to James Banks. He listed accounts and transactions with many merchants in New York, including the merchant families the Beekmans, the Fishers, and the Schuylers.[43] Bancker also shipped goods to the West Indies. In 1735, he received eighty barrels of flour (worth a little more than £52) from three merchants, which he likely shipped to the West Indies.[44] In 1742, similarly, he sent £86 worth of goods to Charles Handler in Jamaica in the ship *Believe*.[45]

Like New York, merchants based in Philadelphia found the markets of the West Indies profitable because the demand for grain was high in the Caribbean, and West Indian trade was cheaper to conduct. From the earliest years of the eighteenth century, Philadelphia shipped a large percentage of its goods to ports in the Caribbean: 51 percent in the 1720s but falling to 30 percent by the 1770s (see Table 14). Though grain and flour dominated Philadelphia's trade after the 1710s, tobacco was initially a major export from the port. In the years 1704–9, roughly 78 percent of the total number of clearances for tobacco shipments were destined for the West Indies (see Table 16). These tobacco shipments may have been reexported to England, but there was also a large market for tobacco since large plantation owners were wealthy enough to buy tobacco.

---

40 Thomas Nicholson Accounts, 1773–74, MHS.
41 Murdock Receipt Book, 1765–71, HSP.
42 Matson, *Merchants & Empire*, 183.
43 Christopher Bancker Journals, 1718–50, NYHS.
44 March 7, 1735, July 9, 1735, Christopher Bancker Journals, 1718–50, NYHS.
45 December 6, 1742, Christopher Bancker Journals, 1718–50, NYHS.

TABLE 16   Distribution of Philadelphia tobacco exports, 1704–9

Destination	# of ships	% of total
Anguilla	3	1%
Antigua	11	5%
Barbados	127	62%
Bermuda	3	1%
Boston	23	11%
Carolina	2	1%
Curaçao and Bonire	12	6%
Nevis	4	2%
Newfoundland	6	3%
New York	12	6%
Rhode Island	2	1%
Total	205	
West Indies	160	78%
North America	45	22%

SOURCE: DUTIES ACCOUNT BOOK, 1704–13, HSP

Barbados was a particularly important island for early Philadelphia trade, as it alone accounted for over 60 percent of tobacco exports in the first decade of the eighteenth century. One may also notice that not a single ship carrying tobacco traveled directly to Britain.

Flour and bread eventually came to dominate the shipping invoices for Philadelphia merchants. Thomas Chalkley was one who consistently sent ships and goods to the West Indies, usually exporting flour and bread and bringing back sugar, molasses, and rum.[46] In just six months, Chalkley received a shipment of rum worth £89, a shipment of molasses, rum, and cotton worth £215, and a shipment of rum worth £37 all from Barbados. As noted in the invoices, all these shipments were paid with profits from flour from Philadelphia, though we do not have the outgoing invoices.[47] By the 1770s, more than ten thousand tons of flour and bread were shipped nearly every year for the West Indies. The

---

46   Thomas Chalkley Account Book, 1718–27, LCP.
47   September 26, 1720, November 20, 1720, February 28, 1721, Thomas Chalkley Account Book, 1718–27, LCP.

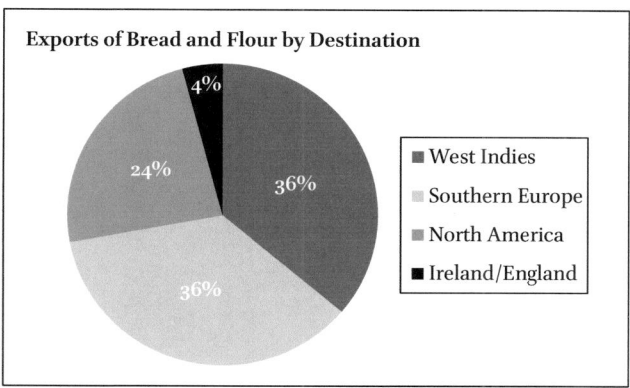

FIGURE 6   Exports of bread and flour from Philadelphia,
1768–1772 (yearly average % of tons)
SOURCE: BASED ON FIGURES IN ARTHUR L. JENSEN,
*THE MARITIME COMMERCE OF COLONIAL
PHILADELPHIA* (MADISON: STATE HISTORICAL
SOCIETY OF WISCONSIN, 1963), 293

only other market that received significant shipments of flour was Lisbon. The British Isles received some 5 to 10 percent of Philadelphia's total flour exports, whereas the exports to the West Indies constituted more than a third of the total (see Figure 6).

Rum was a popular import from the West Indies. By 1772, over a million gallons of rum were being imported into Philadelphia from the West Indies, which amounted to 77 percent of the total imports (See Table 17). However, of those total imports, roughly a quarter each year were reexported to other ports on the coast (See Table 18). Merchants, such as Charles Stewart, created little empires of their own with large networks of merchants, suppliers, and consumers. Most maintained complex account books with merchants from all over the Atlantic. More often than not, the number of each merchant's connections with merchants in London were dwarfed by the number of connections in the West Indies.[48]

Even when using the official British statistics and above-mentioned secondary compilations, it is hard to deny the importance of coastal and West Indian trade for the merchants and producers of Boston, New York, and Philadelphia. Using the 1768–72 data of Shepherd and Walton, a total of £3,737,551 worth

---

48   Charles Stewart Letterbooks, 1751–63, HSP. This is just one example, but many of the account books and letterbooks contain more merchant connections with the West Indies than England, and in those that contain a high number of British connections, most of the invoices and transactions are imports from England rather than exports to England.

TABLE 17   Imports of rum into Philadelphia (Gallons)

Year	West Indies	North America	Total
1768	557,685	168,246	725,931
1769	734,342	167,699	902,041
1770	715,061	237,860	952,921
1771	521,085	204,877	725,962
1772	761,255	256,172	1,017,427

SOURCE: JENSEN, *MARITIME COMMERCE*, 294

TABLE 18   Reexports of West Indian rum to North America (Gallons)

1768	140,636
1769	177,683
1770	209,549
1771	167,864
1772	214,532

SOURCE: JENSEN, *MARITIME COMMERCE*, 294

of goods was exported overseas from the region to various parts of the world during those five years. Of that number, £1,593,152 worth of goods or about 43 percent of the total was exported to the West Indies. Compare this with £643,242 worth of commodities that arrived in Britain. Even if we include the value of goods exported to Ireland (£260,466), the British Isles only constituted 24 percent of total overseas exports or a little more than half of the proportion of West Indian trade. There is little doubt that more than three-quarters of the total value of exports from Boston, New York, and Philadelphia were to ports and markets other than the British Isles. This allowed colonists to make a profit in other parts of the world that could then be used to purchase additional goods from England.

Furthermore, the number of ships going to and from North America and the West Indies was far larger than the number going to the British Isles. Using the port entries and clearances recorded in the *Boston Gazette* and *Pennsylvania*

Gazette, one can get a better picture of the weekly arrivals and exits. In Table 19, the number of clearances and entries is compiled for Boston and Philadelphia for selected years. At no point in the eighteenth century did the British Isles comprise more than 16 percent of the total entries and clearances. Coastal trade accounted for at least twice the number of ships going in and out of both ports, and the same can be said of the West Indian destinations and origins. As the tonnage figures track closely with the customs entries and clearances, it is likely that the breakdown of New York's ship counts would mirror those of Boston and Philadelphia.

As Table 19 shows, the number of ships leaving and entering the region increased every decade, and the biggest increases were in the West Indies and North America, the slowest being the British Isles. Boston experienced a nearly threefold increase in the number of ships arriving from and departing to the West Indies between 1720 and 1739. Philadelphia experienced a doubling of ships going to and coming from the West Indies between the 1730s and the 1750s. Between the 1730s and the 1770s, Philadelphia witnessed a 406 percent and 394 percent increase in entries and clearances. For Boston, the West Indies became more important as a proportion of overall trade, and in Philadelphia, West Indian trade declined in favor of North American. More importantly, Boston's trade with the British Isles was roughly the same as a percentage of overall entries and clearances, but in Philadelphia direct trade with Britain declined from 16 and 14 percent of entries and exits in the 1730s to 10 and 7 percent in the 1770s. This is a further indication that the region solidified and strengthened its position as a key entrepôt for the inter-colonial Atlantic economy.

4 Conclusion

Boston, New York, and Philadelphia imported and exported goods from and to the British Isles. However, these colonial port cities had less to offer in terms of merchandise to the metropolis. Their main products—dried fish, flour, bread—circulated all along coastal North America and the West Indies. These cities served as a nodal center in the Atlantic, as high volumes of goods, especially foodstuffs and provisions, circulating in both North America and the West Indies indicate. In addition to provisions, the region became important for the redistribution of goods imported from Europe (from Britain and continental Europe). While we do not have systematic records of this reexport trade, numerous invoices and bills of lading that included linens, threads, cookware, among others, indicate a region increasing in importance in the Atlantic World

TABLE 19 Origins and destinations of entries and clearances of Boston and Philadelphia for selected years

Destination/Origin	Boston 1720		Boston 1739		Phil. 1730–34		Phil. 1750–54		Phil. 1770–74	
	E	C	E	C	E	C	E	C	E	C
British Isles	21	19	64	54	141	138	264	259	339	273
% Total	5%	4%	8%	5%	16%	14%	13%	12%	10%	7%
North America	282	257	355	599	324	312	913	954	1,522	1,699
% Total	63%	53%	44%	50%	37%	33%	44%	43%	43%	45%
West Indies and South America	103	151	324	469	360	416	686	831	1,220	1,308
% Total	23%	31%	40%	39%	41%	43%	33%	37%	34%	35%
Europe and the Wine Islands	40	54	61	77	48	93	199	182	470	505
% Total	9%	11%	8%	6%	5%	10%	10%	8%	13%	13%
Total	446	481	804	1,199	873	959	2,062	2,226	3,551	3,785

SOURCE: 1720 BOSTON: BOSTON GAZETTE, 18 APRIL 1720–5 JANUARY 1721; AS COMPILED BY HUNTER, PURCHASING IDENTITY IN THE ATLANTIC WORLD, 79. INCLUDES SALEM; 1739 BOSTON: COMPILED BY AUTHOR. INCLUDES SOME NEW YORK ENTRIES. MISSING FOUR ISSUES FROM THE YEAR, SO THE NUMBERS ARE LIKELY A BIT LOWER THAN REAL NUMBER OF ENTRIES AND EXITS; PHILADELPHIA FIVE-YEAR PERIODS: COMPILED FROM THE PENN-SYLVANIA GAZETTE BY JENSEN, MARITIME COMMERCE OF COLONIAL PHILADELPHIA, 290

economy. Most importantly, the inter-colonial trade routes provided ready and willing marketplaces for the goods that all three cities hoped to export, and the trade provided the profits necessary to pay for further imports of European manufactures, easing the pain of chronic currency and specie shortages. The next chapter explores the role of trans-imperial trade in the regional complex of Boston, New York, and Philadelphia, finding that access to the global market may not have been through the proper metropole, as the mercantilist laws of England required, but the chapter also discusses how imperial boundaries could and were more easily crossed within the colonial arena.

CHAPTER 5

Trans-imperial Trade

While the core focus of the maritime economies of Boston, New York, and Philadelphia remained inter-colonial trade, trans-imperial trade, or commerce that transcended imperial boundaries, was as important or more so to the region as trade with the British Isles. Throughout the eighteenth century, British American merchants conducted trade with partners beyond the nominal borders of the British Empire. Despite the efforts of customs officers and imperial administrators to enforce British imperial prohibition, ships and commodities from non-British ports continued to enter these British colonial ports. This is evident from the fairly large number of cases of impounded and captured ships and cargoes at the colonial courts and British Admiralty courts.[1] Regardless of the risk, merchants of Boston, New York, and Philadelphia pursued profit wherever it could be found, irrespective of the imperial borders that crisscrossed the Americas and the Atlantic Ocean.

Trans-imperial trade, perhaps more than any other type of trade in colonial America, was a direct consequence of the limited state capacity to supply enough currency for commerce and a lack of enforcement capability. Colonial merchants simultaneously needed to access non-British markets to find enough consumers and took advantage of the limited enforcement of British mercantilist policies to expand their trade beyond the borders of the British Empire. At a fundamental level, direct trade with the rest of the world placed American merchants in confrontation with the British imperial administration, not to mention the competition they represented to Britain-based merchants.

This chapter examines the mechanisms and importance of trans-imperial trade to the region of Boston, New York, and Philadelphia. First, I explain the ways in which commerce transcended imperial borders between the region and the rest of the world. Next, the chapter explores the legal and illegal channels of trade, the role of East Asian goods in the increasing scale of trans-imperial commerce, and how profit opportunities in non-British markets factored into the decisions of British American merchants. Following the discussion of the mechanics of trans-imperial trade, I describe how inter-colonial trade, especially in the West Indies, provided ample opportunities to conduct

---

1 Dickerson, *Navigation Acts and the American Revolution*, 182–83.

trans-imperial trade. I show that trans-imperial trade occurred on a more substantial scale than most data compilations suggest. Within this discussion, I also compare the trans-imperial networks of trade of the three ports, both in terms of commodities and destinations, highlighting the minor differences that existed between them while still showing how the region shared more in common. In closing the chapter, the case study of Portuguese trade with Philadelphia, between 1765 and 1775, provides further complications to the current literature and data for trans-imperial trade. By the end of the chapter, it will be clear that trans-imperial trade likely exceeded direct trade (especially in the export sector) between the region and Britain.

1 Defining Trans-imperial Trade

The significance and implications of British America's trans-imperial trade for the region's political economy has yet to be fully explored. Past studies have focused on individual port cities and have largely examined it within the larger context of the region's economic and political developments. Perhaps the best examples are April Lee Hatfield's study of seventeenth-century Virginia, and Thomas M. Truxes's book on New York's trade with the French Empire. Hatfield, in her book *Atlantic Virginia*, argues that the key to Virginia's survival, especially in the first few decades of its existence, was its connections with Dutch and Spanish colonies in the West Indies. In addition to inter-colonial dependence, early Virginians traded with anyone who docked at their rudimentary ports regardless of the flag the ships carried. In effect, the eventual success of the Virginia experiment was in no small part due to trans-imperial trade.[2] In *Defying Empire*, Truxes shows how even war did not stop trans-imperial commerce for New York's merchants. New York merchants, according to Truxes, were adept at bypassing the imperial policies that, on paper, prohibited trade between non-British destinations and British Americans. To New York merchants, trans-imperial trade was so important that war intensified trade instead of inhibiting it. In French Canada during the Seven Years' War, for example, New York merchants provided provisions, clothing, and sometimes military supplies for French forces, colonists, and merchants.[3]

---

2 April Lee Hatfield, *Atlantic Virginia: Intercolonial Relations in the Seventeenth Century* (Philadelphia: University of Pennsylvania Press, 2004).
3 Thomas M. Truxes, *Defying Empire: Trading with the Enemy in Colonial New York* (New Haven: Yale University Press, 2008).

Other scholars have discussed trans-imperial trade but have not explored its importance to the economy of British America.[4] John J. McCusker and Russell R. Menard, in their seminal work on the economy of British America, show that trade going to other parts of Europe was important for British America, but they argue that trans-imperial trade is less important than trade with Britain.[5] I offer a different perspective. As explained below, trans-imperial trade was as important, if not more, for British America as trade with its imperial master. Economic connections were created and maintained irrespective of imperial borders, and without understanding how those networks of exchange functioned, we lose the ability to comprehend the nearly constant negotiation and accommodation between colonies and metropole. Moreover, focusing on trans-imperial trade provides an opportunity to explore the roots of revolutionary fervor, which begins to take shape, not coincidentally, in the 1760s.

In this book, trans-imperial trade refers to transactions that moved goods across imperial borders both in continental Europe and in the American colonies. The dynamics of global politics make ascertaining what islands in the Caribbean belong to which European nation difficult at best, so I define each island by the main imperial power that controlled it, even if the island switched imperial hands from time to time.[6] The Canary and other wine islands off the coasts of Africa and the Iberian Peninsula are a special case, as they were generally exempt from British Navigation Acts, likely because of the large population of English merchants and expatriates conducting business.[7] Nevertheless, the goods crossed imperial borders when going to and from those islands, and as the goods were unlikely to have been consumed by British subjects, it is included in the data for trans-imperial trade. In short, if it crosses an imperial border, even between colonies, a transaction or shipment is considered trans-imperial.

---

4 Some examples include Lindert and Williamson, *Unequal Gains*, and Shepherd and Walton, *Shipping, Maritime Trade and the Economic Development of Colonial North America*.
5 McCusker and Menard, *Economy of British America*, 8–9.
6 This is not a perfect system, and when possible, I will note issues as they appear in the source material. Still, it is rare that islands were completely swept clean of one European nation's colonists and replaced with another group of colonists. Instead, business tended to go on as usual, occasionally with additional barriers and rules. By the end of the chapter, it should be clear that it did not matter who owned what island. British Americans sought goods at the cheapest and highest quality to be found, and Caribbean plantation owners and merchants did the same.
7 Leonor Freire Costa, Pedro Lains, and Susana Münch Miranda, *An Economic History of Portugal, 1143–2010* (Cambridge: Cambridge University Press, 2016), 201.

Trans-imperial trade to and from the British American colonies, on the surface, contradicts imperial commercial regulations stipulated in the Navigation Acts that prohibited direct trade with non-British destinations. According to the Navigation Acts passed by the British Parliament in the seventeenth century, no foreign commerce and goods could be imported by British Americans unless one of two things happened: the goods flowed through merchants and ports in England, or the goods were shipped on ships crewed and owned by British subjects based in Britain.[8] Individuals could ship and import goods to and from places outside of the British Empire, but they had to do so through English merchants or on England-based ships and crews. This required partnerships or capital investment from English merchants, and to some extent, this happened frequently but with minor-levels of funding for most English investments. However, it forced America-based merchants to enlist the help of (and therefore share the profit with) metropolitan companies and merchants. This means that goods were not supposed to flow from places outside the imperial boundaries of Britain to British America and vice versa, but the enforcement of these Navigation Acts was limited at best and nonexistent at worst. This is not surprising considering that, until 1760, only five customs offices dotted the coastline of North America. As the coast of North America contains thousands of miles of coastline, not to mention the tens of thousands of miles of shoreline along the many rivers that had access to the ocean, the task was nearly impossible.[9] As a result, many American merchants were able to avoid these acts by landing goods away from the main hubs, forging paperwork, or paying bribes to customs agents.

2 Legal(?) Trade

Colonial merchants used a variety of means to conduct trans-imperial trade. Some of this trade was conducted legally, where merchants, for one reason or another, managed to bring goods into port through the normal process, checking in with customs officials and paying the proper duties on commodities. The official records contain plenty of examples of this trade. Philadelphia customs records include hundreds of bonds paid by captains and merchants agreeing to the conditions of the Navigation Acts, yet many of the very ships

---

8 The Navigation Act of September 13, 1660; The Navigation Act of April 16, 1696, as transcribed in Greene, *Settlements to Society*, 134–36, 210–15.
9 Barrow, *Trade and Empire*, 95–96.

that were forced to swear a bond (paid only when the ship did not abide by the rules) went to places like Lisbon and Amsterdam, destinations clearly beyond the purview of British law. Perhaps the goods they carried were not valuable enough to warrant the energies of the customs agents, or exemptions were made for any number of reasons. Agents were given autonomy to decide each ship's case individually.[10]

Some of the ships that conducted trans-imperial trade legally were either partly owned by English merchants or had enough English sailors to convince port officials to allow legal entry or exit. The bonds and documents collected by customs officials in Philadelphia specified the rules, and merchants could swear a bond specifying the legal status of their cargoes. As resources were limited, rarely were ship cargoes impounded or refused entry if the ships' captains or owners were willing to sign a bond.[11] One of the reasons we know that merchants frequently faked their credentials is the common appearance of court cases regarding ships found to be in violation of the Navigation Acts. One case highlights the scale of the issue as well as the difficulties customs agents faced in preventing illegal entries. A ship aptly named *Fame* arrived in Philadelphia in 1724 bringing in settlers from the Rhine Valley in Europe. The master of the *Fame*, William Lea, was also carrying East Asian and European goods worth roughly £20,000 from Holland. It was not caught initially, but upon further inspection of the ship's papers, the ship was searched again, discovering the illicit goods. Later, during the long court proceedings, the goods were found to be owned by a merchant based in Rotterdam, adding a further violation to the charges. Unfortunately for the customs agents, dozens of individuals, under the protection of darkness, recaptured the *Fame*, cut the ship from its moorings, and moved it down the river where the goods were taken off the ship.[12] The seizure of the *Fame* and the subsequent fallout makes it clear that enforcement was not easy, nor was it accepted by the local merchant community.

Furthermore, customs officials were largely dependent on the good graces of the provincial and city governments that played host. As the number of agents were few until the 1760s, the Navigation Acts were only effective when American merchants willingly abided by the rules, and the evidence suggests that many, if not most, merchants regularly disregarded the acts.[13] Moreover,

---

10   Port of Philadelphia Customs Papers, vol. 3, November 1764–September 1765, HSP. There are several examples throughout the collection, but this volume holds many of those.
11   Port of Philadelphia Customs Papers, HSP.
12   Barrow, *Trade and Empire*, 91–92.
13   Dickerson, *Navigation Acts and the American Revolution*, 69–71.

customs agents were often paid by local governments, either with commissions or with regular pay. Additional income was earned by capturing or seizing illicit cargoes. As the appointments were made by colonial governors, the interest of the governor was usually preeminent, rather than word-for-word enforcement of the law.[14] As the case of the *Fame* in Philadelphia exemplifies, the commission system on prizes was an expensive process to follow, and local courts were not as cooperative as agents wished.[15]

In addition to the inherent difficulties of enforcement, some exemptions were generally allowed by imperial officials. Direct trade between the colonies and Portugal (including the Wine Islands) was tolerated with few restrictions. Though the bonds that individuals signed only exempted the Wine Islands, that exemption was extended to the continental territory of Portugal thanks in no small part to the Methuen Treaty of 1703 signed between Britain and Portugal, which formalized a strong commercial relationship between the empires of Britain and Portugal.[16] Essentially, Portuguese–American trade was allowed since the British and Portuguese were allied economically, politically, and militarily.

Less common yet frequent enough to warrant inclusion, Boston, New York, and Philadelphia outfitted privateers for the many European wars of the eighteenth century. It was a common practice for European nations to grant privateering papers to merchant ships to augment naval fleets during times of war. These privateers were tasked with capturing or sinking (the least desirable option) commercial vessels attempting to trade either with or under the flag of an enemy combatant. This practice was frequently confusing and chaotic, with many nations giving well-known pirates privateering papers when it suited their needs, but in times of peace, governments provided rewards to capture the same pirates-turned-privateers-turned-pirates.[17] British American colonies were no exception, and governors were given the right to give privateer papers to ships. In one example, Massachusetts governor Joseph Dudley provided a privateering commission to Captain Daniel Plowman, a Boston

---

14 Barrow, *Trade and Empire*, 20–35, 94–95.
15 Barrow, *Trade and Empire*, 100–1.
16 Jeremy Land and Rodrigo Dominguez, "Illicit Affairs: Philadelphia's Trade with Lisbon before Independence, 1700–1775," *Ler História* 75 (2019): 179–204. See also: Luiz Felipe de Alencastro, "A rede económica do mundo atlântico português," in *A expansão marítima portuguesa, 1400–1800*, ed. Francisco Bethencourt and Diogo Ramada Curto (Lisbon: Ed. 70, 2010), 133–34.
17 Robert J. Antony, *Pirates in the Age of Sail* (New York: W. W. Norton & Co., 2007), 5.

merchant, and his ship *Charles*, in 1703 during the Queen Anne's War. In this commission, Plowman was given the right

> to War, Fight, Take, Kill, Suppress and Destroy, any Pirates, Privateers, or other the Subjects and Vassals of France, or Spain, the Declared Enemies of the Crown of England, in what Place soever you shall happen to meet them; Their Ships, Vessels and Goods, to take and make Prize of.[18]

Plowman could capture and sell any and all cargoes of ships under the flags of France and Spain.

This method was widely used by merchants to engage in trans-imperial trade, and the port cities of Boston, New York, and Philadelphia were glad to support such activities, as it provided access to goods generally disallowed by British customs. If the altruistic benefit of providing a valuable service to the British Empire was not enough motivation, the promise of profit and glory provided plenty of incentive. It was so profitable that entire ports sponsored privateers during times of war, usually with an amalgamation of investments from local merchants. In 1739, Boston investors outfitted a privateer under the command of Captain Dumaresque to prowl off the coast of Africa and the Wine Islands. The *Boston Gazette* provided regular updates, generally printing excerpts of Dumaresque's letters to the principal investors. The paper referred to the ship as "our privateer" but did not note its actual name. In one update in January 1740, Dumaresque noted that he had captured several vessels, carrying mostly wheat, which he planned to sell in Southern Europe (likely Portugal, as it was at war with Spain). He also planned to sail to Rhode Island and Boston with the ships he had captured to sell to local merchants.[19] In another letter sent through New York, Dumaresque informed Boston citizens that he captured one Dutch and one Swedish ship, together carrying cargoes worth over £6,000.[20]

Other ports also sponsored privateers. Philadelphia sponsored the privateer *St. George* in November of 1739, and the commander, Captain Axon, updated his investors in Philadelphia that he had captured a ship laden with cocoa and a small amount of silver, together valued around £2,000.[21] Newport, Rhode Island (within the port complex and influence of Boston), outfitted a small sloop that cruised the West Indies, usually combining forces with other small privateers to capture larger prizes. Captain Allen, commanding the Newport

---

18 "Captain Plowman's Privateering Commission, 1703," as transcribed in Antony, *Pirates in the Age of Sail*, 59–60.
19 *Boston Gazette*, April 7–14, 1740.
20 *Boston Gazette*, April 14–21, 1740.
21 *Boston Gazette*, April 14–21, 1740.

privateer *Revenge*, sent word through another captain who landed in New York that he had captured three Spanish ships with the assistance of another privateer from Jamaica.[22] New York also sponsored privateers, and all three cities regularly posted updates of the various privateers' progress, successes, and failures.[23] While privateering carried the risks of injury, capture, and death, the profits were more than enough to convince many British Americans to invest in privateering or serve as privateers.

3   Smuggling

Klooster, a historian of the Atlantic World, contends that trans-imperial smuggling was a key segment of the Atlantic economy writ large. Klooster shows that illicit exchange between empires and nations experienced booms and busts that were closely related to the various wars and political struggles that riddled the seventeenth and eighteenth centuries. Smuggling, while important for the overall economies of the Atlantic, was also, for some, a political exercise, providing colonial populations avenues to skirt the imperial laws that bound them to their imperial masters. Furthermore, smuggled goods found ready and willing consumers, and many attempts to bring justice to illicit traders often resulted in resistance from local citizens who wished to purchase those commodities. Especially in British America, efforts to quell illegal commerce were often met with violence against the customs agents tasked with stopping it.[24] Klooster also estimates that at least 75 percent of all commodities consumed and purchased throughout the Atlantic were likely smuggled into their final destinations.[25]

Difficult to quantify, smuggling was an opportunity for goods, ideas, and people to move across national and imperial boundaries, even if empires attempted to place barriers to this trade. Jane T. Merritt argues that in the Atlantic, "imperial restrictions rarely kept Spanish, French, Dutch, Portuguese, and English colonials from trading privately among themselves or with each other."[26] Merritt also explains that tea smuggling was not merely an Atlantic phenomenon, detailing the variety of ways that tea could be acquired in China, shipped from the Indian Ocean to the Atlantic, and finally consumed by tea

---

22   *Boston Gazette*, April 14–21, 1740.
23   *Boston Gazette*, January 1740–October 1741. There are several examples of these updates, but this series includes updates in nearly every issue available.
24   Klooster, "Inter-imperial Smuggling in the Americas," 141–80.
25   Klooster, "Inter-imperial Smuggling in the Americas," 178–79.
26   Merritt, *Trouble with Tea*, 4.

drinkers in British America. At every step along the way, illicit trade occurred. Tea, according to Merritt, easily moved between "permeable imperial boundaries" as easily as a ship could cross the equator.[27]

Many scholars have engaged with the topic of smuggling, and British American scholars frequently discuss the role of smuggling in the colonial experience. Truxes explores how war between empires provided ample opportunity to trade with the so-called enemy. In New York during the Seven Years' War, American merchants frequently traded goods, even military supplies, to French colonists and merchants using the many rivers, bays, and miles of coastline. Of course, not all merchants in New York conducted trade with their sworn enemy, but many did not feel like imperial boundaries should stop them from pursuing profit. In Truxes's perspective, the war increased rather than decreased commercial opportunities for trans-imperial trade.[28] Peter Andreas takes the argument one step further. He argues that the thirteen colonies that eventually became the United States depended upon smuggling for economic success. Furthermore, the skills that smugglers used to conduct trade—establishing trans-imperial connections, moving goods under cover of darkness, using small rivers and creeks efficiently—were crucial in supplying the eventual rebellion. Andreas also shows how Americans did not stop smuggling when the Revolution was over. It was crucial to their identity, and as a result, it became a *Smuggler Nation*, the obvious title for his book.[29] British America was not alone in its dependence on smuggling, as many Spanish colonies were also dependent on illicit commerce to access even bare necessities thanks in large part to neglect from its metropole.[30]

Smuggling clearly was important for British American merchants, and Boston, New York, and Philadelphia were at the center of the illicit Atlantic economy. For instance, much of the sugar, molasses, and rum that traveled through the region was likely smuggled into the three ports from the Caribbean and South America from the many islands and colonies of Spain, France, and the Netherlands.[31] Boston, New York, and Philadelphia were also targeted by the British efforts to control illegal trade. Customs agents in Philadelphia

---

27 Merritt, *Trouble with Tea*, 5.
28 Truxes, *Defying Empire*, 5–7.
29 Peter Andreas, *Smuggler Nation: How Illicit Trade Made America* (Oxford: Oxford University Press, 2013), 43–46.
30 For one such example, see Jesse Cromwell, *The Smuggler's World: Illicit Trade and Atlantic Communities in Eighteenth-Century Venezuela* (Chapel Hill: University of North Carolina Press, 2018).
31 Bailyn, *Atlantic History*, 89–91.

were specifically directed to focus on trade between Boston, New York, and Philadelphia, admitting that the many waterways, miles of shoreline, and abundant access to the ocean provided ample avenues for British Americans to smuggle.[32]

American merchants, therefore, developed myriad ways to import illegal goods. One of the more common yet difficult to track methods to get past customs agents was to pay the officials a bribe. It was extraordinarily common, according to contemporary sources, to find agents willing to accept payments or shares in illegal cargoes. In New York between 1698 and 1702, Chidley Brooke, the customs official in charge of collecting duties, ignored the governor's orders to increase his enforcement of the Navigation Acts, in an unusual case where the colonial governor was more inclined to enforce imperial policy than avoid it. Apparently, it was well known that Brooke was a friend to illicit traders, and the citizens of New York supported him in his confrontation with the governor. Brooke was happy to continue to allow smuggled goods to enter New York as long as those merchants and captains paid him. Though he was given 5 percent of all duties collected plus a salary of £260 per year, it was much lower than the amount he received as bribes.[33] There is no direct evidence of how much he made in bribes, but the New York governor regularly wrote to his superiors in London about the abuses of Brooke and the merchants who sought to avoid customs duties.[34] Also, Brooke and his friends frequently invested in illegal shipments of East Asian and West Indian goods to further supplement their income. Brooke also purchased shares in ships and cargoes that were technically in violation of the Navigation Acts. Since Brooke was the enforcer of those policies, the ships and cargoes he and his friends invested in could conduct business uninhibited.[35]

A more obvious solution, given the geographic possibilities, was that merchants landed goods away from the prying eyes of customs agents whenever possible. New York merchant Waddell Cunningham (as part of his partnership with Belfast merchant Thomas Greg) maintained constant communication with his Dutch compatriots about the situation of illegal shipments of goods. In one letter in 1756, Cunningham informs Isaac and Zachary Hope in

---

32   Port of Philadelphia Customs Papers, HSP. The very first document in the very first volume contains instructions on where to focus customs agents' efforts.
33   *Documents Relative to the Colonial History of the State of New York, 15 Volumes* (Albany: Weed, Parsons and Company, 1853), 4:25.
34   Earl of Bellomont to the Lords of Trade, May 8, 1698, *Documents Relative to the Colonial History of the State of New York*, 4:302–6.
35   Matson, *Merchants & Empire*, 84–86.

Rotterdam that the ship they had sent recently arrived "about Sixty Miles from this place, where his Goods were all safe stored." According to Cunningham, the safety of the cargo was imperiled by "a Number of other Vessels arriving shortly after him from your parts and Copenhagen made so much noise that our Governor is resolved to stop the trade here, if possible."[36] It appears that quite a few ships were attempting to smuggle goods at the same time, sparking suspicion from authorities. Cunningham wrote that he planned to wait a while, then send a smaller sloop to take the goods off the original ship and move them into New York at night.

In the Greg and Cunningham letters, the merchants discuss intricate preparations and routes for illicit trade. In a letter to Herman Van Yzendoorn, also of Rotterdam, Cunningham informs him of all the precautions he took in expectation of another shipment of smuggled goods, already placing men to safely offload the cargo. He also told him the price of rice and logwood, likely goods that Van Yzendoorn requested for the return voyage.[37] Later, Cunningham wrote a letter to Van Yzendoorn to inform him of both good and bad news. One of Van Yzendoorn's shipments sank off the coast of Florida, but another shipment made it safely to Philadelphia, where all goods were sold successfully.[38] These letters indicate that borders were merely obstacles to be overcome. Many of these letters were sent through England, and apparently, the merchants did not fear that their letters would be intercepted.

Accounts and papers of other merchants in the region also show frequent shipments from non-British destinations. In the invoices of a Philadelphia merchant, Tench Francis, multiple shipments from both Lisbon and Amsterdam are mentioned. In one invoice to Francis in May 1760, a shipment of Portuguese wine, priced in Portuguese *reais*, on board the *Britannia* is mentioned.[39] Unfortunately, the only ship named *Britannia* that arrived in that year was from London. There were other ships named Britannia, and there is little evidence to indicate which *Britannia* contained Francis's wine. It appears, however, that the Philadelphia Customs House was not aware of any shipment of Lisbon wine for Francis. There could be two explanations for this. Either the shipment of wine was included in one of the ships named *Britannia* that entered legally, or the shipment was landed out of sight of customs agents.

---

36   Waddell Cunningham to Isaac and Zachary Hope, Rotterdam, May 10, 1756, LGC, 98–99.
37   Waddell Cunningham to Herman Van Yzendoorn, Rotterdam, May 21, 1756, LGC, 122.
38   Waddell Cunningham to Herman Van Yzendoorn, Rotterdam, June 14, 1756, LGC, 141–42.
39   Tench Francis Invoice Book, 1759–61, HSP.

Given the number of smaller docks and offloading points along the Delaware River, the latter was most likely the case.[40]

Wartime offered even greater opportunities for smuggling. In Boston, New York, and Philadelphia, some merchants practiced "flag-trucing," where ships traded merchandise under the premise of prisoner exchanges. This practice began during the War of the Austrian Succession and continued throughout the Seven Years' War, as a greater number of battles and campaigns took place in the Western Hemisphere.[41] As Truxes shows, New Yorkers were especially adept at trading with the non-British actors, even if it meant providing military supplies, provisions, or both to enemy forces. According to an upset citizen: "Scarce a week passes without an illicit trader's going out or coming into this port, under the specious name of flags of truce, who are continually supplying and supporting our most avowed enemies, to the great loss and damage of all honest traders and true-hearted subjects."[42] Dutch islands in the Caribbean frequently became neutral locations for all merchants to conduct trade, without the pesky mercantilist restrictions of the European powers. Curaçao and St. Eustatius were essential in the continuing trans-imperial trade for the merchants of Boston, New York, and Philadelphia.[43] Whenever and wherever illegal goods were traded, the result was the same. Merchants and consumers did not care whether the goods were legal or illegal.

4   Supplying Demand for East Asian Goods

Central to the motivations to conduct trans-imperial trade, legal or illegal, were East Asian goods. Tea, porcelain, and spices were in high demand in British America and especially in the port cities of Boston, New York, and Philadelphia. Though tea did not find a large consumer base until the 1740s, porcelain and

---

40   Port of Philadelphia Customs Papers, vol. 1, 1750–61, HSP; *Pennsylvania Gazette*, June–December 1760. There were multiple ships named *Britannia* with a number of different captains. Some from the West Indies, others from Britain. None listed Lisbon as an origin point. This is not unusual, as ships made multiple stops along the way to a destination.
41   Truxes, *Defying Empire*, 3; Jeremy Land, "Price of Empire: Britain's Military Costs during the Seven Years' War" (MA thesis, Appalachian State University, 2010), 2–3.
42   *New York Gazette, Revived in the Weekly Post-Boy*, June 6, 1748; Truxes, *Defying Empire*, 3.
43   Truxes, *Defying Empire*, 2–6; Klooster, "Inter-imperial Smuggling," 172. Evidence of this can be found in the papers of each city, *New York Mercury*, *Pennsylvania Gazette*, and *Boston Gazette*, to name a few. Numbers of entries and exits to and from Dutch islands tend to increase during wartimes, but they never stop altogether.

spices appeared regularly in the advertisements of newspapers in colonial ports.[44] As detailed earlier, Thomas Greg and Waddell Cunningham regularly smuggled in goods from merchants in Amsterdam and Rotterdam. Many of those shipments contained East Asian goods. In one letter to his colleague in Belfast, Cunningham asks Greg to procure a number of small shipments of tea from Amsterdam and ship them to Rhode Island, away from customs officials.[45] As noted earlier, as much as 75 percent of the tea consumed in British North America was illegally imported from non-British merchants and locations.[46]

In the archives of Boston, New York, and Philadelphia, numerous invoices from places like Amsterdam, Rotterdam, Cádiz, Lisbon, and Hamburg list a wide variety of East Asian goods. One example provides a clear view of many of the mechanisms discussed above. A nine-page invoice from 1760 in the invoice book of a Philadelphia merchant, Tench Francis, details a shipment of tea, porcelain, and German, French, and Dutch manufactures. In this shipment of goods from Amsterdam, Francis received a large quantity of East Asian goods while also bringing in continental goods such as cookware, metalware, and gunpowder. As the cargo was loaded in Amsterdam, prices and shipping charges and insurance costs are given in Dutch guilders, with the total value amounting to 52,128.35 guilders.[47]

While the total is significant, the more intriguing aspects of the invoice are in the details. First, written at the beginning of the invoice is a statement about where the shipment originated, where it was going, and to whom the cargo belonged:

> Invoice of Sundry Goods Ship'd on board the ship St. Graveland Capt'n Joachem Jago bound to Teneriff and Consigned to Mr. Juan Antonio de Franchy y Ponte to be thereine shipped in another Vessel for Philadelphia being ½ acco't with Mess. Francis and Relfe of Philadelphia by order and agreement of Mr. Tench Francis the whole being mark'd and no. as follows.[48]

According to the invoice, the ship was sent first to Tenerife, which is part of the Spanish Canary Islands. Tenerife frequently appears as a destination and origin

---

44   Merritt, *Trouble with Tea*, 4; one can view examples in nearly any issue of the *Boston Gazette*, *New York Mercury*, or *Pennsylvania Gazette*.
45   Waddell Cunningham to Thomas Greg, Belfast, November 12, 1756, *LGC*, 237–38.
46   Klooster, "Inter-imperial Smuggling," 179.
47   Tench Francis Invoice Book, 1759–61, 48–56.
48   Tench Francis Invoice Book, 1759–61, 48. The original spelling is retained.

for ships going to and coming from Boston, New York, and Philadelphia, so it may have been more acceptable than a direct shipment from Amsterdam.[49] They used a middleman, "Juan Antonio de Franchy y Ponte," to ensure that the goods were properly repacked and transported to a Philadelphia-bound ship. Based on documents in the Philadelphia Customs House records, packaging was key. In one case, a ship and its cargo were seized because the soap it was carrying remained packaged in Spanish chests, indicating that the cargo was simply taken off a Spanish ship and placed on the impounded ship.[50] Therefore, Francis's middleman would likely have been careful to package to avoid suspicion. Other Philadelphia merchants frequently included special instructions for smuggled tea, often asking them to be repacked into flour casks with other products placed on top, just in case an agent or naval officer inspected the casks.[51] This appears to have been a regular practice, as another invoice to Francis shows another ship filled with goods from Amsterdam that were to be packed on another ship at Madeira in October of 1761.[52]

Second, the shipment contained a variety of East Asian commodities, of which the most valuable was tea. Francis imported three different types of tea: bohea, hyson, and chausson. Bohea, or black, was the largest portion of the tea shipment, just over 22,700 pounds (weight). The invoice also listed 238 pounds of hyson (dragon pearl green) and 230 pounds of chausson (likely oolong). Altogether, the tea was worth 32,707.9 guilders, and hyson tea carried the highest price per pound. In terms of total weight, this shipment contained more than three times the entire amount of English East India Company tea imported into Pennsylvania between 1731 and 1735 and one thousand pounds less than the yearly average for 1761–65.[53] The second most valuable good on board was porcelain. Likely packed in with the tea though listed separately

---

49   Tenerife is part of the Spanish Canaries, and it may have been slightly more acceptable to show the goods coming from an island that was frequently used as a place to re-provision ships and crews. As we cannot track this particular ship, it may have made at least one more stop before arriving in Philadelphia.
50   Port of Philadelphia Customs Papers, vol. 1, 1750–61, HSP.
51   Merritt, *Trouble with Tea*, 73.
52   Tench Francis Invoice Book, 1759–61, HSP.
53   Merritt, *Trouble with Tea*, table 2.2, 39, and Table 3.1, 69. Between 1731 and 1735, 6,857 pounds of tea were imported into Pennsylvania for the entire period. In the years 1761–65, 122,796 pounds of East India Company tea were imported into Pennsylvania. This works out to an average of just over twenty-four thousand pounds per year during that period. To say that just one ship constituted just one thousand pounds less than the total, legal imports of tea, provides further support to Klooster's assertion that more than 75 percent of tea consumed in the colonies was smuggled. See Klooster, "Inter-imperial Smuggling," 179.

in the invoice, tea sets, cups, saucers, dinner plates, and many more types of porcelain totaled about seven thousand guilders. The shipment also included over forty-eight pounds of saffron, which took up little space but was worth ten guilders per pound, totaling 482.5 guilders. Saffron was likely worth far more in Philadelphia, as it was an extraordinarily rare spice. All told, the Asian goods were worth more than forty thousand guilders, not including shipping or insurance charges, indicating the scale of trans-imperial trade and smuggling normally obscured by efforts to hide such activities.[54] In addition, the porcelain was packed in linens to help prevent damage. Though it does not list these linens as merchandise nor does it indicate the type, these linens could be sold as a bonus once the ship arrived in Philadelphia.

Third, the invoice also lists the various charges that accompanied shipments of this size. Costs to pack, load, and insure the cargo were also itemized. It also shows the various customs duties paid on the goods, though it does not mention where these duties were paid. Most importantly, the itemized charges include two specific entries that are unusual when compared to other similar invoices. The first is listed among the various customs duties paid: "Past ports and Custom House Officers." The amount listed was just over eighty-four guilders, a small amount compared with the sixteen hundred guilders charged just for duties on the tea. The second entry states: "Petty charges to the Officers of Admiralty." It was also a small amount (about eighteen guilders), but considering nearly every other entry is extremely specific, the somewhat vague statement implies a less than honorable meaning. There can be two explanations for these entries. One, the charges might have been administrative charges, such as clerk fees, seals, or other minor costs. Alternatively, the charges are payments (possibly a bribe) to ensure that the goods were cleared for shipment to the intended destination. It is unclear exactly where the payments were made, but it seems unlikely those payments were made in Philadelphia, as no evidence exists of a ship from Tenerife arriving in Philadelphia within the expected period of time.[55] Given that the goods were sent to one destination, offloaded, repacked on another ship, and sent to Philadelphia, the entries might have helped grease the wheels of commerce.[56]

Regardless, the invoice is notable for several reasons. It shows the scale of trans-imperial trade, whether legal or illegal. It highlights the importance of Asian goods in motivating British American merchants to conduct trade across

---

54 Tench Francis Invoice Book, 1759–61, 48–56.
55 *Pennsylvania Gazette*, 1760–61.
56 Tench Francis Invoice Book, 1759–61, 48–56.

imperial borders, not to mention the large quantity of European goods, which included gunpowder and guns.[57] The shipment also describes how a cargo moved through the clearly permeable barriers between empires and colonies, mentioning the specific mechanisms used to avoid detection. In this case, the true nature of the shipment was obscured by multiple ships, repackaging, and multiple agents and consignees. In essence, this invoice provides a glimpse into what must have been a massive, illicit economy, hidden from posterity by individuals wishing to avoid detection.

British Americans were not merely content to wait for European middlemen and merchants to bring goods from the Indian Ocean to North America. They also traded with pirates and privateers, who ventured into the Indian Ocean and prowled its waters. In one case in the 1690s, the *Charles* was given privateering papers by New York's governor, but otherwise, the captain was a notorious pirate. However, in the 1690s, war convinced the governor and New York's merchants that trading with pirates could be profitable. The *Charles* arrived in Madagascar in 1693 to offload a shipment from New York of English manufactures, rum, and other provisions. The witness does not list the goods it carried back to New York, but it likely picked up East Asian goods or Spanish silver and gold from ships it captured while in the Indian Ocean.[58] Several ships from British America joined with the *Charles* to sail into the Red Sea. Two ships, the *Portsmouth Adventure* and the *Pearle*, were outfitted in Rhode Island. The *Amity* traveled from New York; the *Dolphin* was a repurposed Spanish ship based near Philadelphia. Yet another ship arrived from Boston, though the deponent did not name the ship. In all cases, the crews were largely from North America, and all planned to return to North America laden with gold, silver, and luxury items.[59]

Some of the more famous Boston merchants made their fortunes from smuggling East Asian goods. John Hancock is likely the most famous, but Thomas Boylston and his family, whose surname adorns major roads and squares in present-day Boston, earned a large portion of his wealth from smuggling East

---

57 Tench Francis Invoice Book, 1759–61, 48–56. The presence of gun barrels and the various ingredients for gunpowder, all of which came from either France or Germany, is likely due to the Seven Years' War, which raged throughout the world in 1760. However, why a Philadelphia merchant would risk importing military supplies from France *and* German states, since they were at war, remains an unanswered question.

58 Deposition of Adam Baldridge, May 5, 1699, transcribed in Antony, *Pirates in the Age of Sail*, 67–69.

59 John Dann's Testimony against Henry Every, transcribed in Antony, *Pirates in the Age of Sail*, 70–75.

Asian goods from Dutch traders. His sons grew up in a wealthy house filled with exotic goods. The Boylstons enjoyed East Asian goods so much that Thomas's son Nicholas commissioned a painting of himself and wore East Asian clothing for his sitting. As Phyllis Whitman Hunter writes, "Far from showing any semblance of a Yankee trader, Boylston's pose of indolence, draped in silk and velvet, leaning languidly on closed ledgers, summoned images of a Middle Eastern pasha. He donned a silk gown called a 'banyan,' from a Hindi word that means 'merchant' or 'trader.'"[60] It is highly doubtful that the gown chosen for the painting was a mistake. In fact, Boylston's choice of attire was likely deliberate, overtly refusing to resemble an English merchant.

At the root of Boston, New York, and Philadelphia's trans-imperial trade, profit was more important than imperial boundaries and mercantilist policies. Prices of British American goods were often higher in continental Europe than in Britain, especially dried fish and flour, largely because demand was low in Britain. Prices of dried fish, for example, remained nearly double the acquisition price in the colonies throughout the 1760s and up until the outbreak of the Revolutionary War. In Boston and Salem alone, merchants (not including fishermen's profits) pocketed more than £111,000 in 1767.[61] Flour also commanded higher premiums in the Iberian Peninsula, and New York and Pennsylvania averaged more than £250,000 in profits per year between 1768 and 1772 in the grain trade with Southern Europe.[62]

As ensuring maximum profit was of the highest priority, much of the communication between merchants in Boston, New York, and Philadelphia focused on sharing prices, news of droughts or gluts, and hazards that might prevent a ship from arriving, including war, pirates, weather, or increased customs enforcement. In a letter to a Boston merchant, Caleb Davis, written in December 1774, Davis's partner in Gibraltar wrote:

> The failure of the last Harvest in many parts of this Country (particularly to the Eastward) has caused a pretty brisk demand for Foreign Grain, but we are of the opinion even the present price will advance after Xmas, both here & at the neighboring Ports, as that time the effect of the War between the Moors & Spaniards must be felt. The high price in England deprives us of any supplies from thence, therefore our sole dependence

---

60   Hunter, *Purchasing Identity in the Atlantic World*, 149.
61   James G. Lydon, *Fish and Flour for Gold, 1600–1800: Southern Europe in the Colonial Balance of Payments* (Philadelphia: Program in Early American Economy and Society, Library Company of Philadelphia, 2008), 79–81.
62   Lydon, *Fish and Flour for Gold*, 134.

is upon those may drop in from your Quarter, which enhances the value of that Article.⁶³

In short, Davis's partner explained that the poor harvest in the Iberian nations, especially Spain, had created an opportunity for North American grains to find better prices than usual. The merchant even anticipated a higher return, as he thought prices would go up after Christmas and once the effects of war took hold. Frankly cold and calculated, profit was preeminent to ensuring that consumers were able to access grain affordably.

5 Transcending Imperial Borders in the Colonial Arena

European colonies in the West Indies and, to a lesser extent, North America provided easy access to goods such as sugar products and European manufactures. Proximity and a general lack of oversight provided Boston, New York, and Philadelphia merchants and captains the ability to move goods largely unimpeded by British authorities. As long as merchants and captains loosely adhered to British trade policies, commerce between Britain's colonies and the colonies of its rivals remained an important source of profit and capital.

The West Indies offered ample opportunities for merchants to conduct business across imperial boundaries. While British colonies were the most commonly listed origins and destinations customs reports did not list the actual number of islands that a ship might have visited while in the West Indies. Perhaps like no other place in the Atlantic Ocean, imperial borders were blurred and essentially meaningless in the Caribbean, and American merchants and captains took advantage of the proximity between islands (and therefore empires). No single empire could claim absolute authority in the West Indies, greatly limiting the ability of every empire to control or limit trans-imperial commerce. Captains frequently reported their destination as the "West Indies," as merchants provided flexibility for captains to land goods and sell them at the best price. Many times, the stated destination was only the first stop. In the case of Barbados, it was one of the easiest islands to reach and find buyers, but captains were given instructions to continue sailing to other islands if Barbados was not the best option.⁶⁴ In 1739, the *Boston Gazette*

---

63 Robert Anderson to Caleb Davis, December 15, 1774, Caleb Davis Papers, Box 7, December 1774 Folder, MHS.
64 Pares, *Yankees and Creoles*, 48–50; evidence of this can also be found in Caleb Davis Papers, MHS.

records 151 clearances for the "West Indies," but no ship lists just the "West Indies" as its origin. This is clearly indicative of this practice, as many of the listed origins of vessels do not have many reported clearances (see Table 20). Listing "West Indies" as the destination was also an easy way to hide trans-imperial destinations from customs officers. In one invoice in Davis's papers, the sloop *Hope* was "bound for the West Indies" in December 1774 carrying codfish, mackerel, whale oil, iron hoops, and wooden staves. The sloop, however, sailed to Môle-Saint-Nicolas in Saint-Domingue, a French sugar colony. In the same folder of papers, a bill for provisions purchased by the sloop's captain includes items procured in Môle-Saint-Nicolas, and the bill of lading that Davis kept in his possession listed the destination as "St. Nicholas Mole," providing further proof of the true nature of the shipment.[65]

Iberian colonies were important for British American merchants, as much of the contraband imports from Latin America were gold and silver.[66] In Table 20 below, the Customs House of Boston listed twenty-four entries from Spanish colonies in the Caribbean in 1739. Boston merchant Nicholas Oursel attempted to establish regular shipments to and from Brazil between 1709 and 1715.[67] Though silver and gold were highly desirable, imports of slaves from Spanish and Portuguese colonies were also part of the trade between Boston, New York, and Philadelphia. By 1742, black slaves accounted for 8.5 percent of Boston's population, and the consistent arrivals from Ibero-America, such as Hispaniola, usually contained a small number of slaves in addition to commodities such as sugar, precious metals, and logwood (from Honduras in particular).[68]

French West Indian islands were especially important to British American merchants. According to Klooster, merchants in the French Caribbean preferred to do business with British American merchants because they were reliable and offered reasonable prices and higher quality goods compared with English and continental merchants. St. Eustatius, a Dutch island, was a neutral port for the region's trade with French merchants, especially during war years.[69] In 1739, at least nine ships arrived from St. Eustatius (see Table 20).

---

65   Folder December 1774, Box 7, Caleb Davis Papers, MHS.
66   Peggy K. Liss, *Atlantic Empires: The Network of Trade and Revolution, 1713–1826* (Baltimore: Johns Hopkins University Press, 1983), 27.
67   Nicholas Oursel Account Book, 1709–15, Amory Family Papers, MHS.
68   Liss, *Atlantic Empires*, 27–28; Nash, *Urban Crucible*, 106–8.
69   Klooster, "Inter-imperial Smuggling," 172–73.

TABLE 20   Entries and clearances in Boston Gazette, 1739

Destination/origin	Entries	Clearances
English	204	302
Antigua	30	36
Bahamas	1	1
Barbados	30	89
Bermuda	19	5
Jamaica	56	96
Leeward Islands	2	54
Montserrat	4	1
New Providence	4	7
St. Kitts	27	12
Virgin Islands	31	1
Dutch	66	3
Bonaire	1	0
Curacao	22	2
St. Eustatius	9	0
St. Martins	29	1
Surinam	5	0
Spanish	24	1
Dominico	1	0
Hispaniola	3	1
Honduras	20	0
West Indies	0	151
Total	294	457

SOURCE: *BOSTON GAZETTE*, JANUARY–DECEMBER 1739. COMPILED BY AUTHOR. SOME ISSUES ARE MISSING

Furthermore, Saint-Domingue was the most profitable sugar-producing colony in the Western Hemisphere, so it is not surprising that British American merchants sought to conduct trade in Saint-Domingue. Caleb Davis, a preeminent Boston merchant, established his brother, Nathanial, as an agent in Môle-Saint-Nicolas, on the other side of Saint-Domingue's main port, Port-au-Prince. Nathanial Davis worked with French plantation owners and merchants to acquire sugar and molasses, which he regularly shipped back to Boston.

Caleb Davis, as explained above, hid the obviously illicit trade in the official documentation but kept records to ensure that he paid his brother the proper commissions and shares of profits.[70]

Boston, New York, and Philadelphia merchants traded on a substantial scale with the Dutch West Indies. As demonstrated by the 1739 breakdown of entries and clearances in Table 20, ships coming from Dutch islands accounted for 22 percent of all entries from the West Indies into Boston. Suriname, on the coast of South America, was an important destination for the region's merchants. In one bill of lading, Oswald Peel, a Philadelphia merchant, sent a small shipment of one hundred shoes to Antonio Wolfe, a merchant in Suriname.[71] Many other shipments to Suriname included provisions, such as flour, bread, and beer.[72] Gerard Beekman, a New York merchant, collaborated with a fellow merchant in Rhode Island to gather more than a thousand bushels of salt to send to St. Martin in 1754. According to Beekman, the demand was high in St. Martin's, and the schooner he planned to send was already cleared out. This likely means that the ship was cleared for a different destination, but as the ship was already cleared by customs, it could easily carry additional merchandise.[73]

Exemplifying the trans-imperial nature of the intra-Caribbean economy, the account book of Thomas Nicholson, a captain and merchant based in Boston, is full of examples of trans-imperial commerce in the West Indies. While Nicholson conducted trade in the West Indies from the 1760s to the 1780s, the best example of his trans-imperial activities is his account book of 1773–74. Most of the entries in this book are transactions with non-British ports, namely Môle-Saint-Nicolas, Suriname, and Cayenne (northwestern coast of South America). The voyage begins with a load of codfish loaded in Salem and Boston.[74] The cargo of fish belonged to multiple merchants, and he lists the shares of profits at the end of the account book. In February 1773, Nicholson stops first at Môle-Saint-Nicolas in Saint-Domingue, where he sold some of the fish to several merchants, including Nathanial Davis, brother of Caleb Davis. Nicholson then purchased sugar and molasses, much of which was purchased with his own money (or profits from the initial cargo of fish), using mostly

---

70   Folder December 1774, Box 7, Caleb Davis Papers, MHS.
71   Bill of Lading from Oswald Peel to Antonio Wolfe, December 3, 1746, Port of Philadelphia Bills of Lading, 1716–72, vol. 1, HSP.
72   Port of Philadelphia Bills of Lading, 1716–72, vol. 2, HSP. See also, Imports into American Ports and Exports to Great Britain, British and Foreign West Indies, Southern Europe, Wine Islands, 1771–72, HSP.
73   Gerard Beekman to Samuel Fowler, April 29, 1754, *BMP*, 1:213.
74   He lists both ports as origin points, but as Salem was within the greater port complex of Boston, it is likely that he picked up fish from several locations in Massachusetts.

French *livres*. He also picked up additional barrels of fish to sell to Nathanial Davis at his subsequent stops. Nicholson then sailed to Cayenne in French Guiana, where he arrived in March 1773. He sold some of his cargo of fish and purchased cocoa and wine worth six hundred *livres* and 160 *livres* respectively. From Cayenne, Nicholson traveled to Suriname, a Dutch colony just up the coast from Cayenne, where he sold his cargo and procured sugar, cocoa, and wine during March–May 1773. In Suriname, he conducted trade in Dutch guilders, using the currency of each destination as the accounting currency.[75]

Nicholson's account book contains several intriguing entries. First, he conducted trade in multiple currencies, and his summaries of transactions at the end of the account book have scribblings in the margins where he converted *livres* and guilders into English pounds. Second, he picked up his own cargoes in non-British islands in addition to acquiring cargoes for other merchants back in Boston. Third, he regularly sold provisions to other captains, and he occasionally traded goods outright between ships. Fourth, and possibly more interesting, Nicholson recorded multiple loans to other captains and merchants in the Caribbean. In one instance, he lent eleven guilders to Captain Minot, and in another, he lent 250 guilders to Captain Walker. He appears also to have exchanged currencies for captains who were coming from either British America or English islands and wished to trade in Suriname or other non-British destinations.[76] In effect, Nicholson was at once a ship captain, a merchant, and a banker who conducted trade on behalf of himself and others in at least two continents.

Coastal and regional trade also offered plenty of opportunities to conduct illicit, trans-imperial trade. Customs agents, on the whole, paid less attention to the large number of small sloops, ships, and coastal skiffs that plied the waters between ports and hinterlands. In fact, customs agents did not take great care to fully detail the cargoes, nor the origins of the cargoes moving between the ports of North America.[77] French Canada was a popular destination for all three ports. Massachusetts, during the early decades of the eighteenth century, developed a robust commercial relationship with Quebec, Montreal, Louisbourg, and smaller French colonial fishing and trapping towns along

---

75 Account Book, 1773–74, Thomas Nicholson Navigation and Logbooks, 1766–1813, MHS.
76 Account Book, 1773–74, Thomas Nicholson Navigation and Logbooks, 1766–1813, MHS. The entries do not note whether the loans were repaid, but there is a good chance many of these loans were repaid in merchandise, as later summaries in the account book list his cargo on the way back to Boston.
77 Shepherd and Williamson, "Coastal Trade of the British North American Colonies," 784–85.

the North Atlantic coastline. Massachusetts merchants such as Peter Faneuil and William Pepperell frequently shipped goods to French Canada, picking up European manufactures and furs to bring back to Boston.[78] Sometimes, these merchants also arranged cargoes of dried fish, collected and processed by French fishermen, to be sent to Spain, Portugal, and France. In other cases, Boston ships picked up furs and fish in French Acadia and voyaged south to French islands in the Caribbean, acquiring French sugar and molasses to bring back to Boston.[79]

Many goods that were imported into British America from non-British islands in the West Indies were distributed all over the port complex and the hinterlands. Those goods were then repacked onto smaller coastal skiffs, frequently changing containers as well, which were then carried into major ports.[80] Philadelphia merchant Thomas Riche used New Bern, North Carolina, as a stopover destination for goods he planned to export to French Guiana. He instructed a partner merchant to post a bond that the ship carrying provisions was destined for Barbados. He ultimately failed in the ruse, but he continued his efforts to smuggle goods to and from French destinations.[81] Merchants frequently used small Spanish ports along the North American coastline such as St. Augustine to gain access to goods from Mexico and the Spanish Caribbean, at least until 1763, when Spanish lands in North America were ceded to the British.[82]

With entries and clearances from all three cities, we can also separate the origins and destinations into four groups—Britain and Ireland, British intercolonial, trans-imperial, and West Indies—providing a different view of the importance of trans-imperial trade for the region. Table 21 shows the breakdown of entries and clearances in Boston, New York, and Philadelphia at two points in the eighteenth century: 1740 and 1770. In all three cities, the proportion of ships going to and coming from trans-imperial locations grew between 1740 and 1770, with one exception, namely Boston's clearances in 1770. This is likely due to the British military occupation that began in 1768.[83] Philadelphia experienced a major increase in the number of trans-imperial entries, which resulted in Britain substantially falling as a percentage from 10 percent of

---

78 Invoice no. 123, Peter Faneuil Invoice Book, 1725–37, Peter Faneuil Ledger, etc., MHS; Chard, "Massachusetts–Louisbourg Trade, 1713–1744," 146–50.
79 Chard, "Massachusetts–Louisbourg Trade, 1713–1744," 148–50.
80 Matson, *Merchants & Empire*, 85.
81 Doerflinger, *Vigorous Spirit of Enterprise*, 146–48.
82 Liss, *Atlantic Empires*, 27.
83 More on this in the next chapter.

entries in 1740 to just 5 percent in 1770. Even when including Ireland as part of the British Isles, the proportion of ships going to the British Isles does not change much over time. Most importantly, at least a quarter of the ships going to and from all three cities in 1770 are from or going to trans-imperial ports, indicating a heavier integration with non-British markets than with the British market.

Boston newspapers only reported the names of captains and ships leaving and did not report the size or tonnage of the ship, unlike the New York and Philadelphia papers. However, the proportions of tonnage generally align with the breakdowns of entries and clearances. We do know that transatlantic ships were generally larger, so if anything, ships destined for both Southern Europe and the British Isles would have been larger than those going to the West Indies or coastal destinations. Still, the West Indies and North America composed the largest percentage of tonnage (appendix A, Tables A.5–A.7). Given that we know ships frequently visited more than one island while in the West Indies and captains were given enormous latitude to land where the best prices were offered, total trans-imperial trade can only be higher. Furthermore, most shipments of illicit goods were likely not included in these records, further adding weight to the importance of trans-imperial trade for Boston, New York, and Philadelphia.

While the entire region regularly conducted trans-imperial commerce, both legally and illegally, each of the major ports slightly differed in the diversity and proportion of its business with trans-imperial destinations. For Boston, salted cod and other types of fish fueled most of its trans-imperial trade. Portugal and Spain were the top destinations for the highest quality catches, and the West Indies served as the largest market for the lesser qualities of dried fish. In exchange for dried fish, Boston and its feeder ports imported mostly wine and salt, and occasionally small quantities of lemons and other goods. The figures for Boston's trade with Southern Europe are likely understated, primarily because many of the ships that left Massachusetts for Portugal or Spain departed from Salem, which was closer to the large cod fisheries.[84] Nevertheless, the official statistics indicate a range of 4–9 percent of total Boston exports went to Southern Europe, and this number declined substantially during the occupation of Boston from 1768 to 1775 (see appendix A, Table

---

84   See Table 22 for source. Salem primarily exported fish, with most Boston merchants handling the arrangements and supplying the capital necessary for outfitting and loading for both outgoing and return cargoes. As many of these ships returned with salt, it was natural for them to arrive at Salem rather than Boston, since much of that salt was used to process fish.

TABLE 21 Breakdown of entries and clearances in Boston, New York, and Philadelphia in 1740 and 1770

Designation	Philadelphia				New York				Boston			
	1740		1770		1740		1770		1740		1770	
	E	C	E	C	E	C	E	C	E	C	E	C
Britain	30	7	37	25	24	14	39	40	58	46	53	48
% of Total	10%	2%	5%	3%	9%	5%	8%	7%	9%	8%	9%	9%
Ireland	27	42	26	43	12	15	19	32	4	2	0	0
% of Total	9%	14%	4%	6%	5%	6%	4%	6%	1%	0%	0%	0%
Inter-Colonial	196	205	407	483	173	169	252	318	468	421	372	389
% of Total	65%	66%	58%	67%	65%	66%	49%	58%	73%	69%	65%	71%
Trans-Imperial	49	57	226	170	57	60	208	155	113	139	147	113
% of Total	16%	18%	32%	24%	21%	23%	40%	28%	18%	23%	26%	21%
Total:	302	311	696	721	266	258	518	545	643	608	572	550

SOURCE: PHILADELPHIA: 1740, 1770, *PENNSYLVANIA GAZETTE*; NEW YORK: 1740, *NEW YORK WEEKLY JOURNAL* AND 1770, *NEW YORK GAZETTE*; BOSTON: 1740, *NEW ENGLAND WEEKLY JOURNAL* AND *BOSTON NEWS-LETTER* AND 1770, *BOSTON WEEKLY NEWSLETTER*, *BOSTON POST BOY*, AND *BOSTON GAZETTE*

TABLE 22   Fishing vessels entering and clearing bilbao, Spain, 1763–75

Origin	Imports			NCL	Exports		
	Vessels	Value	% of Value	Vessels	Vessels	Value	% of Value
Newfoundland	257	447,555	27%	200	57	33,749	11%
Canada	33	53,936	3%	21	12	22,021	7%
New England	437	995,595	60%	197	240	236,567	76%
Britain	73	100,168	6%	45	28	10,158	3%
Iberia	27	52,843	3%	19	8	6,818	2%
Unknown	5	9,440	1%	3	2	406	0%
Totals	832	1,659,537		485	347	309,719	

SOURCE: LYDON, *FISH AND FLOUR FOR GOLD*, 109. NCL INDICATES NUMBER OF VESSELS THAT WAS NOT FOUND IN CLEARANCES

A.5). Still, we see an increasing diversification of Boston's trade in both goods and trading partners, with new destinations like West Africa appearing more frequently.

Whatever the actual proportion of trade that can be defined as transimperial, Iberians relied on New England fish imports to fulfill dietary needs. In Bilbao, Spain, New England vessels far outnumbered the vessels coming from anywhere else between 1763 and 1775. This is remarkable considering the Boston occupation of 1768–75. As shown in Table 22, New England fish accounted for 60 percent of all fish imported into Bilbao. Only Newfoundland challenged New England at 27 percent. Many of the vessels from Newfoundland were also ships based in Salem or Boston, meaning that much of Newfoundland's exports to Spain were profiting New England owners and merchants, as more vessels cleared Boston for Newfoundland than entered, showing an increasing diversification and reorientation of the region's maritime trade.[85] Spanish diets depended upon British American merchants and fishermen in the eighteenth century, and the profit earned from those ventures provided Boston merchants the capital necessary to increase their own political, economic, and social power.

85   *Boston Gazette*, December 1739–December 1741.

Boston merchants were also active participants in direct trade with Africa and the Indian Ocean. William Pepperell, a famous Boston merchant, regularly received updates from the coast of Madagascar at the beginning of the eighteenth century. According to small snippets of letters, Pepperell conducted business in the Indian Ocean, sending goods to and bringing shipments into Boston directly from the Indian Ocean.[86] Throughout the eighteenth century, Boston merchants regularly sent cargoes of provisions, largely rum and dried fish, to coastal areas of West Africa. In general, Boston customs agents only marked down "Africa" as the destination for most of these ships. There were not a large number, but thirteen ship clearances from Boston to Africa are listed in the *Boston Gazette* for the year 1739.[87] In all likelihood, Boston ships were destined for islands off the coast of Africa, provisioning ships and slavers with rum and food. Boston ships took part in the triangular trade of the Atlantic by picking up slaves to exchange for sugar and molasses in the West Indies.[88]

Though tea and other East Asian goods were commonly smuggled, molasses from the many sugar islands in the Caribbean were just as desirable. In the words of John Adams, "I know not why we should blush to confess that molasses was an essential ingredient in American independence."[89] In the official port records of Boston, 384 hogsheads of molasses were listed as arriving in 1754. The rum distilleries needed about forty thousand hogsheads to produce rum in that year. Those distilleries functioned quite well, which indicates that a large part of imported molasses was smuggled into the region.[90] Some of this illicit trade may have originated in British islands, as smuggling British sugar allowed merchants to avoid customs duties, but most of the illegally imported sugar products likely arrived from non-British islands.[91] Regardless of the types of goods, smuggling hurt British revenue streams. As early as 1700, customs

---

86   Papers, 1664–1745, William Pepperrell Papers, 1664–1782, MHS. Many of these letters are damaged and only portions can be read.
87   *Boston Gazette*, January–December 1739.
88   Shepherd and Walton, *Shipping, Maritime Trade and the Economic Development of Colonial North America*, 49–50.
89   As quoted in Andreas, *Smuggler Nation*, 15.
90   Bailyn, *Atlantic History*, 90.
91   While avoiding duties may have been the overarching reason for smuggling British sugar, much of the smuggled British sugar may have been necessary as ships regularly stopped at several islands in the West Indies. Therefore, ships may have acquired sugar from several colonies from two or more empires. As a result, importers may have chosen to secretly unload cargoes rather than try to legitimize sugar from outside of the British Empire, which carried heavier import duties and restrictions. See discussion of Thomas Nicholson and the West Indian trade earlier in the chapter.

agents estimated the yearly loss of duties due to illicit trade at £60,000 just in Massachusetts, an amount that had surely increased by 1775.[92]

Well after the formal British takeover of New York in 1664, New York merchants carried on trade with the Netherlands and its colonies.[93] As noted earlier, Waddell Cunningham regularly smuggled goods in from Amsterdam and Rotterdam. Other major merchants that imported goods directly from the Netherlands include Philip Cuyler, John Waddell, and John Ludlow. Many of the illicit cargoes contained tea, and some of those cargoes were brought through smaller ports in New England. Until 1740, furs brought into New York from its hinterland and French Canada were then sent to the Netherlands or Dutch colonies in the West Indies to help gain access to European manufactures and East Asian goods, like those listed in the Tench Francis invoice discussed earlier. After 1740, when British officials sought to end the illegal trade with French fur trappers, potash, ginseng, and eventually flour helped merchants to continue their commercial relationship between New York and the Netherlands.[94] On average, at least 11 percent of New York's exports were sent to trans-imperial destinations in Europe (see appendix A, Table A.6).

Non-British West Indian islands were important trade destinations for New York merchants. Much of the West Indian rum that found its way into New York came through the trade of flour to French and Spanish islands.[95] The reason for this is due to French prohibitions against the importation of West Indian rum into France in an attempt to protect brandy producers. These prohibitions remained in place from 1688 to 1729. This left French sugar plantation owners with little choice but to expand trade with British North America to find a market for rum. At least until 1729, merchants regularly reported wholesale prices for sugar, molasses, and rum in French islands to be lower by more than 25 percent than in the British West Indian islands.[96] Grains of all kinds were frequently sent to non-British islands in the Caribbean. In one case, Gerard Beekman sent at least two ships to the West Indies with instructions to find French brandy in exchange for the rye and flaxseed Beekman shipped south. Though the letters do not list the ships' destinations, it would have been easier to find French brandy in the French West Indies than in Jamaica or Barbados.[97]

---

92 Bailyn, *New England Merchants in the Seventeenth Century*, 153.
93 Matson, *Merchants & Empire*, 139–40.
94 Matson, *Merchants & Empire*, 208–9.
95 Christopher Bancker Journals, vol. 1, 1718–39, NYHS.
96 Matson, *Merchants & Empire*, 186–87.
97 Gerard Beekman to Francis Brown, April 14, 1753, and Beekman to John Bennit, May 25, 1753, *BMP*, 1:174, 176.

Both New York and Philadelphia relied on trans-imperial trade for their grain exports. So much so that during the Seven Years' War, merchants in both New York and Philadelphia conspired to conduct trade between French fleets and ships from both cities using "flag-trucing." In one instance, Philadelphia merchants wrote to Jacob Van Zandt, in New York, asking for French prisoners of war to be acquired and sent to Philadelphia. The plan was to meet French traders in the West Indies under a white flag to "exchange prisoners." They were successful in conducting business with French merchants but were later captured by the British Navy on their way back to Philadelphia and New York.[98]

For Philadelphia, exports of grain and flour to Southern Europe were key to the overall economy. In the official British records, 18 percent of Philadelphia's exports went to Southern Europe, matching exactly the proportion of goods going to Britain and Ireland (see appendix A, Table A.7). In the account books of Isaac Norris, three separate shipments of flour and bread were sent to Spain and Portugal within a few months of one another in 1738–39. In the first one, 347 casks of medium-grade flour and nine casks of fine flour were shipped to Cádiz. In the second, 179 casks of fine flour along with £129 worth of staves were sent to Lisbon and Madeira. In the third shipment, 171 casks of fine flour were shipped to Lisbon.[99] In June 1762, Thomas Riche, Tench Francis, and John Searle shared a shipment of flour, raw grain, and corn to Madeira. There the three partners split the profit (2,362 *reais*) from sales of grains in Madeira.[100]

6   Lisbon–Philadelphia Trade

Philadelphia also provides an excellent case study to show the true scale of trans-imperial trade. As mentioned earlier, British American trade with Portugal was a special situation, in that the longstanding treaties between Britain and Portugal opened the door for direct trade between Philadelphia and Portugal. When using Portuguese sources, Philadelphia figures more prominently in the transatlantic grain trade with Portugal. There are large numbers of observations indicating a longstanding trade between Lisbon and Philadelphia throughout the eighteenth century, and it made regular appearances in official port records.[101] This suggests that British officials were aware of the trade and

---

98   Truxes, *Defying Empire*, 94.
99   Isaac Norris Accounts, 1735–40, Account Books (Isaac Norris), LCP.
100 Account Sale of Sundries, Madeira, June 28, 1762, Tench Francis Invoice Book, 1759–61, HSP.
101 Port of Philadelphia Customs House Papers, 1704–89, vol. 1, HSP.

apparently gave their blessing to the growing relationship between the two ports. In the port registry of Lisbon, one entry is quite confusing considering the nature of eighteenth-century imperial relationships. In that entry, a French-owned and crewed ship apparently made regular trips between Philadelphia, Lisbon, and sometimes a French colony in the Caribbean. In Philadelphia, it picked up a shipload of flour, proceeded to unload that cargo in Lisbon, then continued in ballast (empty) to the Caribbean.[102] It is unclear what, if anything, the ship picked up in the Caribbean. We do not have documents to track this ship, but it is highly unlikely that it completed the journey without any merchandise on board. Passing through several islands off the coast of Africa, it may have picked up new cargoes, perhaps slaves, to carry to the Caribbean.

From the other side of the Atlantic, however, Lisbon's trade with Philadelphia may possibly have been far more robust than the current literature and British records indicate. As seen in Table A.9 in appendix A, records from the British Customs House in Philadelphia printed weekly in the *Pennsylvania Gazette* show that 419 ships left Philadelphia to go to Lisbon between 1769 and 1774. Lisbon records, however, show that 725 ships entered from Philadelphia in the same time frame, a 73 percent increase on the figures recorded by the British.[103] This indicates that, when we use source material from other empires, the region's trans-imperial trade could be much higher than we currently see in the literature. Furthermore, the example of the French ship maintaining a regular route between Philadelphia and Lisbon is not an isolated case. There are several other ships, owned and crewed by other empires, such as Spanish or Dutch ships, consistently moving American goods to and from Lisbon. In effect, the current estimates need to be adjusted, especially as new sources become available such as those from Lisbon.[104] In Figure 7, we can see that Philadelphia's main exports to Lisbon were grain and corn products. Flour made up 51 percent of total entries into Lisbon, and Portugal's appetite for Philadelphia's flour provided a substantial amount of capital by which mill owners increased their capacity.

---

102 Lisbon Municipal Archive, Historical Archive, Collection "Taxes," Tonnage Tax Fund, Tonnage Tax Book of Entries, refs. AML-AH-MN.
103 Sources: 1769–74, *Pennsylvania Gazette*. Lisbon Municipal Archive, Historical Archive, Collection "Taxes," Tonnage Tax Fund, Tonnage Tax Book of Entries. Compiled by author.
104 Lisbon Municipal Archive, Historical Archive, Collection "Taxes," Tonnage Tax Fund, Tonnage Tax Book of Entries. Lisbon's archives pre-1755 were destroyed in the catastrophic 1755 Lisbon earthquake that decimated the city and its infrastructure. They are still being reconstructed by archivists and historians in Portugal. For more on this special relationship between the colonies and Portugal, see Land and Dominguez, "Illicit Affairs," 179–204.

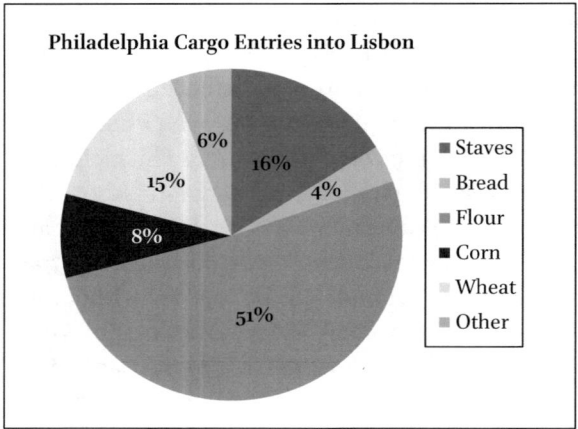

FIGURE 7   Philadelphia cargo entries into Lisbon
SOURCE: BASED ON TRADE DATA CONTAINED IN THE LISBON MUNICIPAL ARCHIVE, HISTORICAL ARCHIVE, COLLECTION "TAXES," TONNAGE TAX FUND, TONNAGE TAX BOOK OF ENTRIES, REFS. AML-AH-MN

7   Conclusion

Though inter-colonial trade was prominent in the total maritime trade of Boston, New York, and Philadelphia, trans-imperial trade was quite significant and more important than the direct trade with Britain and Ireland. The region's continued trade with non-British ports throughout this period reveals that the Navigation Acts and imperial prohibitions on British American trade were not so effective as is generally assumed. In addition, the growing number of vessels and merchants sailing throughout the Atlantic Ocean began to worry many in the British Isles about where the real competition for Atlantic trade lay. There were political repercussions from the growing reliance on trans-imperial trade for access to both luxuries and necessities. British officials responded at various points in the eighteenth century to growing concerns in England that American merchants were overstepping their place in the British Empire. By the middle of the 1760s, Britain took concrete steps to limit or outright stop direct trade between British America and destinations outside of its empire. These reinvigorated efforts were instrumental in creating the conditions for the political turmoil of the 1770s.

CHAPTER 6

"Salutary Neglect" and the Origins of Independence

Throughout the eighteenth century, merchants and consumers in Boston, New York, and Philadelphia confronted numerous challenges and obstacles, both economic and political, that threatened their livelihoods. At the core of these difficulties was the relationship between these colonies and the metropolis, which created both impediments to and opportunities for economic growth. Often precisely because of its economic growth, British imperial officials sought to curtail the region's mercantile capacity and mobility in favor of the metropole. Instead of a story of "salutary neglect," British efforts to impose a mercantilist vision on its colonies came in waves with varying levels of success, and each wave was met with resistance from merchants and consumers in Boston, New York, and Philadelphia. Yet by the 1770s, Britain was still unable to muster enough state capacity to enforce the mercantilist policies that nominally prohibited trade to non-British destinations, providing ample opportunities for trans-imperial trade as seen in the previous chapter. The virtual lack of enforcement, at least until the late 1760s, allowed the region to become an economic nodal center within both the British Empire and the Atlantic economy, greatly empowering its merchants to confront British efforts to control the three cities' trade.

This chapter explores the growing political and economic power and its implications for the economy of Boston, New York, and Philadelphia. The first section explores the ways in which the region's merchants conducted trade up until the 1750s and the extent to which the British Empire was able to regulate this trade. A key question is whether there was a general "salutary neglect" or if the empire had the capacity to effectively control the region's trade. In the second section, I examine the dynamics of the region's economic growth in the eighteenth century and how the colonies' merchants and their commercial aspirations affected the relationship between the colonies (Boston, New York, and Philadelphia) and Britain. I will then discuss the repercussions of the Seven Years' War for the region by focusing on the challenges and opportunities that the war created as well as merchants' responses to Britain's trade policies in the Atlantic. Most importantly, I examine the economic consequences of the war for Boston, New York, and Philadelphia, and how the war's outcomes altered the trans-imperial nature of the region's trade. Finally, I conclude the chapter with a discussion of the post-war developments and Britain's efforts to hold on to its expanded North American empire. To what extent did war debt influence

British decisions to enact new revenue measures and increase enforcement of the Navigation Acts? In the end, Britain lost thirteen of its North American colonies in the 1770s, and merchants in Boston, New York, and Philadelphia played a major role in the eventual independence of those colonies.

1   "Salutary Neglect" and Imperial Control

Traditional narratives of colonial America tend to assume that the bilateral economic relationship between British Americans and Britain was the most important for American merchants and consumers. Historians treat the colonies as having a metropolitan focus. They assume that the mercantilist aspirations of the British Empire were largely fulfilled, effectively treating non-British trade as the exception rather than the rule.[1] The substantial trans-imperial trade carried out by merchants of these colonies and a nearly constant endeavor by British imperial officials to restrict any trade with non-British ports and stamp out smuggling show that any narrative centered on the colony–metropolis trade alone is inadequate to fully understand the dynamics of the commercial economy of these colonies. If the colonial balance of trade was far in favor of Britain, why would British officials frequently express dismay at being unable to stop the flow of non-British goods into British American ports and the export of American products to other European empires?

More recent research into the nature and activity of European empires in the Atlantic has highlighted a constant discourse between colony and metropole where negotiation and accommodation were more important than imperial dictates. Antoinette Burton, for example, argues that "the very character of imperial power was shaped by its challengers and by the trouble they made for its stewards."[2] In other words, hegemony depended upon local and/or indigenous acquiescence to imperial policy. Without it, the empire was forced to negotiate to find a route toward compliance, and only in rare cases did colonial

---

1 In general, the older the history the more dominant the British Empire appears. Some examples include but are not limited to: Oliver Morton Dickerson, *American Colonial Government, 1696–1765: A Study of the British Board of Trade in Its Relation to the American Colonies, Political, Industrial, Administrative* (New York: Russell and Russell, 1912); Ralph Davis, *The Rise of the Atlantic Economies* (Ithaca, NY: Cornell University Press, 1973); and McCusker and Menard, *Economy of British America*. Of these three, McCusker and Menard make clear that the role of non-British trade was important, but they still rely on the high negative balance of trade between the colonies and England to indicate economic dependence.
2 Antoinette Burton, *The Trouble with Empire: Challenges to Modern British Imperialism* (Oxford: Oxford University Press, 2015), 1.

subjects immediately obey metropolitan edicts. This is especially true for the British Empire in the seventeenth and eighteenth centuries. Abigail Swingen shows how the early struggle for local autonomy and access to unfree labor in the British Caribbean shaped the overall structure and character of British imperial policy. When local elites faced a nearly constant shortage of labor for their fledgling plantations, they sought to find access to slaves regardless of the empire to which the slave ships belonged. This placed British colonial subjects in direct conflict with the imperial-backed monopoly of the Royal African Company to provide slaves to Jamaica, Barbados, and other British islands. Even though Britain occasionally used naval and military threats and blockades to force colonial compliance, British imperial policy often failed to prevent British plantation owners from purchasing slaves from non-British suppliers, compelling British imperial officials to accommodate the needs and wants of the colonies.[3] If negotiation and accommodation were still not enough to satisfy colonial subjects, merchants and others circumvented and, at times, outrightly disregarded imperial policies. Smuggling and extra-legal activity frequently provided opportunities for profit and subsistence for many European colonies, utilizing the trans-imperial nature of Atlantic commerce to their advantage.[4]

Scholars of British America have frequently cited the period before 1763 as a period of "salutary neglect" wherein imperial officials, despite having various Navigation Acts legally prohibiting free trade in the colonies, largely turned a blind eye to the maritime commerce of British America. Most treat the period before 1763 as a period of virtual laissez-faire with limited interruptions to British America's free trade.[5] So common is it in the historiography that Andreas, in his study of illicit trade in America, also emphasizes the importance of this period as essential to the development and growth of smuggling in the colonies, while at the same time discussing the many court cases involving illegal traders who were caught in the act.[6] How could it have been a period of "neglect" if a constant stream of cases filled the court dockets of British America?

---

3 Swingen, *Competing Visions of Empire*.
4 For more on how illegal commerce became common in the Atlantic, see Andreas, *Smuggler Nation*, and Cromwell, *Smuggler's World*.
5 One of the oldest and most influential works is Arthur Meier Schlesinger, *The Colonial Merchants and the American Revolution, 1763–1776* (New York: Longmans, Green and Company, 1918). Other examples are Dickerson, *Navigation Acts and the American Revolution*, and Benjamin L. Carp, *Rebels Rising: Cities and the American Revolution* (Oxford: Oxford University Press, 2007).
6 Andreas, *Smuggler Nation*, 15–18.

Instead of treating the period before 1763 as one devoid of imperial enforcement of mercantilism, this study shows that there were alternating phases of strict enforcement of imperial regulations, neglect or a hands-off attitude, and accommodation. This was primarily because Britain's commercial ambitions were incompatible with the local realities, the ambitions of local merchants and the limited state and fiscal capacity of the imperial state. The British administration did not lack the desire to control colonial trade, but the empire was not capable of controlling trade due to limited resources and the huge geographic size of Britain's North American empire. Even within Britain's borders, the state was unable to fully realize the fiscal opportunities that the burgeoning economic power of the British Empire offered. The first few decades of the eighteenth century witnessed a struggle over the structure and depth of the empire's power to tax its citizens.[7] It was not even successful in stemming the flow of illegal goods into the British Isles, as the Swedish East India Company was very successful in smuggling tea into Scotland and England.[8] Britain, therefore, outsourced regulation and administration to colonial governments and officials. Britain expected that local, colonial institutions and private citizens would enforce and abide by the mercantilist ideals of the mother country. At times, this was successful, but the vast area that the imperial structure needed to cover prevented a full enforcement, no matter how much imperial agents tried.

As the empire provided the British American colonies the ability to create governments, British administrators initially believed that the colonies could control their own citizens and that imperial laws would be enforced properly. To that end, the Commissioners of the Customs charged colonial governments

---

7   John Brewer, *The Sinews of Power: War, Money and the English State, 1688–1783* (Cambridge, MA: Harvard University Press, 1988), xviii–xx. Brewer portrays a government in a continual struggle to obtain ever greater powers to tax its empire before the loss of the American colonies. Increasing amounts of financial resources were necessary due to the nearly constant state of warfare between England and France, and as a result, England became a more bureaucratic and efficient state, though it did cost it thirteen colonies of its North American empire.

8   Leos Müller, "Svenska ostindiska kompaniet och den europeiska marknaden för te," in *Sverige och svenskarna i den ostindiska handeln II: Strategier, sammanhang och situationer*, Bertil S. Olsson and Karl-Magnus Johansson (Riksarkivet, Landsarkivet i Göteborg, 2019), 237–61. For more on Swedish tea smuggling into Britain and throughout the Atlantic see: Hanna Hodacs and Leos Müller, "Chests, Tubs, and Lots of Tea: The European Market for Chinese Tea and the Swedish East India Company, c. 1730–1760," in *Goods from the East, 1600–1800: Trading Eurasia*, ed. Felicia Gottman et al. (New York: Palgrave Macmillan, 2015), 277–93; and Hanna Hodacs, *Silk and Tea in the North: Scandinavian Trade and the Market for Asian Goods in Eighteenth-Century Europe* (London: Palgrave Macmillan, 2016).

with setting the fees and commissions provided to customs officers and collectors. On the surface, it seemed like a great idea considering that any seizures or criminal charges would be tried in local, colonial court systems. As we have already seen, however, colonial governments were often composed of and sympathetic to merchants, especially in Massachusetts, New York, and Pennsylvania. By the 1710s, colonial governments had lowered fees and commissions to such low levels that few individuals desired to work for the customs service. Of the forty-two permanent positions in the customs service from Newfoundland to Bermuda, most experienced significant turnover, and some remained open throughout most of the first half of the eighteenth century.[9] According to one customs official, prosecuting smugglers in a place where "they hate to have their trade inspected" was nigh impossible.[10]

Local resistance to customs enforcement, like that of the *Fame* in Philadelphia, was a common occurrence not only among the merchants of the colonies but also among colonial governors and assemblies. In South Carolina in 1715, the governor, Charles Craven, frequently commandeered ships that had been impounded by customs officials on the "pretext that it was required for the public service." The ship would then sail out to sea on a clearly superfluous mission and return without the illicit cargo on board. In other cases, Craven claimed seized goods as his own, no doubt protecting his merchant friends. One crisis nearly threatened outright war between the British Navy and South Carolina when Craven ordered the Charleston port to fire on the customs and naval vessels attempting to search visiting ships.[11]

In one court case in 1708, Boston merchants petitioned the imperial government to prevent a shipment from being impounded by the customs officials in Boston. The ship in question had visited Lisbon and Bilboa before arriving in Boston. With their petition, they included excerpts of a letter written by an official in Lisbon remarking that the goods were shipped on "English vessels with such passes for better security," attempting to give legitimacy to the goods according to the Navigation Acts.[12] The records do not indicate the success or failure of the petition, but the fact that multiple people spoke on behalf of the accused smugglers and that the court included such documents shows the willingness of the court and local government to include nearly anything that might legitimize a ship and its cargo. This also highlights the incompatibility between imperial ambitions and local realities.

---

9   Barrow, *Trade and Empire*, 93–96.
10 As quoted in Barrow, *Trade and Empire*, 95.
11 Barrow, *Trade and Empire*, 93.
12 Petition by Boston Merchants, April 1708, MHS.

Negotiation between colonial governors and the crown often limited the enforcement of customs regulations. In New York in the 1710s, Governor Richard Ingoldesby insisted that New Yorkers be allowed to ship flour and wheat to the Spanish West Indies because both farmers and merchants would be "impoverished" without that trade. By the 1730s, New Yorkers were still importing logwood and Spanish American silver into the port, and customs and colonial officials often turned a blind eye for a few pieces of that silver.[13] Smuggling was so important to the economies of Boston, New York, and Philadelphia that merchants could insure goods against seizure by customs officers. In the records of a Boston insurance underwriter, Ezekiel Price, there are examples of insurance policies that contain additional clauses protecting ships even if caught importing illegal goods. In 1760, the ship *Fly* was insured against "seizures by ships of his Majesty's Britannia Navy."[14]

Merchants were undeterred by the prospect of seizure, and merchant communities, especially in Boston, New York, and Philadelphia, often helped other merchants conduct illicit trade. Cornelius Cuyler, a New York merchant, provided a substantial amount of latitude to his captains to visit non-British islands in the West Indies and regularly sent his son to Amsterdam to procure bohea tea.[15] Merchants used complicated paperwork and multiple stops to obscure the true nature of their goods. In 1735–36, New York merchant Philip Livingston sent New York wheat to Barcelona but had his captain send payments to London creditors while in Barcelona. From there, Livingston's ship sailed to Amsterdam, where the captain was instructed to use the remaining profits to buy tea, Dutch manufactures, paper, glass, and other items.[16] Because of the multiple stops and large variety of return goods, customs officials were often unable to prevent the importation of non-British tea or other merchandise.

Sometimes merchants and local citizens responded with violence toward efforts to stifle smuggling. In 1723, Boston customs officials drew a summons in the Admiralty Court for the master of the ship *William and Mary*, W. Whipple, and his crew who had sailed into Boston from Lisbon carrying salt. The comptroller, William Lambert, discovered that the ship had secretly stopped along

---

13   Matson, *Merchants & Empire*, 212.
14   Ezekiel Price Papers, MHS. For more on the insuring of illegal goods, see John W. Tyler, *Smugglers and Patriots: Boston Merchants and the Advent of the American Revolution* (Boston: Northeastern University Press, 1986), 14–17.
15   Matson, *Merchants & Empire*, 210.
16   Matson, *Merchants & Empire*, 210.

the coast of Massachusetts to unload Spanish leather and oil without declaring those goods at port. Only two of the crew appeared in court to testify, and the supporters of the defendants threatened and shoved the witnesses so violently that the court was forced to adjourn for the day.[17] Lambert described the group of merchants and captains as a mob who continued to make violent threats and assaults on the customs officials and even the local sheriff. The governor of Massachusetts was able to quell the riots and subdue the mob, but customs officials were hesitant to make further seizures or prosecutions.[18]

Though English officials wished to increase the size and effectiveness of the customs service, no more than fifty-eight permanent positions were created in all of British America until 1760, which included the West Indies. Most of those positions were support positions for the various customs houses, four of which were located within the region of Boston, New York, and Philadelphia. Local governments resisted new efforts to increase the number of enforcement officers, and because of the reliance on local governments to provide proper fees and commissions, imperial officials were unable to create an efficient force. The issue became so pronounced that, in 1725, the Commissioners of the Customs received a report that suggested that payments to various customs agents and officials were too high and needed to be reduced, largely because they were not bringing in enough revenue. The Commissioners reduced the expenses of the customs services mainly due to the continuous resistance that the customs service faced from colonial merchants, governors, and consumers. The expense of the customs service in the colonies under the original agreement amounted to about £4,000, and the 1725 plan reduced the number of positions and wages so that they only cost £2,660. In view of the substantial resistance to enforcement in the colonies, the board chose not to enforce the regulations to assuage colonial merchants' concerns. Whatever the case may be, the plan represented a serious effort to both reduce imperial expenses and cool the growing colonial resentment to imperial policies.[19]

---

17   In colonial courts, a literal bar separated the audience, witnesses, and defendants from the judges, juries, and lawyers trying cases. This resulted in witnesses surrounded by members of the public, often with limited or nonexistent protection. In this particular instance, the witnesses were so pressed up against the bar that they had difficulty speaking and breathing. In addition, those opposed to the witness statements could shout directly in the ear of the witnesses and whisper threats to their persons or families. In effect, the court was certainly not a safe place for witnesses to provide testimony, and it was common for witnesses to avoid appearing if at all possible.
18   Barrow, *Trade and Empire*, 89–90.
19   Barrow, *Trade and Empire*, 106–8.

2   Colonial Merchants as Competitors with English Merchants

Colonial merchants, in large part due to their ability to avoid imperial policies, earned a significant amount of profit from both legal and illegal trade. As a result, British merchants began to fear that American merchants would challenge their preeminence in the Atlantic economy. Whether a real threat or an imagined one, English merchants and imperial officials sought to limit the commercial capacity of British American merchants, especially in Boston, New York, and Philadelphia.

Merchants and government officials in Britain feared colonial competition as early as the late seventeenth century. The revised Navigation Act of 1673 was introduced into Parliament for the explicit reason that New England threatened to become a powerful center of trade. In meetings of the Privy Council's Committee on Plantation Commerce, commonly referred to as the Lords of Trade, several members expressed concern about the growing mercantile capacities of New England, and specifically Boston. A year before the Navigation Act was even introduced in Parliament, one council member stated that New England "dayly grew more destructive to the trade of Kingdome," and that the government should "hinder theire growth as much as can be."[20] After the passage of the act, Lord Culpeper, an influential leader of the Lords of Trade, remarked that the Parliament seemed to direct the act toward merchants in New England. The Navigation Act's objectives were to limit British American trade between colonies, England, and foreign merchants. More specifically, colonial trade must solely benefit England and English merchants. Revenue was not a main objective, but the Parliament hoped it would turn a tidy profit for the public coffers.[21]

Their fears were not unfounded, as Boston, New York and Philadelphia certainly grew into commercial centers. While London remained the largest and wealthiest port in the Atlantic throughout the eighteenth century, the American colonies substantially increased their purchasing power and consumption during this period. Using English imports as a measure of consumption, Table 23 shows the yearly average for each decade of the eighteenth century. English imports are the only types of imports for which there is data for the entire century, and while we are certain that imports from elsewhere in the Atlantic were substantial (see Chapter 5), legal imports of goods also show an increase in purchasing power. Between the first decade of the eighteenth

---

20   As quoted in Barrow, *Trade and Empire*, 9.
21   Barrow, *Trade and Empire*, 8–10.

TABLE 23 Ten-yearly average values of english imports into colonies by decade (£ sterling, constant value)

Decade	Total Thirteen Colonies	Regional Total	Regional % of Total
1700–9	272,371	126,220	46%
1710–19	363,038	190,791	53%
1720–29	449,624	259,654	58%
1730–39	618,541	338,546	55%
1740–49	804,775	409,072	51%
1750–59	1,447,546	901,062	62%
1760–69	1,866,542	1,082,750	58%
1770–74	1,381,053	835,330	60%

Notes: Regional Total includes New England, New York, and Pennsylvania which were dominated by the ports of Boston, New York, and Philadelphia. The year 1775 is not included as hostilities began between Britain and the colonies which resulted in a severe drop in English imports.

SOURCE: S. B. CARTER, ET AL, CHAPTER EG, HISTORICAL STATISTICS OF THE UNITED STATES: MILLENNIAL EDITION (CAMBRIDGE: CAMBRIDGE UNIVERSITY PRESS, 2006), 5: 710–13

century and the 1760s, total imports of goods from Britain increased by 685 percent, and the region of Boston, New York, and Philadelphia increased its consumption by 857 percent, outpacing the rest of the thirteen colonies. By the 1770s, the region accounted for over 60 percent of total consumption in the British American colonies. These figures do not include exports and imports to and from places other than England, and therefore, based on the data presented in the previous chapters, it may be argued that the levels of consumption and purchasing power were much higher.

In Table 24, Shepherd and Walton indicate a strong domestically owned merchant marine that, on the surface, may have threatened the dominance of British merchants in the Atlantic Basin. Compared with McCusker and Menard's figures (see Table 5, Chapter 2), the percentages are similar. When one considers that there is a vast discrepancy between the owners of tonnage engaged in trade with colonies south of Pennsylvania, one must conclude that the ports of Boston, New York, and Philadelphia were largely in a league of

TABLE 24 Percentage of ship tonnage entering and clearing colonial ports owned by colonial residents in overseas trade, 1768–72

Origin/Destination	Colonial-Owned	
	Entries	Clearances
Great Britain and Ireland	63%	72%
Southern Europe and the Wine Islands	76%	75%
West Indies	84%	80%
Africa[a]	100%	100%

a The number of observations for destinations and origins in Africa are quite few, and given the growing levels of direct trade between the colonies and Africa, especially for Boston, it appears that the primary investors in direct trade with Africa were solely based in the British American colonies
SOURCE: JAMES F. SHEPHERD AND GARY M. WALTON, "ESTIMATES OF 'INVISIBLE' EARNINGS IN THE BALANCE OF PAYMENTS OF THE BRITISH NORTH AMERICAN COLONIES, 1768–1772," *JOURNAL OF ECONOMIC HISTORY* 29, NO. 2 (JUNE 1969): 230–63, AT 240–41.

their own, as residents in those three cities owned more than 70 percent of their total tonnage, whereas colonial residents in the Southern colonies owned less than 35 percent of tonnage employed in trade. More importantly, colonial merchants owned more than 75 percent of the total tonnage employed in the direct trade with Southern Europe. This was well known to imperial officials, as the figures above are derived from the official statistics of the empire. Considering the discrepancy between entries and clearances just between Lisbon and Philadelphia and that many ships landed away from the eyes of customs officials, the real percentage must be higher. Based on these figures, it may be argued that colonial merchants were capable of challenging British primacy in the Atlantic maritime economy.

If the tonnage was largely owned by colonial merchants, then colonial merchants had the lion's share in trade. As Boston, New York, and Philadelphia dominated the region (in the data divided between New England and the Middle Colonies), the largest proportion of maritime profits were earned by the merchants in and around Boston, New York, and Philadelphia. In Table 25, between 81 and 84 percent of British American shipping profits went to the region. This disparity holds true for nearly every category, excepting the West Indies, where the region's merchants received more than 87 percent. For Africa, New England vessels and merchants were the only ones regularly shipping goods (usually rum) to the west of the continent. As discussed in the previous chapter, the profits from Southern European trade were likely substantially higher than have been estimated by Shepherd and Walton. As profits are hard to track, Shepherd and Walton used commodity prices and the ownership figures they and McCusker produced to determine where and how much profit found a home.[22] The main reason for the huge disparity between the region of Boston, New York, and Philadelphia and the rest of British America was that most of the tonnage engaged in the region's trade was owned by merchants based in that area. Therefore, most of the costs to ship goods stayed in the hands of colonial merchants, captains, and shipowners.

As we have already seen in Chapter 5, there were only a few examples of direct trade between British America and South and East Asia and usually with the assistance of pirates and less scrupulous individuals. This was, however, not because of any lack of effort on the part of American merchants. William Allen and Benjamin Franklin, both of Philadelphia, bankrolled three attempts to find a Northwest Passage to China. The ship *Argo* sailed north in 1751, 1753, and 1754 to find rivers, lakes, and oceans to access the Pacific. Explicitly in opposition to the Navigation Acts, London authorities expressed major concern about colonial merchants finding their own way to China. Though unsuccessful in finding a way to China, the *Argo* was successful in establishing a fruitful trade with fishermen and trappers in Labrador, but this too placed the venture of Allen and Franklin in competition with the Hudson's Bay Company, which held a monopoly in the region.[23] Whatever the result, English merchants and, especially, monopolistic companies were concerned about the economic reach of the region's merchants and sought to pressure imperial officials to limit the capacity and freedom of American commerce.[24]

Again, British Americans consistently imported East Asian goods from non-British ports, especially from the Netherlands and Portugal, often by way of the West Indies and other stopover locations. Tenerife, Madeira, St. Eustatius, Saint-Domingue, and other non-British islands were popular stops for merchants

---

22 James F. Shepherd and Gary M. Walton, "Estimates of 'Invisible' Earnings in the Balance of Payments of the British North American Colonies, 1768–1772," *Journal of Economic History* 29, no. 2 (June 1969): 230–63.

23 The Hudson's Bay Company was formed in 1670 to monopolize the English fur trade in and around the Hudson's Bay in the North Atlantic. It was formed by a group of fur traders with investment capital from merchants in Boston to expand access to furs in the northeasternmost part of what is now Canada. In fact, as of 2022 it still functions as a clothing company.

24 Jonathan Goldstein, *Philadelphia and the China Trade, 1682–1846: Commercial, Cultural, and Attitudinal Effects* (University Park: Pennsylvania State University Press, 1978), 23.

TABLE 25   Estimated shipping profits, 1768–72 (thousands of £ sterling)

Colonial Region	Overseas Area				
	1768	1769	1770	1771	1772
Great Britain and Ireland					
Northern Colonies	1	1	1	2	2
New England	55	62	66	60	60
Middle Colonies	61	57	59	66	55
Southern Colonies	27	27	25	30	28
Florida, Bahamas, and Bermuda	0	0	0	0	0
Total	*144*	*147*	*151*	*158*	*145*
Southern Europe					
Northern Colonies	3	4	5	10	8
New England	39	46	42	55	48
Middle Colonies	39	52	51	36	40
Southern Colonies	28	43	28	16	20
Florida, Bahamas, and Bermuda	0	0	0	0	0
Total	*109*	*145*	*126*	*117*	*116*
West Indies					
Northern Colonies	1	2	2	2	2
New England	193	195	205	225	235
Middle Colonies	62	64	75	69	83
Southern Colonies	36	37	39	40	44
Florida, Bahamas, and Bermuda	1	1	1	1	1
Total	*293*	*299*	*322*	*337*	*365*
Africa					
Northern Colonies	0	0	0	0	0
New England	3	4	4	2	5
Middle Colonies	0	0	0	0	0
Southern Colonies	0	0	0	0	0
Florida, Bahamas, and Bermuda	0	0	0	0	0
Total	*3*	*4*	*4*	*2*	*5*
Total Overseas Areas					
Northern Colonies	5	7	8	14	12
New England	290	307	317	342	348
Middle Colonies	162	173	185	171	178
Southern Colonies	91	107	92	86	92
Florida, Bahamas, and Bermuda	1	1	1	1	1
Total	*549*	*595*	*603*	*614*	*631*

SOURCE: SHEPHERD AND WALTON, "ESTIMATES OF 'INVISIBLE' EARNINGS IN THE BALANCE OF PAYMENTS OF THE BRITISH NORTH AMERICAN COLONIES, 1768–1772," 250

from Boston, New York, and Philadelphia.[25] British merchants and imperial officials were aware and concerned about the frequent use of stops to obscure the origin of imports into the area. Even when officials attempted to reduce or eliminate the taxes on legal imports of tea, they were still unable to stop smuggling.[26] A Philadelphia merchant, Samuel Wharton, noted in 1773 that smuggling was still preferred because "the ports of Holland and Portugal in Europe and St. Eustatius in America, as they know, they are always open for the reception of their flours, corn, and etc."[27] For many merchants in America, trading with merchants in non-British destinations provided an easier way to obtain tea and other East Asian goods because those areas maintained a steady demand for American products like flour and dried fish. In this way, they could overcome the constant shortage of hard specie that was too often demanded by British companies and merchants. This greatly lowered their transaction costs by reducing the amount of capital necessary to obtain items to export since so many merchants in Boston, New York, and Philadelphia provided merchandise credit in exchange for agricultural goods and commodities. This reality can be seen in contemporary discussions of tea smuggling. Philadelphia merchant John Kidd remarked in 1757 that "not more than 16 chests of tea legally imported from England have been consumed in Pennsylvania in two previous years, although total yearly consumption must have been ca. 200 chests."[28]

It was precisely because of East Asian goods that customs agents maintained employment. In Philadelphia, the customs officers received instructions from the Commissioners of Customs to ensure that Asian goods did not arrive in Philadelphia and its feeder ports. In a 1750 letter to William Peters, customs collector in Philadelphia, an unknown customs official in Virginia explained his orders from the Commissioners and wrote:

> Upon an information that great quantities of European and East Asian commodities, particularly Linnen & Tea, are run into His Majesty's Plantations in America by the French, Dutch, & others, the Commissioners have directed me to use my utmost endeavors, to prevent these Frauds for the Future. I therefore most earnestly recommend it to you, to be

---

25 See Chapter 6 for a more complete discussion, but some of the key examples can be found in Caleb Davis Papers, 1684–1831 and Thomas Nicholson Navigation and Logbooks, 1766–1813, MHS; Thomas Chalkley Account Book, 1718–27, LCP; and Tench Francis Invoice Book, 1759–61, HSP.
26 Goldstein, *Philadelphia and the China Trade*, 15–20.
27 Samuel Wharton, "Observations on Consumption of Teas in North America," *Pennsylvania Magazine of History and Biography* 25, no. 1 (1901): 139–41.
28 As quoted in Goldstein, *Philadelphia and the China Trade*, 18.

particularly careful, that no foreign vessel touching in your District, land any Tea, Linnen, or any other European or Asiatick commodities.[29]

Later in the letter, the Virginia official wrote that Philadelphia and areas north (likely meaning New York and Boston) were certainly engaged in smuggling with other European powers, especially the French. He went a step further to express that he had yet to find such illegal trade in his district, and therefore, Peters should focus on vessels and merchants in and around Philadelphia, as it was well known that illegal imports were finding their way into the hinterlands.[30]

By the 1750s, individual English merchants began expressing concern about the growing commercial power of British American merchants, especially of those based in Boston, New York, and Philadelphia. Some wrote letters to the Parliament desiring new laws or, at least, stronger enforcement of old laws to limit competition from American merchants. In the port of Philadelphia customs records, several letters between customs agents contain references to letters received from London-based merchants desiring increased patrols or deterrence against smugglers.[31] In the 1760s and 1770s, the Treasury received formal protests begging Treasury officials, who oversaw the Commissioners of Customs, to make significant efforts to prevent further injury to the interests of English merchants. In one case, a handful of London merchants sought to increase the number of naval vessels off the coast of Virginia to counteract the increased smuggling of European goods by both American and Dutch ships. They claimed "that there are six or eight Smuggling Vessels constantly employed between Holland and the Coast of Norfolk, some of them stout cutters, and as he has heard with Guns, and unless some Measures taken to scour the Norfolk Coast of them some Mischief must ensue."[32] More to the point, they complained that these smuggling cutters were taking legitimate cargoes away from the coast and importing illegal commodities, hurting the profits of merchants based in England. Clearly, London-based merchants perceived British American merchants as competitors and tried to minimize the competition by invoking the authority of British imperial officials to inhibit trade with non-British ports and smuggling.

---

29   Letter to William Peters, July 20, 1750, vol. 1, Port of Philadelphia Customs Papers, HSP.
30   Letter to William Peters, July 20, 1750, vol. 1, Port of Philadelphia Customs Papers, HSP.
31   Vol. 1, Port of Philadelphia Customs Papers, HSP.
32   William Bursons et al. to the Excise Office, May 13, 1773, Treasury Papers, T/501, Public Record Office, British National Archives.

3 The Seven Years' War and the 1760s

Until the mid-eighteenth century, Britain had failed to fully implement its policies of controlling colonial commerce in North America. Merchants based in Boston, New York, and Philadelphia took advantage of this and developed their economic and political power. However, the way in which the British Empire engaged with its North American colonies and their trans-imperial trade drastically changed with the outbreak of the Seven Years' War, which was caused by the escalation of a global political struggle between European empires in the mid-1750s.

In 1754, Virginia sent a colonel named George Washington with a military contingent to survey and treat with French fur trappers in the Ohio Valley in an effort to increase the size of its western territory. A significant reason for Virginia's desire to expand its territory was to increase the available land for plantations and its access to the riverways that fed the Mississippi River and the Great Lakes region. Washington's excursion resulted in a skirmish between his soldiers and French militia and their Native American allies. Washington was forced to surrender and retreat to Virginia, but the Virginia colonial government sought military and diplomatic assistance from the British Empire. By 1756, however, France and England were at war once again, dragging much of the European continent and its colonies throughout the world into a global conflict.[33]

In many previous imperial wars, North America was a peripheral theater to the main continental and oceanic campaigns of France and Britain. But, in the Seven Years' War, the northwestern Atlantic was one of the theaters of war where Britain and France fought for their North American possessions. In Britain's view, the conflict began because of the proximity of French colonies to British colonies in North America. Given what we know about the scale of smuggling between French Canada and British America, it is logical to assume that Britain wished to control American commerce. North America, therefore, became a major theater of war for the first time in colonial history, wherein Britain committed substantial military and financial resources to North America.[34]

English imports into the colonies increased during the war. During 1756–60, total English imports into British America grew from £1.35 million to £2.61 million. As these years were the most active war years, it is not surprising that

---

[33] Walter Borneman, *The French and Indian War: Deciding the Fate of North America* (New York: Harper Collins Publishers, 2006), 20–26. For a more complete history of the Seven Years' War, see Fred Anderson, *Crucible of War* (New York: Alfred A. Knopf, 2000).

[34] Land, "Price of Empire," 1–5.

more goods and commodities would accompany the troops and supplies coming into the major ports of British America. This bump in trade fell back to just under £2 million by 1765, but overall, trade between the colonies and the British Isles increased substantially during the war.[35] Moreover, much of that new tonnage coming into Boston, New York, and Philadelphia was owned by local merchants, creating even more profits for American merchants.

Similarly, illicit trade increased along with legal commerce. While we do not have similar data to adequately show this quantitatively, qualitative data abounds in the literature and sources. War time provided substantial distractions for imperial and military officials in all empires, giving cover for illicit activities like "flag-trucing," or trading under flags of truce and prisoner exchange. New York was the epicenter of illegal commerce between French and English subjects. New York merchants were especially well connected to West Indian islands, and substantial numbers of New York ships made stops to sell food and supplies, at substantial markups, to French settlements and plantations in exchange for cheap sugar and molasses. One ship from New York, the *Sea Flower*, carried salted meat and flour to Monte Cristi to obtain sugar, molasses, indigo, and coffee, and instead of sailing back to New York, chose to sail to Hamburg, where prices were much higher for the French goods.[36] For Tench Francis, a Philadelphia merchant, the war years provided ample opportunity to trade with non-British merchants. During 1759–61, Francis imported more than seventeen million *reis* worth of cargoes from Portuguese locations, at least 125,872 guilders worth of Dutch goods, 16,551 *reals* of Spanish products, and a little more than 6,600 *liras* of Italian commodities. Though his records of exports are incomplete, Francis made just under 12.5 million *reis* of profits in Portuguese destinations and 14,302 guilders in Dutch ports.[37]

Colonists also contributed to the war effort. American merchants, just as they did in previous wars, financed privateers to help the British war effort and to bring in cargoes and ships to the region. In February 1758, the *Pennsylvania Gazette* reported that a privateer from New York had captured a French packet ship and was carrying it into New York.[38] In December 1762, another New York privateer named *Mars* captured a ship called the *Active*, which carried a cargo of "131 hogsheads, 46 tierces, and 35 barrels best white sugars, 75 tierces of coffee, and 5 tierces of indigo."[39] Pennsylvania, like its neighbors, issued a large

---

35   Carter et al., *Historical Statistics of the United States: Millennial Edition*, 5:710–13.
36   Truxes, *Defying Empire*, 75.
37   Tench Francis Invoice Book, 1759–61, HSP.
38   February 23, 1758, *Pennsylvania Gazette*.
39   December 2, 1762, *Pennsylvania Gazette*.

increase in currency or "bills of credit" to help finance local war efforts. In 1755, Pennsylvania only had about £96,000 of its paper bills in circulation. By 1760, that number had jumped to over £400,000.[40] Much of this influx of paper money was financed by colonial merchants, who were enticed to buy early forms of bonds to help add financial backing to the enormous sums of new currency being issued by the colonies.[41]

4 Economic Implications of Renewed Imperial Control

Following the formal conclusion of the Seven Years' War in 1763, imperial policies shifted to a stronger enforcement of the longstanding Navigation Acts and expanding tax revenues from the colonies by adding duties on popular commodities, such as tea and sugar. In addition to their efforts to increase revenue, Britain also had to consolidate an even larger empire, further stretching the capacities of the colonial customs administration. Naturally, British American merchants, especially in Boston, New York, and Philadelphia, were annoyed by these new efforts to limit and tax their trade. Some imperial officials too were worried about the legitimacy of the new revenue acts. By the end of the 1760s, American merchants found solidarity in resistance to imperial "oppression," and many subscribed to citywide, regional, and continental non-importation agreements, or promises to stop importing British goods, to strike hard at the profits of the British Empire and its merchants.

Due to the global nature of the war, Britain was forced to take on an unprecedented amount of debt to finance its war efforts. Britain subsidized the German armies of Frederick the Great to conduct war against France on the continent, so that the British Navy and Army could be spread around the world in India, North America, and throughout the oceans. At the outset of the war, Britain's national debt stood at just over £74.6 million, but by 1763, the debt had gone up to £132.6 million. Sticker shock prevailed among British politicians, elites, and administration officials, leading to a succession of public debates regarding repayment of that debt. Eventually, the British government settled on a plan to consolidate its now larger empire in both North America and India and raise new revenues in the colonies.[42]

---

40   Grubb, "Circulating Medium of Exchange in Colonial Pennsylvania," 335.
41   Michener, "Money in the American Colonies."
42   Jari Eloranta and Jeremy Land, "Hollow Victory? Britain's Public Debt and the Seven Years' War," *Essays in Economic and Business History* 29, no. 1 (2011): 110–12.

In North America, one of the first things British officials did was to expand Britain's customs department to include the newly acquired French ports in Canada. Within a few months of Britain's capture of Quebec and Montreal, the Philadelphia Customs House received regular reports on the arrivals and departures of ships and goods in and from the two Canadian ports. Taxes were collected and sent on to London. During 1759–63, Philadelphia functioned as the de facto center of Britain's efforts to consolidate its control over the commerce of British North America. After 1763, it appears that the records no longer went through Philadelphia, but Philadelphia still received regular reports from other ports throughout the British Empire such as Bridgetown in Barbados.[43] In 1768, Boston became the central office for the customs service in America following the creation of the new Customs Board for the North American colonies by the Commissioners of Customs Act of 1767 (discussed in more detail later in this chapter). Nothing substantial changed in the function of the revenue system with the exception that the British military and navy now helped enforce collection and enforcement of the same laws, a transitioned facilitated by the military occupation of Boston in 1768.[44]

Imperial efforts to end longstanding practices of illicit trade usually had negative consequences for both colonial subjects and the empire. For example, Spanish colonists in what is now Venezuela conducted illegal trade with non-Spanish merchants and consumers throughout the Caribbean and beyond in order to obtain European goods and foodstuffs in exchange for their cacao. As cacao did not find a large market in Spain and the officially sanctioned convoys of ships rarely stopped in Caracas, local Spanish colonists developed strong ties with neighboring Dutch and English islands to gain access to much needed food and manufactures, in stark opposition to Spanish imperial law. But when Spain decided to end this illicit trade, it nearly bankrupted and starved the colony, fundamentally altering the longstanding networks of economic production and exchange.[45] A similar situation occurred in British America. In no small part due to the English inability to fully control trade prior to 1763, efforts to inhibit trans-imperial trade and to force adherence to the stipulations of

---

43   Port of Philadelphia Customs House Papers, 1704–89, HSP.
44   The Customs House in Boston became the lead office in British America and increasingly gained oversight responsibility with Boston's officials frequently writing to officials in other American ports to convey orders given by imperial officials in London. We can see an increasing number of letters and documents collected by Boston agents then transmitted (either in original or copy form) to London to Treasury officials. Evidence of this can be found in the Treasury Papers, T/501 and T/505, Public Record Office, British National Archives.
45   Cromwell, *Smuggler's World*, 88–91.

the Navigation Acts of the late seventeenth century met with considerable resistance in the colonies, especially in the ports of Boston, New York, and Philadelphia.[46]

Between 1763 and 1770, a series of new taxes and restrictions were passed aimed at raising revenues and updating the long-neglected Navigation Acts of the late seventeenth century. The Sugar Act of 1764, the Stamp Act of 1765, and the Townshend Acts were by far the most controversial, nearly all of which were aimed at limiting or taxing the maritime trade of British America. Resistance to the acts was quick and severe. Many colonial merchants viewed the acts as oppressive, even those who professed loyalty to the Crown. Of the acts, the Stamp Act of 1765 received the most vitriol from merchants and consumers. The law forced merchants and captains to obtain and purchase a stamp for all documents involved in shipping, including but not limited to bills of lading, bonds, clearances, and any document detailing the cargo or cargoes of the ship. On average, the stamps cost roughly £2 for each clearance, not accounting for the bills of lading. Because ships frequently carried multiple cargoes for multiple merchants to multiple destinations, the tax burden would have increased tremendously for every single bill of lading.[47] In Boston and New York especially, ships going to and from the West Indies usually contained a half dozen or more separate cargoes.[48]

Perhaps the most impactful of the new revenue acts was the Sugar Act of 1764. The act taxed the importation of foreign sugar, molasses, coffee, indigo, East Asian and European silks and linens imported from England, and wines (from both foreign and English ports). In addition, the act taxed the imports of coffee and pimento imported from British colonies. Of all, this was the most revenue-generating act, but it was also the one that adversely affected the merchants in Boston, New York, and Philadelphia. In Table 26 below, the Sugar Act supplied, in many years, 85 percent or more of the total revenue from post-1763 acts. The Sugar Act installed a one-pence per gallon tax on the import of foreign molasses.[49] In 1765 Philadelphia, the average wholesale price of molasses

---

46   Most histories of the American Revolution note the substantial resistance of colonial Americans to British imperial policies in the 1760s. Some of the better studies of this resistance include: Carp, *Rebels Rising*; Alfred F. Young, *Liberty Tree: Ordinary People and the American Revolution* (New York: New York University Press, 2006); and Tyler, *Smugglers and Patriots*.
47   Dickerson, *Navigation Acts and the American Revolution*, 191–92.
48   Matson, *Merchants & Empire*, 392n34; Hunter, *Purchasing Identity in the Atlantic World*, 78–80.
49   Dickerson, *Navigation Acts and the American Revolution*, 172, 185.

TABLE 26   Imperial taxes collected under selected British revenue laws, 1765–74 (£ sterling)

Year	Sugar Act (1764, 1766)	Stamp Act (1765)	Townshend Revenue Act (1767)	Total post-1763 Revenue Acts	Navigation Acts (1673)
1765	14,091	3,292	-	17,383	2,954
1766	26,696	-	-	26,696	7,373
1767	33,844	-	197	34,041	3,905
1768	24,659	-	13,202	37,861	1,160
1769	39,938	-	5,561	45,499	1,294
1770	30,910	-	2,727	33,637	1,828
1771	27,086	-	4,675	31,761	1,446
1772	42,570	-	3,300	45,870	1,490
1773	39,531	-	2,572	42,103	2,517
1774	27,074	-	921	27,995	672

SOURCE: CARTER ET AL., *HISTORICAL STATISTICS OF THE UNITED STATES: MILLENNIAL EDITION*, 5:707

was 1.76 shilling per gallon, making the duty on molasses about 5 percent of the price for which merchants could reasonably expect to sell their cargoes. Most likely, this cost was passed on to consumers, including distillers and farmers. In Philadelphia in the same year, brown sugar was priced at about fifty-six shillings per hundredweight.[50] With a tax of five shillings per hundredweight, nearly 10 percent of the price, merchants were forced to increase the sale price and pass the burden on to the consumers.

The impact was especially severe on the merchants of Boston, New York, and Philadelphia. Boston shouldered the heaviest burden of the new taxes, as Boston distilleries regularly required substantial imports of both British and foreign molasses. As we can see in Table 27, Boston alone accounted for 29 percent of the yearly average of the total duties collected in all of British America, which includes West Indian ports; Philadelphia and New York together provided 37 percent of the total duties. Merchants in the region were understandably perturbed by the imperial drain on their profits.

---

50   Anne Bezanson, Robert D. Gray, and Miriam Hussey, *Prices in Colonial Pennsylvania* (Philadelphia: University of Pennsylvania Press, 1935), 423.

"SALUTARY NEGLECT" AND THE ORIGINS OF INDEPENDENCE

TABLE 27   Tax collected under the Sugar Act of 1766 at four major ports (£ sterling)

Port	1769	% of Total	1770	% of Total	1772	% of Total
Boston	9,975	25%	8,393	27%	14,476	34%
New York	7,244	18%	5,927	19%	6,437	15%
Philadelphia	7,054	18%	7,511	24%	7,651	18%
Charleston	3,660	9%	2,087	7%	2,436	6%
Total	27,933	70%	23,918	77%	31,000	73%
Total All Ports	39,938		30,910		42,570	

Note: Percentages have been rounded, so the total may not equal one hundred. Salem is included in the Boston figures
SOURCE: OLIVER M. DICKERSON, *THE NAVIGATION ACTS AND THE AMERICAN REVOLUTION* (PHILADELPHIA: UNIVERSITY OF PENNSYLVANIA PRESS, 1951), 186.

The Townshend Acts were a series of laws quickly passed in 1767–68 under the English Exchequer, Charles Townshend. Composed of the New York Restraining Act, the Revenue Act, the Indemnity Act, the Commissioners of Customs Act, and the Vice Admiralty Court Act (1768), the Townshend Acts, or "duties" as they were often called, significantly altered the way commercial laws were enforced and substantially damaged relations between the colonies and the British government. The New York Restraining Act (1767) forbid the New York colonial government from implementing any new laws or policies until it complied with the Quartering Act of 1765, which forced colonists to house and feed British troops stationed in the colonies. The Revenue Act (1767) added new duties on paper, glass, paints, and other minor goods, but it also gave broader authorities to customs agents to search private property for smuggled goods. This act was despised by colonists more for the nearly limitless authority to conduct searches than the taxes it imposed. The Indemnity Act (1767) lowered taxes on tea imported into England by the East India Company, making it cheaper for consumers everywhere. However, the law also forced all goods, no matter where they were produced, to be shipped to England first and then reexported to the colonies, which raised both wholesale and retail prices. This placed yet another burden on the merchants and consumers of Britain's colonies, especially in Boston, New York, and Philadelphia, as they had become a key nodal center for trade in the Atlantic. This law, perhaps more than any other, fully embraced the principle of mercantilism. The Commissioners of Customs Act (1767) further inflamed tensions by establishing a new board of customs to be headquartered in Boston. This was intended to help increase enforcement and limit smuggling, but instead, the act sparked resistance and demonstrations against the new board in Boston, leading the British government to send military and naval units to help establish the board and assist enforcement of the new acts.[51]

While the revenue produced from the acts never equaled the revenue from the Sugar Act, the Vice Admiralty Court Act became a major source of friction between British American merchants and the Crown. The Sugar Act of 1764 essentially moved prosecution of smugglers out of colonial governments and into an expanded number of Admiralty Courts. Prior to 1764, only one such court, adjudicated by Royal Navy captains and their subordinates, existed, and it was located in Halifax, some distance away from the most active centers of trade, Boston, New York, and Philadelphia. However, the Vice Admiralty Court Act created three new Admiralty Courts in Boston, Philadelphia, and Charleston. This decision infuriated both merchants and colonial governments as it removed judicial authority effectively out of local courts and into the hands of London appointees. Furthermore, not only were smuggling offenses moved to naval courts but all trespasses or crimes against the empire were placed under the jurisdiction of the Royal Navy, including any violence or obstruction against customs officials.[52]

Seizures of ships and cargoes were particularly destructive of the region's commerce. In large part due to the combined efforts of the customs department and the British Navy, the value of seized property rapidly increased, all of which was a net loss to merchants in the colonies. During 1768–74, customs officers in the colonies seized goods and ships valued at £30,400, and the Royal Navy captured £30,556 worth of cargoes and vessels. All told, increased enforcement of imperial policies against smuggling led to mercantile losses of £60,956, most of which were borne by merchants in and around Boston, New York, and Philadelphia.[53]

Merchants sought and frequently received assistance from colonial governments and courts to overturn and recover the seized assets and cargoes. In one case in Rhode Island in 1774, Nathanial Shaw, a Newport merchant within the port complex of Boston, brought a case against Charles Dudley, the customs collector of Newport, charging him for illegally seizing and selling Shaw's cargo of molasses and coffee. The case records do not indicate where the molasses

---

51   Barrow, *Trade and Empire*, 217–26.
52   Dickerson, *Navigation Acts and the American Revolution*, 181–83.
53   Dickerson, *Navigation Acts and the American Revolution*, 202.

and coffee were obtained, but Robert Keeler, a captain in the Royal Navy, and his ship the *Mercury* captured and impounded Shaw's ship and cargo on October 10, 1772. Shaw was suspected of importing 109 casks of molasses and two casks of coffee worth £1,090. The Admiralty Court condemned the goods, which were then sold at a public auction with the proceeds divided between Keeler, Dudley, and another customs officer. Even though the Admiralty Court had ruled against Shaw, the Rhode Island Superior Court decided that the seizure was unlawful and ruled against Dudley. In the thirteenth point of the final ruling, the court explained that the Admiralty Court's declaration "does not contain any lawful Cause of Action But is in all its parts frivolous vexations insensible unissuable and wanting in Form and Substance."[54] While they were speaking directly to this particular ruling, it can be assumed that the justices were speaking largely to the Sugar Act of 1764, which expanded the laws regarding the import of both molasses and coffee. In effect, the court judged that the act itself was unlawful, and therefore, any seizure or condemnation would also be illegitimate. Thus, the court ordered Dudley to pay Shaw £871, the amount that he and the other two officials had pocketed.[55] Two things stand out in this case. First, the willingness of colonial institutions to challenge the legitimacy of imperial laws and institutions, including the Royal Navy, provides further evidence of increasing political distance between the colonies and the Crown. Second, many of these cases involving seizure of ships and cargoes and complaints against them dragged on for many months and years, greatly limiting the effectiveness of enforcement and providing yet another reason for imperial officials to consider alternatives to cracking down on illegal trade. In no way were these acts completely successful, as smuggling and overall trade continued to increase. However, compared with the earlier period, Britain was more effective in enforcing the imperial agenda during the war, as the seizure of ships and cargoes and collection of additional revenues suggest.

Resistance was not limited to colonial merchants and institutions; imperial officers and supporters frequently voiced their objections to renewed and expanded efforts to bring British American trade under control. In 1772, James Allen, a lawyer who helped prosecute seizures by the Royal Navy in Philadelphia, wrote in his diary that his schedule was filled with prosecutions

---

54 Superior Court of Rhode Island Judgment in Nathanial Shaw v. Robert Dudley, February 21, 1774, Treasury Papers, T/505, vol. 2, 227–52, Public Record Office, British National Archives.

55 Superior Court of Rhode Island Judgment in Nathanial Shaw v. Robert Dudley, February 21, 1774, Treasury Papers, T/505, vol. 2, 227–52, Public Record Office, British National Archives.

against merchants and captains who had broken navigation and revenue laws. In complaining about how much of his time was devoted to these prosecutions, he wrote, "I am doing, as a Lawyer what I would not do as a politician; being fully persuaded of the oppressive nature of those laws. I have however refused to prosecute two or 3 persons on the penal clauses, as thinking it invidious & rigid."[56] Allen, while in the service of the Crown, chose not to pursue criminal charges against several individuals as a result of his dissatisfaction with the laws he was hired to enforce.

In February 1773 in Boston, customs officials wrote to the Treasury in order to protest a proposed law forcing masters of ships to immediately check in at the customs house and submit to inspection. In their dissent, the customs agents suggested that the new rules would be difficult at best to enforce in places with large coastlines and river access, particularly in Boston and Philadelphia. Additionally, they suggested that areas such as Virginia and North Carolina could not possibly force masters to appear at customs house locations as few such places existed close to where trade was conducted. Finally, they wrote, "We must expect that every Difficulty and Embarrassment will be thrown in the way of the Officers in the execution of any new Laws that may not be agreeable to the ... temper of the People [ellipsis in original text]." The agents, in what appears to be a sarcastic tone, suggested that the merchants and consumers would do all they could to avoid and prevent enforcement of any additional regulations. They concluded by recommending that the Lordships avoid any new attempts at regulation, "until some more effectual Provision be made for supporting the Authority of Parliament and carrying the Acts of Trade and Revenue into execution."[57] No matter its efficacy, every new law was met with resistance at all levels, not just from the merchants who wished to conduct illicit trade.

Even when customs enforcement was successful in one port or area, other customs officials in other ports were less successful. In January 1773, the customs officers in Boston led by William Burch wrote to the Lords Commissioners of the Treasury to complain about the inefficient collection efforts in Philadelphia and New York, implying that the customs agents of Philadelphia and New York were negligent. Burch explained that more than £27,000 were remitted to Britain's Treasury in October 1772 for the previous year's duty collection in

---

56   James Allen, "Diary of James Allen, Esq. of Philadelphia, Counsellor-at-Law, 1770–1778, Part I," *Pennsylvania Magazine of History and Biography* 9, no. 2 (July 1885): 176–96, at 179.
57   Custom House Boston to the Lords Commissioners of His Majesty's Treasury, February 11, 1773, Treasury Papers, T/501, Public Record Office, British National Archives.

all of British America, but more than £11,000 was spent in wages and incidental costs in prosecuting illicit traders. Furthermore, most of the duties were obtained in Boston, and the amounts collected in New York and Philadelphia were far lower than anticipated. To this point, Burch wrote: "The Ports of New York and Philadelphia have fallen very short on their receipt of Duties by this Act. We have frequently enjoined our Officers in these Ports to exert themselves in their Duty, but we are sorry to observe to your Lordships that it has not been attended with the desired effect." In effect, the receipts did not meet expectations, nor did Burch believe that the officers were acting appropriately. He continued: "For we have no doubt of a clandestine Trade being carried on in those Ports with the foreign Ports in Europe in the Article of Teas and other Goods to a great extent."[58] Burch conveniently failed to mention that Boston was under nearly complete blockade and occupation by the Royal Army and Navy, greatly assisting the efforts to control illegal trade, but he does highlight the inefficiencies of the customs service, even in the best of times.

5   Regional Merchants and Collective Resistance

When merchants grew tired of the renewed efforts, in their view, to oppress colonial commerce, many entered into local non-importation agreements with the stated goal of forcing British merchants to intercede in Parliament on their behalf by hurting English profits. There were real documents to which merchants subscribed, usually voluntarily but occasionally through peer pressure. These documents resembled the legal partnerships or "articles of agreement" that most merchants signed with their commercial partners. This resemblance no doubt was deliberate as it was intended to be enforceable, if not by law, then by other merchants.

Sparked by the punishing nature of the Stamp Act of 1765, groups of merchants gathered to discuss options for resisting the universally despised act. Initially centered in Boston, New York, and Philadelphia but later spreading to other cities and ports throughout British America, non-importation agreements were signed by many of the top merchants in British America. The first non-importation movement, composed of dozens of non-importation agreements, was successful as it forced the government to repeal the Stamp Act in 1766. Emboldened by this success, merchants exerted their collective strength

---

58   William Burch et al. to the Lords Commissioners of His Majesty's Treasury, January 19, 1773, Treasury Papers, T/501, Public Record Office, British National Archives.

and used non-importation agreements to protest the government's policies and trade regulations throughout the late 1760s and early 1770s.[59]

In both verbiage and form, the documents list the terms of the agreement, much like the terms of partnerships, to which individual merchants signed their names. One agreement in Boston read:

> We the subscribers inhabitants of the Town of Boston being desirous to concur with the Merchants and Traders of said Town in their late Laudable Agreement not to Import any of the Manufactures of Great Britain, do hereby faithfully promise and engage that we will abide by the following Resolutions:
>
> First. That we will not, either by ourselves or any for or under us purchase any Goods whatever from any Person or Persons who have or may Import any of said Manufactures contrary to the spirit of said Agreement.
>
> Secondly. That we will not either by ourselves or any for or under us purchase any of such Manufactures from any Factor or Factors who now do or may hereafter expose the same for Sale.
>
> Thirdly. We are determined to assist the said Merchants and Traders in any further Measures that may be taken for the better carrying their Resolution into Execution.[60]

Agreements such as these dotted the port cities throughout British America, and most of the merchant groups sent copies of agreements to other ports and cities, creating what amounted to a non-military continental blockade against the importation of British goods. In effect, these merchants participated in collective resistance against the British imperial policy of mercantilism by exerting economic pressure on the trade and profits of British merchants. These agreements are yet another example of the mercantile community's long-term effort to circumvent and disregard the British Empire's mercantilist agenda.

Unlike partnerships, non-importation agreements did not have any legal ground for enforcement, but the merchants who agreed to non-importation worked in tandem to track down and ostracize merchants who refused to sign the agreements. In 1768, merchants from Boston, New York, and Newburyport proposed that copies of the agreement be sent to all merchants engaged in importing goods from England. They then listed more than two dozen names

---

59   Matson, *Merchants & Empire*, 298–300.
60   Non-importation Agreement, July 31, 1769, MHS.

of merchants who were not present and were known to import English commodities.[61] This was done with the hopes that all would sign and agree, and those that would not were pressured, largely by cutting off business ties and, occasionally, with violence.[62] While some merchants consistently and effectively refused to sign non-importation agreements, such as those whose businesses involved imports from Britain, the movement against the importation of British goods continued to gain traction between 1765 and 1774.

Merchants were eventually joined by consumers, who signed non-consumption agreements, in creating a coastal community opposed to the "oppressive" acts and regulations imposed by British authorities. The non-consumption agreements resembled the non-importation agreements wherein individuals would sign and promise to avoid buying or consuming goods imported from Britain. This could be East India Company tea or British clothing, but if tea was clearly imported from Amsterdam, for example, then the tea could be consumed. Women, in particular, were key in enforcing both non-importation and non-consumption agreements, as some groups, such as the Daughters of Liberty, regularly shamed men and women for drinking tea imported from Britain or for wearing English-produced clothing.[63] In both the non-importation and non-consumption agreements that spread throughout the Atlantic port cities of British America, shared goals brought a diverse group of colonies and port cities into greater alignment. These cooperative pacts also brought colonial governments in closer agreement, as many of the agreements succeeded in forcing a change of imperial policies including repeal of new regulations. In the end, the ports of Boston, New York, and Philadelphia convinced thirteen colonies of British America to pursue independence as a plausible means to prevent further inhibitions to maritime trade.

6 Britain's Military Occupation of Boston and the Sparks of War

In October 1768, the growing tension, resentment, and resistance to British efforts to control colonial trade culminated in the arrival of five thousand British troops and several naval vessels in Boston. Though troops had been stationed in and around Boston for decades prior to 1768, the arrival of troops was clearly in response to American resistance to Parliament's attempts at imposing

---

61 Non-importation Agreement, March 4, 1768, Samuel P. Savage Papers, Box 1, MHS.
62 Merritt, *Trouble with Tea*, 106–8.
63 Merritt, *Trouble with Tea*, 68.

new taxes and control over the colonies. Members of Parliament frequently mentioned the resistance of Bostonians as warranting occupation. Some even viewed it as an open conflict, especially following the Boston Massacre in 1770. For example, Edmund Burke explained that the "first thing [Britain] did in this military arrangement [was] to beat down the port of Boston."[64] Thomas Gage also viewed his army's role as imposing discipline and policing. In a letter to his superiors, Gage explains that almost immediately after the beginning of the occupation, some leaders who were responsible for the disturbances were already being tried in Admiralty Courts.[65]

Naturally, many Boston civilians viewed the presence of soldiers as reprehensible. Silas Deane commented that the occupation of Boston was "one operation of the general plan long since concerted, for subjugating the colonies," continuing to describe how troops were nothing more than enforcers and symbols of Parliamentary power.[66] There was a good reason to perceive the soldiers as enforcers. In December of 1768, British troops were used to take possession of a vessel that was suspected of smuggling sugar. Though they discovered that the sugar had been reported to the Customs House as required by law, a newspaper journalist who reported the incident expressed his surprise and disdain for the use of soldiers in everyday operations of royal officials.[67]

The situation continued to escalate with a growing number of violent incidents of either mob violence or confrontations between customs agents, soldiers, merchants, and laborers. For example, a couple of men and a young boy were walking home and were called to halt by the soldiers on guard. For whatever reason, they refused to stop and were approached by the soldiers. According to *The Boston Evening Post*, the soldier then thrust a bayonet at one of the men who was able to avoid a blow to the head but was badly cut in the process, "grievously wounded in divers [sic] parts of his body."[68] General Gage even argued that the Boston Massacre in 1770 began as a scuffle between

---

64   Lords Proceedings and Commons Debate, March 7, 1774, printed in Simmons and Thomas, *Proceedings and Debates of the British Parliament Respecting North America*, 27–31, 36–51.

65   Major General Gage to the Earl of Hillsborough, November 3, 1768, printed in Thomas Gage et al., *Letters to the Ministry from Governor Benard, General Gage, Commodore Hood, and also Memorials to the Lords of the Treasury from the Commissioners of the Customs with Sundry Letters and Papers Annexed to Said Memorials* (Boston: Edes and Gill, 1769), 77–78.

66   Silas Deane to the Committee of Correspondence, Boston, June 13, 1774, printed in *Correspondence and Journals of Samuel Blachley Webb*, ed. Worthington C. Ford (New York: New York Times and Arno Press, 1969), 1:26–29.

67   Dickerson, *Boston under Military Rule*, 40.

68   Dickerson, *Boston under Military Rule*, 17–18.

soldiers and common laborers.[69] John Rowe, Boston merchant, wrote of two congregations of people on consecutive nights in 1774 who were upset about the blockade. He explained that they intended to find a certain official who was alleged to have committed crimes against the people. More importantly, he explained that it was a large group of people that included not just merchants and middle-class citizens but workers and other segments of the population. He claimed that over 1,200 people (nearly 10 percent of the civilian population of Boston) had attended the nights' events. On the second night, the crowd was out for blood, or at least tar and feathers. They were looking for a particular person of public infamy but "could not find him, [which was] very lucky for him."[70] These incidents highlight the importance of maritime trade to the cities of Boston, New York, and Philadelphia, as much of the port cities' population was directly affected by the trade restrictions discussed above.

In 1773, the British government faced a choice of either ending the Boston occupation or adding further punishment to Boston for its resistance against imperial policies. During the night of December 16, 1773, colonists dumped more than three hundred chests of East India Company tea into Boston Harbor, protesting the many policies described above. Parliament responded by passing a series of new acts (the Intolerable Acts) that further inflamed tensions and colonial resistance. Of the Intolerable Acts, the Boston Port Act and the Massachusetts Government Act were the most important. The Boston Port Act closed the port of Boston to all trade, and the Massachusetts Government Act ended the colonial charter for Massachusetts and brought the government under the auspices of the British government. In essence, it placed the entire colony of Massachusetts under the direct rule of the British Parliament and the Crown.[71] The results of these acts are well known. The following year, 1775, the first shots of the American Revolution were fired in Lexington and Concord, two small towns on the outskirts of Boston.

Britain's military occupation of Boston was the first salvo in a battle for equal access to global markets. Parliament was not solely focused on Boston. As the War for Independence escalated, both New York and Philadelphia were key targets of the British military. While American troops pushed British forces out of Boston in 1775, New York was subsequently attacked and occupied until the end of the war in 1783, and Philadelphia was occupied by British forces

---

69 General Thomas Gage to Lord Hillsborough, April 10, 1770, printed in *The Correspondence of General Thomas Gage with the Secretaries of State, 1763–1775*, ed. Clarence Edwin Carter (New Haven: Yale University Press, 1931), 1:248–51.
70 Cunningham, *Letters and Diary of John Rowe*, 261.
71 Barrow, *Trade and Empire*, 248–52.

for roughly nine months between September 1777 and June 1778. All three cities were the main focus of the British military campaign to end the American rebellion until the focus shifted to the south with Lord Cornwallis's campaign beginning with the capture of Charleston in 1780 and ending with Cornwallis's surrender at Yorktown in 1781.[72] Both Americans and the British government viewed Boston, New York, and Philadelphia as the center of a developing competitor for global markets, and the American Revolution was the culmination of a century-long process of the region's growing economic and political power.

7 Conclusion

From the beginning of the eighteenth century until the start of the war between Britain and its colonies, the century was defined by a push and pull between colonial merchants and the British Empire. Until 1750, the British government was unable to muster the resources and capacity necessary to fully enforce the mercantilist intentions and laws of the metropole, nor did it adequately support the economic growth and function of its empire in North America. As a result, British American merchants became enmeshed in trans-imperial networks that produced a tidy profit for colonial merchants in Boston, New York, and Philadelphia. During the Seven Years' War, the region's merchants took advantage of the global war effort to increase their own profits and economic power, often to the disadvantage of Britain. When the war ended, however, Britain faced an unprecedented war debt and looked to its colonies to help refill its coffers. To that end, the British government believed the colonies were overdue for true enforcement of the Navigation Acts and were prosperous enough to shoulder additional financial burdens for the good of the empire. These new efforts were met with a resistance that initially stunned metropolitan politicians, forcing some concessions, but ultimately, the increasing friction between the increasingly wealthy colonies of British America and their imperial master sparked yet another global and expensive struggle for control over the oceans and global marketplaces.

---

72   For more on the American Revolution, see John Ferling, *Almost a Miracle: The American Victory in the War of Independence* (Oxford: Oxford University Press, 2007).

Conclusion: Revolution or a Battle for Free Trade?

Boston, New York, and Philadelphia played a prominent role in the maritime trade of the British Empire as well as in the larger Atlantic economy in the eighteenth century. The extensive trade networks created by merchants of these port cities enabled them to trade on a large scale in and outside of the empire. They brought wealth and prosperity to the region and caused economic growth and political empowerment. Together, the three port cities and their hinterlands formed a region, which served as a nodal center in British North America and in the maritime trade of the western Atlantic Ocean. By the middle of the eighteenth century, all three cities had developed multilateral shipping routes and shuttle patterns that provided merchants with increasingly diverse economic opportunities. By the 1770s, more local merchant-owned ships operated in inter-colonial and trans-imperial trade than British-owned ships. This shows that most of this region's coastal, West Indian, and transatlantic trade was handled by colonial merchants.[1] Boston, New York, and Philadelphia conducted trade primarily with ports and destinations in the Atlantic Ocean and occasionally with ports in the western Indian Ocean. However, the commodities the merchants imported or reexported were global. Whether directly or indirectly, Chinese tea, porcelain, and silks, Indian spices and textiles, Southeast Asian spices, and myriad other goods from all over the world found their way into the proverbial hands of the region's merchants and consumers.

This book shows that throughout the eighteenth century, the volumes and values of this region's inter-colonial and trans-imperial trade exceeded those of the direct trade with Britain. Colonial economies thrived on trade with British and non-British American colonies and continental European markets and were less dependent on the metropole. As British American merchants found better consumer markets for dried fish, rum, and grains in places like Portugal, Spain, and Amsterdam, they went for it even at the risk of violating British laws, which prohibited direct trade between the colonies and other European empires. The British called it smuggling, but the American merchants considered it necessary and natural. Whether necessary or not, smuggling was an act of resistance against the mercantilist policies of the empire, and it was endemic in the Atlantic World. In the British North American colonial arena,

---

[1] Shepherd and Walton, *Shipping, Maritime Trade and the Economic Development of Colonial North America*, 51.

trade and profit reigned supreme, and colonial merchants continuously circumvented and subverted the British Empire's attempts to control trade and restrict their access to global markets. Americans did not suddenly find the British Empire distasteful and injurious to their freedom of thought, action, and beliefs in the 1770s. The conflict that has become known as the American War for Independence was the culmination of more than a century of negotiations and accommodations (or lack thereof) between the British Empire and its colonies in North America.

Despite substantial limitations to imperial capacity that failed to provide enough specie to conduct business, colonial merchants found alternative ways to conduct business, thriving where others failed. Moreover, the lack of capacity provided opportunities to expand their trade at the expense of the British mercantilist vision, greatly improving their ability to profit and overcome the lack of fiscal support. Though war between the colonies and Britain was not inevitable, the growing economic capacity of the region and the competition it represented forced the British Empire to either embrace economic realities and remove the limitations on American commerce or double down on its eighteenth-century mercantilist imperial visions. Britain chose the latter, which intensified resistance and resentment against British rule. Britain's occupation of Boston and the subsequent occupations of New York and Philadelphia serve as a stark reminder that the region was an important nodal center for the British Empire. While many factors contributed to thirteen American colonies declaring independence from Britain, the colonial merchants of Boston, New York, and Philadelphia certainly helped lead others to the conclusion that independence could provide more and better opportunities to trade and profit. America's war for independence was not simply a war for political autonomy but a final battle to win free access to global commodities and markets.

During and after the Revolution, American merchants continued to build their networks of exchange, capital, and credit. Though made increasingly difficult by the growing conflict, communication between American merchants and their European partners specifically addressed risk mitigation and limiting the impact of the global war on their businesses and profits. For British merchants, the war greatly concerned them, and many, such as Daniel Eccleston, diversified their connections by establishing partners in the West Indies in an effort to remain tied to the American market, even if indirectly.[2]

---

2   Carolyn Downs, "Networks, Trust, and Risk Mitigation during the American Revolutionary War: A Case Study," *Economic History Review* 70, no. 2 (2017): 509–12.

American merchants sought to turn their mercantile networks into military supply routes during the war. John Carter and Jeremiah Wadsworth used their expansive networks throughout the Atlantic to supply the fledgling American military with guns, ammunition, and cannon, taking greater than usual risks in the process. As a result, American merchants, like Carter and Wadsworth, leaned on the Continental Congress and later Constitutional Convention to develop safeguards and laws that protected free trade.[3] Whether one examines the networks before or after independence, interaction between merchants, whether competitive or cooperative, indicates a shared effort to earn a profit, improve the region's economy, and gain a greater foothold in the global economy. Once granted independence from Britain, these networks supplied both the capital and partnerships necessary to exploit the newly legal access to East Asia and the Indian Ocean.

Ironically, American political leaders and merchants immediately found themselves in disagreement over whether the new nation should regulate and/or tax maritime trade. Eventually, the first American Congress under the new United States Constitution passed tariffs that targeted foreign merchants and ships that imported foreign goods into the United States. At the forefront of the debate was whether the US government could or should limit access to foreign markets such as China and India. As East Asian goods were of primary interest to both American consumers and merchants, merchants were quick to begin commercial ventures in Indian Ocean markets nearly immediately following the conclusion of war.[4] Tea was one of the first commodities to be targeted by tariffs, installing higher tariffs on non-American merchants who sent tea to the United States, encouraging American merchants to trade directly with China.[5]

Even before Congress approved the tariffs, American merchants capitalized on the newfound freedom to conduct direct trade with East Asia. Their first efforts were to sail east around the Cape of Good Hope into the Indian Ocean. The first ship carrying the US flag to touch the Indian Ocean was the *Harriet* in April 1784, based in Boston. It arrived at the Cape of Good Hope with a cargo of American ginseng and, instead of continuing to China, traded the ginseng for tea from European ships heading home to Europe before it returned to Boston.[6] Following close on the heels of the *Harriet*, the *Empress of China* set

---

[3] Tom Cutterham, "The Revolutionary Transformation of American Merchant Networks: Carter and Wadsworth and Their World, 1775–1800," *Enterprise and Society* 18, no. 1 (March 2017): 1–31, at 5–6.
[4] John R. Haddad, *America's First Adventure in China: Trade, Treaties, Opium, and Salvation* (Philadelphia: Temple University Press, 2013); Fichter, *So Great a Proffit*.
[5] Merritt, *Trouble with Tea*, 127–28.
[6] Fichter, *So Great a Proffitt*, 37.

out from New York for China, arriving at the Cape of Good Hope in May 1784 and at Canton in September 1784, where it offloaded its cargo of ginseng and Spanish silver in exchange for tea and other goods.[7] While the original plan of the *Empress of China* was to sail west around South America and across the Pacific Ocean, it chose a more well-known route. The *Columbia*, on the other hand, traveled the Pacific route, focusing on taking furs from North America's west coast to China instead of ginseng. It was financed largely by Joseph Barrell, a Boston merchant, who received advice from his friend Thomas Randall, the supercargo for the *Empress of China*, on how to handle negotiations with Chinese merchants.[8] These voyages were just a few of many such expeditions to expand the commercial networks of merchants in Boston, New York, and Philadelphia, showing the continued importance of the region to the mercantile success of the new United States.

Much like their European counterparts, American merchants consistently sought greater access to the globe's ever-growing mercantile networks. The speed with which Americans turned to direct trade with East Asia is not surprising when one considers their sustained efforts to expand the scale and scope of their commercial enterprise and take it beyond the confines of oceans and empires. Other countries soon recognized the importance of the region in the Atlantic economy. Sweden placed its first two consulates in Boston and Philadelphia in 1783—the year American independence was assured.[9] Others followed suit, and the United States began its young history as a nation looking to the oceans for its success.

---

7   Haddad, *America's First Adventure in China*, 9–17.
8   Oakley, "Columbia at Sea," 112–16, 135–40.
9   Leos Müller, *Consuls, Corsairs, and Commerce: The Swedish Consular Service and Long-Distance Shipping, 1720–1815* (Uppsala: Uppsala University Press, 2004), 45.

Appendices

Appendix A

Data on the Trade of Boston, New York, and Philadelphia

TABLE A.1 Destinations of shipping clearing Boston, New York, and Philadelphia annually for selected years, 1750–1772 (in Tons)

Port of Origin	Years	Destination							
		British Isles		Non-British Isles					
		Great Britain	Ireland	Southern Europe	North America	West Indies	Total	% Non-British Isles
Boston	1753–54	3,000	200	2,200	11,500	10,300	27,200	88%
	1765–66	5,100	200	1,600	12,800	8,200	28,000	81%
	1772	6,200	200	1,000	24,500	10,700	42,500	85%
New York	1754	2,200	1,500	500	2,500	6,000	12,700	70%
	1765–66	2,900	2,000	3,500	3,000	8,400	19,800	75%
	1772	4,300	1,600	2,700	11,900	8,100	28,600	80%
Philadelphia	1750–54	1,100	2,500	1,700	12,700	7,200	25,200	86%
	1765–66	1,800	4,800	4,800	14,600	13,500	39,500	83%
	1772	3,100	2,500	8,400	15,100	15,700	45,800	88%

Note: Figures are rounded to the nearest one hundred, and the totals do not always equal the sum of the various parts
SOURCE: MCCUSKER AND MENARD, *ECONOMY OF BRITISH AMERICA*, 195–97.

APPENDICES

TABLE A.2 Commodity exports from Massachusetts, 1768–72 (value in £ sterling)

1768–72

Commodity	Unit	England Quantity	England Value	Ireland Quantity	Ireland Value	Southern Europe* Quantity	Southern Europe* Value	West Indies Quantity	West Indies Value	Africa Quantity	Africa Value
Beeswax	lb.	18,252	914	–	–	23,340	1,168	–	–	–	–
Beef and Pork	bbl.	945	1,804	–	–	213	431	8,183	17,045	–	–
Bread and Flour	ton	2	18	–	–	513	5,280	1,125	11,855	–	–
Candles, spermaceti	lb.	–	–	–	–	36,792	2,485	316,220	21,364	6,513	442
Cotton	lb.	9,672	472	–	–	–	–	–	–	–	–
Deerskins	lb.	1,800	225	–	–	–	–	–	–	–	–
Fish, dried	quintal	2,011	1,024	–	–	570,110	284,178	743,188	371,192	–	–
Flaxseed	bu.	27,867	5,590	11,470	1,462	–	–	–	–	–	–
Grain, corn	bu.	100	9	–	–	28,529	3,024	13,337	1,294	–	–
Grain, rice	bbl.	120	303	–	–	326	854	303	743	–	–
Grain, wheat	bu.	–	–	–	–	19,348	4,319	–	–	–	–
Indigo	lb.	1,790	270	–	–	–	–	–	–	–	–
Hoops	1,000	–	–	–	–	–	–	3,503	7,092	–	–
Iron, bar	ton	13	205	–	–	–	–	1	18	–	–
Iron, pig	ton	278	1,388	–	–	–	–	–	–	–	–

TABLE A.2 Commodity exports from Massachusetts, 1768–72 (value in £ sterling) (cont.)

1768–72

Commodity	Unit	England Quantity	England Value	Ireland Quantity	Ireland Value	Southern Europe* Quantity	Southern Europe* Value	West Indies Quantity	West Indies Value	Africa Quantity	Africa Value
Livestock, cattle	no.	-	-	-	-	-	-	1,037	6,222	-	-
Livestock, horses	no.	-	-	-	-	-	-	910	9,100	-	-
Naval stores, pitch	bbl.	1,644	678	-	-	-	-	-	-	-	-
Naval stores, tar	bbl.	33,420	12,727	-	-	-	-	-	-	-	-
Naval stores, turpentine	bbl.	6,726	3,099	-	-	-	-	-	-	-	-
Oil, whale	ton	14,363	172,358	-	-	53	637	417	5,009	-	-
Potash	ton	3,597	90,203	-	-	-	-	-	-	-	-
Rum, American	gal.	20,040	1,278	3,174	194	100,228	6,210	-	-	417,649	25,992
Rum, West Indian	gal.	882	88	-	-	5,634	559	-	-	360	37
Wine	ton	-	-	1	2	-	-	6	361	-	-
Wood products, pine boards	1,000 ft.	6,379	9,497	48	102	1,290	1,950	55,403	84,948	-	-
Wood products, staves/headings	1,000 ft.	2,934	8,748	32	92	928	2,717	3,790	11,008	-	-
Total Value			310,898		1,852		313,812		547,251		26,471

APPENDICES

TABLE A.2 Commodity exports from Massachusetts, 1768–72 (value in £ sterling) (*cont.*)

Commodity	Unit	Total 1768–72		Yearly Average	
		Quantity	Value	Quantity	Value
Beeswax	lb.	41,592	2,082	8,318	416
Beef and Pork	bbl.	9,341	19,280	1,868	3,856
Bread and Flour	ton	1,640	17,153	328	3,431
Candles, spermaceti	lb.	359,525	24,291	71,905	4,858
Cotton	lb.	9,672	472	1,934	94
Deerskins	lb.	1,800	225	360	45
Fish, dried	quintal	1,315,309	656,394	263,062	131,279
Flaxseed	bu.	39,337	7,052	7,867	1,410
Grain, corn	bu.	41,966	4,327	8,393	865
Grain, rice	bbl.	749	1,900	150	380
Grain, wheat	bu.	19,348	4,319	3,870	864
Indigo	lb.	1,790	270	358	54
Hoops	1,000	3,503	7,092	701	1,418
Iron, bar	ton	14	223	3	45
Iron, pig	ton	278	1,388	56	278
Livestock, cattle	no.	1,037	6,222	207	1,244
Livestock, horses	no.	910	9,100	182	1,820

TABLE A.2 Commodity exports from Massachusetts, 1768–72 (value in £ sterling) (*cont.*)

Commodity	Unit	Total 1768–72		Yearly Average	
		Quantity	Value	Quantity	Value
Naval stores, pitch	bbl.	1,644	678	329	136
Naval stores, tar	bbl.	33,420	12,727	6,684	2,545
Naval stores, turpentine	bbl.	6,726	3,099	1,345	620
Oil, whale	ton	14,834	178,004	2,967	35,601
Potash	ton	3,597	90,203	719	18,041
Rum, American	gal.	541,091	33,674	108,218	6,735
Rum, West Indian	gal.	6,876	684	1,375	137
Wine	ton	7	363	1	73
Wood products, pine boards	1,000 ft.	63,120	96,497	12,624	19,299
Wood products, staves/headings	1,000 ft.	7,684	22,565	1,537	4,513
Total Value			1,200,284		240,057

SOURCE: SHEPHERD, "COMMODITY EXPORTS FROM THE BRITISH NORTH AMERICAN COLONIES," 12–53

APPENDICES

TABLE A.3 Commodity exports from New York, 1768–72 (value in £ sterling)

		1768–72							
		England		Ireland		Southern Europe*		West Indies		Africa	
Commodity	Unit	Quantity	Value	Quantity	Value	Quantity	Value	Quantity	Value	Quantity	Value
Beeswax	lb.	89,426	4,471	243	2,565	59,522	2,977	-	-	-	-
Beef and Pork	bbl.	115	226	-	-	379	782	14,182	29,551	-	-
Bread and Flour	ton	3,052	29,846	456	4,585	8,242	91,178	21,241	231,442	-	-
Candle, spermaceti	lb.	-	-	-	-	9,375	646	58,170	3,936	-	-
Cotton	lb.	45,890	1,968	-	-	-	-	-	-	-	-
Deerskins	lb.	15,750	1,679	-	-	-	-	-	-	-	-
Fish, dried	quintal	-	-	-	-	1,519	767	10,821	5,402	-	-
Flaxseed	bu.	15,910	2,841	576,842	104,114	-	-	-	-	-	-
Grain, corn	bu.	2,937	229	225	17	174,563	18,290	160,796	16,552	-	-
Grain, rice	bbl.	1,867	4,480	-	-	1,487	3,879	456	1,382	-	-
Grain, wheat	bu.	25,829	4,814	36,050	6,517	264,047	51,987	124	29	-	-
Indigo	lb.	1,135	171	-	-	-	-	-	-	-	-
Hoops	1,000	-	-	-	-	-	-	1,097	2,218	-	-
Iron, bar	ton	3,833	57,688	198	2,900	-	-	344	5,311	-	-
Iron, pig	ton	4,609	22,954	-	-	-	-	-	-	-	-

TABLE A.3 Commodity exports from New York, 1768–72 (value in £ sterling) (cont.)

1768–72

Commodity	Unit	England Quantity	England Value	Ireland Quantity	Ireland Value	Southern Europe* Quantity	Southern Europe* Value	West Indies Quantity	West Indies Value	Africa Quantity	Africa Value
Livestock, cattle	no.	–	–	–	–	–	–	360	2,160	–	–
Livestock, horses	no.	–	–	–	–	–	–	909	9,090	–	–
Naval stores, pitch	bbl.	532	214	–	–	–	–	–	–	–	–
Naval stores, tar	bbl.	11,609	4,329	–	–	–	–	–	–	–	–
Naval stores, turpentine	bbl.	5,601	2,621	–	–	–	–	–	–	–	–
Oil, whale	ton	954	11,449	2	18	–	–	82	984	–	–
Potash	ton	2,220	56,896	8	177	–	–	–	–	–	–
Rum, American	gal.	36,998	2,477	29,100	1,980	32,710	2,248	–	–	55,756	3,810
Rum, West Indian	gal.	349	37	4,463	457	2,695	266	–	–	1,000	104
Wine	ton	–	–	–	–	–	–	95	5,737	–	–
Wood products, pine boards	1,000 ft.	452	707	65	99	321	484	4,548	7,190	–	–
Wood products, staves/headings	1,000 ft.	1,373	4,238	2,153	6,426	1,617	4,707	6,958	20,889	–	–
Total Value			214,335		129,855		178,211		341,873		3,914

APPENDICES

TABLE A.3 Commodity exports from New York, 1768–72 (value in £ sterling) (cont.)

Commodity	Unit	Total 1768–72 Quantity	Total 1768–72 Value	Yearly average Quantity	Yearly average Value
Beeswax	lb.	149,191	10,013	29,838	2,003
Beef and Pork	bbl.	14,676	30,559	2,935	6,112
Bread and Flour	ton	32,991	357,051	6,598	71,410
Candle, spermaceti	lb.	67,545	4,582	13,509	916
Cotton	lb.	45,890	1,968	9,178	394
Deerskins	lb.	15,750	1,679	3,150	336
Fish, dried	quintal	12,340	6,169	2,468	1,234
Flaxseed	bu.	592,752	106,955	118,550	21,391
Grain, corn	bu.	338,521	35,088	67,704	7,018
Grain, rice	bbl.	3,810	9,741	762	1,948
Grain, wheat	bu.	326,050	63,347	65,210	12,669
Indigo	lb.	1,135	171	227	34
Hoops	1,000	1,097	2,218	219	444
Iron, bar	ton	4,375	65,899	875	13,180
Iron, pig	ton	4,609	22,954	922	4,591
Livestock, cattle	no.	360	2,160	72	432
Livestock, horses	no.	909	9,090	182	1,818

TABLE A.3 Commodity exports from New York, 1768–72 (value in £ sterling) (cont.)

Commodity	Unit	Total 1768–72		Yearly average	
		Quantity	Value	Quantity	Value
Naval stores, pitch	bbl.	532	214	106	43
Naval stores, tar	bbl.	11,609	4,329	2,322	866
Naval stores, turpentine	bbl.	5,601	2,621	1,120	524
Oil, whale	ton	1,038	12,451	208	2,490
Potash	ton	2,228	57,073	446	11,415
Rum, American	gal.	154,564	10,515	30,913	2,103
Rum, West Indian	gal.	8,507	864	1,701	173
Wine	ton	95	5,737	19	1,147
Wood products, pine boards	1,000 ft.	5,386	8,480	1,077	1,696
Wood products, staves/headings	1,000 ft.	12,101	36,260	2,420	7,252
Total Value			868,188		173,638

SOURCE: SHEPHERD, "COMMODITY EXPORTS FROM THE BRITISH NORTH AMERICAN COLONIES," 12–53

APPENDICES

TABLE A.4 Commodity exports from Pennsylvania, 1768–72 (value in £ sterling)

Commodity	Unit	England		Ireland		Southern Europe*		West Indies		Africa	
		Quantity	Value	Quantity	Value	Quantity	Value	Quantity	Value	Quantity	Value
Beeswax	lb.	124,547	6,228	-	-	58,269	2,913	-	-	-	-
Beef and Pork	bbl.	672	1,326	-	-	447	916	19,503	40,523	-	-
Bread and Flour	ton	2,240	22,570	2,826	28,497	52,626	555,207	52,631	560,975	-	-
Candle, spermaceti	lb.	-	-	-	-	6,925	469	55,300	3,733	-	-
Cotton	lb.	1,480	65	-	-	-	-	-	-	-	-
Deerskins	lb.	65,407	5,997	-	-	-	-	-	-	-	-
Fish, dried	quintal	-	-	-	-	288	144	6,270	3,124	-	-
Flaxseed	bu.	5,433	1,012	391,328	71,902	-	-	-	-	-	-
Grain, corn	bu.	2,527	195	304	27	379,841	36,934	136,626	13,840	-	-
Grain, rice	bbl.	4,092	11,155	21,048	3,641	4	10	1,647	4,108	-	-
Grain, wheat	bu.	20,683	3,976	12,707	2,582	566,558	109,661	803	157	-	-
Indigo	lb.	732	122	-	-	-	-	-	-	-	-
Hoops	1,000	-	-	-	-	-	-	855	1,731	-	-
Iron, bar	ton	972	14,148	40	574	-	-	609	9,072	-	-
Iron, pig	ton	5,095	25,290	-	-	-	-	-	-	-	-
Livestock, cattle	no.	-	-	-	-	-	-	46	276	-	-
Livestock, horses	no.	-	-	-	-	-	-	102	1,020	-	-

TABLE A.4 Commodity exports from Pennsylvania, 1768–72 (value in £ sterling) (cont.)

Commodity	Unit	England		Ireland		Southern Europe*		West Indies		Africa	
		Quantity	Value	Quantity	Value	Quantity	Value	Quantity	Value	Quantity	Value
Naval stores, pitch	bbl.	1,387	584	-	-	-	-	-	-	-	-
Naval stores, tar	bbl.	6,911	2,776	-	-	-	-	-	-	-	-
Naval stores, turpentine	bbl.	9,307	4,386	-	-	-	-	-	-	-	-
Oil, whale	ton	180	2,158	0	2	-	-	158	1,897	-	-
Potash	ton	168	4,209	1	18	-	-	-	-	-	-
Rum, American	gal.	15,791	1,062	9,594	643	3,395	226	-	-	21,978	1,472
Rum, West Indian	gal.	26,564	2,603	33,425	3,450	3,542	347	-	-	-	-
Wine	ton	-	-	-	-	-	-	92	5,832	-	-
Wood products, pine boards	1,000 ft.	782	1,701	91	189	65	139	7,201	16,280	-	-
Wood products, staves/headings	1,000 ft.	2,180	6,446	5,843	17,234	3,372	9,845	13,858	41,460	-	-
Total Value			118,009		128,759		716,811		704,028		1,472

TABLE A.4 Commodity exports from Pennsylvania, 1768–72 (value in £ sterling) (cont.)

Commodity	Unit	Total 1768–72		Yearly average	
		Quantity	Value	Quantity	Value
Beeswax	lb.	182,816	9,141	36,563	1,828
Beef and Pork	bbl.	20,622	42,765	4,124	8,553
Bread and Flour	ton	110,324	1,167,249	22,065	233,450
Candle, spermaceti	lb.	62,225	4,202	12,445	840
Cotton	lb.	1,480	65	296	13
Deerskins	lb.	65,407	5,997	13,081	1,199
Fish, dried	quintal	6,558	3,268	1,312	654
Flaxseed	bu.	396,741	72,914	79,348	14,583
Grain, corn	bu.	519,298	50,996	103,860	10,199
Grain, rice	bbl.	26,791	18,914	5,358	3,783
Grain, wheat	bu.	600,751	116,376	120,150	23,275
Indigo	lb.	732	122	146	24
Hoops	1,000	855	1,731	171	346
Iron, bar	ton	1,622	23,794	324	4,759
Iron, pig	ton	5,095	25,290	1,019	5,058
Livestock, cattle	no.	46	276	9	55
Livestock, horses	no.	102	1,020	20	204

TABLE A.4 Commodity exports from Pennsylvania, 1768–72 (value in £ sterling) (cont.)

Commodity	Unit	Total 1768–72		Yearly average	
		Quantity	Value	Quantity	Value
Naval stores, pitch	bbl.	1,387	584	277	117
Naval stores, tar	bbl.	6,911	2,776	1,382	555
Naval stores, turpentine	bbl.	9,307	4,386	1,861	877
Oil, whale	ton	338	4,057	68	811
Potash	ton	168	4,227	34	845
Rum, American	gal.	50,758	3,403	10,152	681
Rum, West Indian	gal.	63,531	6,400	12,706	1,280
Wine	ton	92	5,832	18	1,166
Wood products, pine boards	1,000 ft.	8,139	18,309	1,628	3,662
Wood products, staves/headings	1,000 ft.	25,253	74,985	5,051	14,997
Total Value			1,669,079		333,816

SOURCE: SHEPHERD, "COMMODITY EXPORTS FROM THE BRITISH NORTH AMERICAN COLONIES," 12–53

APPENDICES

TABLE A.5 Tonnage clearing from Boston to specified destinations at selected years, 1714–72

Date	Great Britain	% Total	Ireland	% Total	Southern Europe[a]	% Total	West Indies	% Total	Africa	% Total	Coastal	% Total	Total
1714–17[b]	3,985	0.19	-	-	1,185	0.06	11,146	0.53	-	-	4,613	0.22	20,929
1754	2,510	0.09	165	0.01	2,465	0.09	10,781	0.40	75	0.00	10,673	0.40	26,669
1755	2,975	0.14	100	0.00	1,853	0.09	8,075	0.38	-	-	8,292	0.39	21,295
1766	5,822	0.19	-	-	1,350	0.04	7,806	0.25	-	-	16,236	0.52	31,214
1767	6,257	0.19	-	-	754	0.02	9,079	0.27	-	-	17,115	0.52	33,205
1768	6,428	0.19	170	0.01	1,333	0.04	10,095	0.30	-	-	15,669	0.47	33,695
1769	6,707	0.18	60	0.00	1,081	0.03	9,190	0.25	495	0.01	19,512	0.53	37,045
1770	5,819	0.16	-	-	813	0.02	8,348	0.23	415	0.01	21,570	0.58	36,965
1771	5,750	0.15	-	-	1,113	0.03	9,531	0.24	267	0.01	22,334	0.57	38,995
1772	6,178	0.15	170	0.00	555	0.01	10,988	0.26	420	0.01	24,195	0.57	42,506
Total	52,431	0.16	495	0.00	12,502	0.04	95,039	0.29	1,672	0.01	160,209	0.50	322,348

Notes:
a Includes the Wine Islands.
b Indicates a yearly average.
Blank spaces indicate no recorded or available data. However, it is not entirely certain that no trade occurred.
SOURCE: CHAPTER 2, "COLONIAL STATISTICS," 5:719. FORMATTING OF THE TABLE INSPIRED BY MANCALL, ROSENBLOOM, AND WEISS, "EXPORTS FROM THE COLONIES AND STATES OF THE MIDDLE ATLANTIC REGION 1720–1800," 267

TABLE A.6 Tonnage clearing from New York to specified destinations at selected years, 1715–72

Date	Great Britain	% Total	Ireland	% Total	Southern Europe[a]	% Total	West Indies	% Total	Africa	% Total	Coastal	% Total	Total
1715	1,461	0.20					3,790	0.52	40	0.01	1,406	0.19	7,327
1726	988	0.13			630	0.09	3,468	0.45			2,761	0.36	7,732
1727	1,030	0.13			515	0.07	4,309	0.54			2,138	0.27	7,942
1733	690	0.09	160	0.02	465	0.06	3,937	0.53			2,349	0.32	7,411
1734	645	0.10	160	0.03	275	0.04	2,881	0.47	60	0.01	1,959	0.32	6,180
1735	838	0.12	200	0.03	475	0.08	2,941	0.41			2,321	0.32	7,204
1739	795	0.08	820	0.09	904	0.13	4,431	0.46			2,451	0.26	9,537
1754	2,085	0.16	1,615	0.12	1,040	0.11	6,486	0.49	130	0.01	2,076	0.16	13,117
1763	2,079	0.14	1,460	0.10	725	0.06	7,657	0.52	70	0.00	2,450	0.17	14,716
1764	2,952	0.19	1,882	0.12	1,000	0.07	8,221	0.52	140	0.01	1,495	0.09	15,777
1765	5,165	0.29			1,087	0.07	7,825	0.45			2,988	0.17	17,570
1766	4,907	0.25			1,592	0.09	8,385	0.42			3,090	0.16	19,862
1767	5,588	0.28			3,480	0.18	6,697	0.34			3,770	0.19	19,875
1768	5,130	0.24	2,522	0.12	3,820	0.19	7,220	0.34	35	0.00	3,754	0.18	21,021
1769	3,955	0.16	2,515	0.10	2,360	0.11	5,628	0.23	205	0.01	9,068	0.37	24,649
1770	4,665	0.20	2,692	0.12	3,278	0.13	7,244	0.31	98	0.00	5,655	0.24	23,274
1771	4,830	0.22	2,476	0.11	2,920	0.13	7,996	0.36	115	0.01	4,968	0.22	22,414
1772	4,280	0.17	1,610	0.06	2,029	0.09	8,248	0.32	260	0.01	8,859	0.34	25,706
Total	52,083	0.19	18,112	0.07	2,449	0.10	107,364	0.40	1,153	0.00	63,558	0.23	271,314

Notes:
a Includes the Wine Islands.
Blank spaces indicate no recorded or available data. However, it is not entirely certain that no trade occurred.
SOURCE: MANCALL, ROSENBLOOM, AND WEISS, "EXPORTS FROM THE COLONIES AND STATES OF THE MIDDLE ATLANTIC REGION 1720–1800," 267

APPENDICES

TABLE A.7 Tonnage clearing from Philadelphia to specified destinations at selected years, 1715–72

Date	Great Britain	% Total	Ireland	% Total	Southern Europe[a]	% Total	West Indies	% Total	Africa	% Total	Coastal	% Total	Total
1720	520	0.12			270	0.06	2,190	0.52	–	–	1,210	0.29	4,190
1721	650	0.17			480	0.13	1,680	0.45	–	–	910	0.24	3,720
1722	560	0.15			420	0.11	1,770	0.48	–	–	930	0.25	3,680
1723	450	0.13			420	0.13	1,870	0.56	–	–	600	0.18	3,340
1724	290	0.07	140	0.03	660	0.16	2,300	0.57	–	–	650	0.16	4,040
1725	690	0.15			740	0.16	2,410	0.51	–	–	910	0.19	4,750
1726	990	0.16			1,110	0.18	3,570	0.57	–	–	610	0.10	6,280
1727	730	0.14	50	0.01	470	0.09	3,120	0.61	–	–	760	0.15	5,130
1728	1,150	0.21			790	0.14	2,480	0.45	–	–	1,130	0.20	5,550
1729	1,580	0.22			1,300	0.18	3,230	0.44	–	–	1,190	0.16	7,300
1730	1,170	0.15			790	0.10	4,280	0.56	–	–	1,410	0.18	7,650
1731	1,310	0.15	240	0.03	1,450	0.17	4,170	0.48	–	–	1,430	0.17	8,600
1732	620	0.10	620	0.10	830	0.14	2,930	0.48	–	–	1,140	0.19	6,140
1733	890	0.09	1,440	0.14	950	0.09	5,070	0.50	–	–	1,820	0.18	10,170
1734	1,400	0.13	1,460	0.13	2,130	0.19	4,160	0.38	–	–	1,880	0.17	11,030
1735	1,090	0.11	1,180	0.12	2,420	0.25	3,240	0.33	–	–	1,830	0.19	9,760
1736	790	0.09	1,690	0.19	2,100	0.23	2,750	0.31	–	–	1,630	0.18	8,960
1737	1,110	0.11	870	0.08	2,740	0.27	3,430	0.33	–	–	2,090	0.20	10,240

TABLE A.7 Tonnage clearing from Philadelphia to specified destinations at selected years, 1715–72 (cont.)

Date	Great Britain	% Total	Ireland	% Total	Southern Europe[a]	% Total	West Indies	% Total	Africa	% Total	Coastal	% Total	Total
1738	780	0.08	1,060	0.11	1,690	0.18	3,590	0.37		-	2,460	0.26	9,580
1739	570	0.05	1,450	0.14	3,580	0.33	3,450	0.32		-	1,660	0.15	10,710
1750	1,136	0.04	2,491	0.10	1,739	0.07	12,682	0.50		-	7,204	0.29	25,252
1765	5,161	0.14		-	3,345	0.09	12,340	0.33		-	17,004	0.45	37,850
1766	1,830	0.05	4,830	0.13	4,455	0.12	14,053	0.39	300	0.01	10,834	0.30	36,302
1767	8,263	0.20		-	6,408	0.16	13,371	0.33		-	13,061	0.32	41,103
1768	4,134	0.12	3,482	0.10	7,255	0.21	12,119	0.35		-	8,116	0.23	35,106
1769	4,049	0.10	3,170	0.08	12,040	0.30	11,114	0.28	30	0.00	9,085	0.23	39,488
1770	3,208	0.07	4,791	0.11	10,940	0.24	14,043	0.31		-	12,370	0.27	45,352
1771	3,222	0.08	3,470	0.08	7,110	0.17	13,757	0.33	90	0.00	13,655	0.33	41,304
1772	3,123	0.07	2,491	0.06	8,415	0.20	16,081	0.37	20	0.00	12,872	0.30	43,002
Total	51,466	0.11	34,925	0.07	87,047	0.18	181,250	0.37	440	0.00	130,451	0.27	485,579

Notes:
a Includes the Wine Islands.
Blank spaces indicate no recorded or available data. However, it is not entirely certain that no trade occurred.
SOURCE: MANCALL, ROSENBLOOM, AND WEISS, "EXPORTS FROM THE COLONIES AND STATES OF THE MIDDLE ATLANTIC REGION 1720–1800," 267

TABLE A.8 Average annual values of selected commodities in the coastal trade of British America, 1768–72 (£ sterling)

Commodity	Newfoundland Exports	Newfoundland Imports	P.E. Island Exports	P.E. Island Imports	Quebec Exports	Quebec Imports	Nova Scotia Exports	Nova Scotia Imports	Massachusetts Exports	Massachusetts Imports
Corn	-	300	-	-	-	300	-	1,100	1,400	21,800
Wheat	-	-	800	-	2,900	-	100	100	100	10,600
Rice	-	200	-	-	-	300	-	300	600	4,000
Molasses	-	1,500	-	700	-	1,800	-	3,700	25,900	1,600
Brown Sugar	100	800	-	400	-	400	20	1,500	4,600	2,500
Bread and Flour	-	800	-	3,600	400	4,700	300	7,500	5,600	43,100
Dried Fish	2,300	-	2,500	-	3,200	-	12,300	200	4,900	21,400
New England Rum	-	600	-	2,300	-	13,000	100	700	44,900	1,500
West Indian Rum	-	800	-	700	100	1,400	-	800	4,500	2,200
Pitch	-	200	-	-	-	-	-	-	200	900
Tar	-	200	-	-	-	-	-	100	300	5,600
Turpentine	-	-	-	-	-	-	-	-	100	1,200
Potash	-	-	-	-	-	-	-	-	100	3,700
Pine Boards	-	700	-	100	-	200	200	200	3,300	200
Train Oil	-	100	300	300	100	200	1,100	200	16,800	3,900
Total	*2,400*	*6,200*	*3,600*	*8,100*	*6,700*	*22,100*	*14,120*	*16,400*	*113,300*	*124,200*

TABLE A.8 Average annual values of selected commodities in the coastal trade of British America, 1768–72 (£ sterling) (*cont.*)

Commodity	New Hampshire		Rhode Island		Connecticut		New York		New Jersey	
	Exports	Imports	Exports	Imports	Exports	Imports	Exports	Imports	Exports	Imports
Corn	100	2,600	600	3,300	3,200	200	600	1,500	100	200
Wheat	-	600	1,300	1,500	3,900	100	200	4,000	-	200
Rice	-	100	400	3,100	-	200	700	4,700	-	-
Molasses	1,800	500	11,400	200	7,600	1,400	2,500	13,000	-	600
Brown Sugar	600	300	2,600	300	2,000	700	4,800	1,800	200	-
Bread and Flour	400	4,300	1,300	17,900	2,600	2,100	30,800	1,900	1,500	-
Dried Fish	300	1,400	600	8,400	300	5,300	100	1,000	-	-
New England Rum	4,000	500	14,900	200	1,000	1,400	8,100	5,000	100	900
West Indian Rum	3,100	200	10,700	500	14,200	1,500	2,400	17,300	100	1,100
Pitch	-	100	-	200	-	100	200	400	-	-
Tar	100	400	100	1,100	-	200	200	1,600	-	-
Turpentine	-	100	-	600	-	100	100	800	-	-
Potash	600	-	-	100	4,600	-	100	1,100	-	-
Pine Boards	1,800	-	100	3,400	100	1,500	300	100	100	-
Train Oil	300	100	3,600	9,600	600	1,200	100	2,900	-	-
Total	*13,100*	*11,200*	*47,600*	*50,400*	*40,100*	*16,000*	*51,200*	*57,100*	*2,100*	*3,000*

TABLE A.8 Average annual values of selected commodities in the coastal trade of British America, 1768–72 (£ sterling) (cont.)

Commodity	Pennsylvania		Delaware		Maryland		Virginia		North Carolina	
	Exports	Imports	Exports	Imports	Exports	Imports	Exports	Imports	Exports	Imports
Corn	900	2,300	-	-	8,400	300	16,200	-	10,000	-
Wheat	-	11,500	-	200	8,100	100	13,400	100	1,100	-
Rice	700	6,800	-	-	-	100	-	-	400	-
Molasses	1,800	11,000	-	-	10	4,900	-	4,100	300	2,300
Brown Sugar	1,900	2,700	-	-	100	2,300	300	1,600	100	600
Bread and Flour	73,500	300	-	-	13,400	200	5,100	900	300	700
Dried Fish	-	1,300	-	-	-	200	-	100	-	100
New England Rum	7,200	11,500	-	-	100	11,500	500	9,000	200	4,100
West Indian Rum	9,800	5,200	-	-	200	5,600	1,300	2,600	300	900
Pitch	-	300	-	-	-	-	-	-	2,100	-
Tar	-	1,700	-	-	-	300	300	300	10,800	-
Turpentine	100	1,100	-	-	-	100	400	100	4,100	-
Potash	-	-	-	-	-	-	-	-	-	-
Pine Boards	100	300	-	-	100	100	100	100	300	-
Train Oil	100	5,500	-	-	-	200	-	200	100	200
Total	96,100	61,500	-	200	30,410	25,900	37,600	19,100	30,100	8,900

TABLE A.8 Average annual values of selected commodities in the coastal trade of British America, 1768–72 (£ sterling) (cont.)

Commodity	South Carolina		Georgia		Florida		Bahamas		Bermuda	
	Exports	Imports	Exports	Imports	Exports	Imports	Exports	Imports	Exports	Imports
Corn	3,000	1,600	800	100	100	800	-	600	-	6,200
Wheat	-	-	-	-	-	-	-	-	-	-
Rice	15,000	4,300	6,300	200	100	600	-	300	-	600
Molasses	300	700	100	100	-	100	200	-	100	-
Brown Sugar	400	1,200	200	200	200	300	1,300	1,600	400	-
Bread and Flour	1,200	700	-	2,200	100	5,200	-	2,100	-	1,400
Dried Fish	-	100	-	-	-	-	-	-	-	-
New England Rum	1,700	10,100	200	2,700	800	2,800	-	400	100	100
West Indian Rum	2,500	1,300	300	800	400	2,100	200	700	600	-
Pitch	400	-	-	-	-	-	-	-	-	-
Tar	200	400	-	-	-	-	-	-	-	100
Turpentine	100	200	-	-	-	-	-	-	-	-
Potash	-	-	-	-	-	-	-	-	-	-
Pine Boards	100	400	100	-	-	100	-	300	-	900
Train Oil	-	300	-	-	-	-	-	-	-	-
Total	24,900	21,300	8,000	6,300	1,700	12,000	1,700	6,000	1,200	9,300

SOURCE: SHEPHERD AND WILLIAMSON, "COASTAL TRADE OF THE BRITISH NORTH AMERICAN COLONIES," 808–9

TABLE A.9 Philadelphia–Lisbon entries and clearances, 1769–74

Port of Record	Origin/Destination	1769		1770		1771		1772		1773		1774		1769–74	
		E	C	E	C	E	C	E	C	E	C	E	C	E	C
Philadelphia	Lisbon	61	105	101	93	31	45	43	52	41	50	32	74	309	419
		C	E	C	E	C	E	C	E	C	E	C	E	C	E
Lisbon	Philadelphia	119	135	148	153	71	83	95	115	102	94	122	145	657	725
# Difference (Lisbon-Philadelphia)		58	30	47	60	40	38	52	63	61	44	90	71	348	306
% Difference v Philadelphia Records		95%	29%	47%	65%	129%	84%	121%	121%	149%	88%	281%	96%	113%	73%

Note: Percentages are rounded
SOURCES: 1769–74, *PENNSYLVANIA GAZETTE*. LISBON MUNICIPAL ARCHIVE, HISTORICAL ARCHIVE, COLLECTION "TAXES," TONNAGE TAX FUND, TONNAGE TAX BOOK OF ENTRIES. COMPILED BY AUTHOR

Appendix B

Sectoral Population Breakdown of Boston, New York, and Philadelphia

Sector	Boston (1790)	Philadelphia (1774)	New York (1795)
I. Government	68 (2.75%)	58 (1.53%)	9 (3.49%)
A. Federal or Congressional	11		4
B. State or Provincial	13	23	
D. Local and Law Enforcement	44	34	5
E. Military		1	
II. Service Sector	1,115 (45.01%)	1,856 (48.9%)	146 (56.59%)
A. Professional	102 (4.12%)	129 (3.4%)	10 (3.87%)
1. apothecary, druggist	17	10	
2. architect	1		
3. dentist	1		
4. doctor, physician	26	38	
5. lawyer, attorney	21	17	
6. minister	20	13	
7. schoolmaster	16	43	
8. surveyor		1	
B. Retailers and Local Wholesalers	243 (9.81%)	301 (7.94%)	30 (11.67%)
1. auctioneer	7	7	
2. bookseller	2	2	
3. cyderman, cider cooper		1	
4. grocer	33	17	
5. hardware, ironmonger, iron dealer	12	1	
6. hosier			
7. jeweler	3	3	
8. lemon-lime dealer/seller	10	1	
9. lumber or board merchant	5	5	
10. milkman		11	

APPENDICES   211

Sector	Boston (1790)	Philadelphia (1774)	New York (1795)
11. oysterman		1	
12. peddler, huckster	10	39	
13. retailer, shopkeeper	133	195	
14. shoe dealer	6		
15. slop-shop keeper	4		
16. stationer	5		
17. tallow chandler		11	
18. trader, dealer, jobber	13	2	
19. wine cooper, liquor seller		1	
C. "Retail" Crafts	201 (8.11%)	495 (13.05%)	23 (8.91%)
1. bacon smoker	1		
2. baker, biscuit baker	64	124	
3. butcher	10	121	
4. confectioner	1	1	
5. mustardmaker		1	
6. bookbinder	3	9	
7. furrier	3		
8. tailor	100	190	
9. tobacconist, snuffmaker	17	20	
D. Building Crafts	250 (10.09%)	428 (11.28%)	39 (15.11%)
1. carpenters	140	278	
2. contractor, head builder	5		
3. glazier	12	2	
4. mason, bricklayer	44	70	
5. paver	34	27	
6. plasterer		19	
7. plumber		2	
8. sawyer, woodcutter	7	20	
9. stonecutter, marble quarrier	3	13	
10. wharfbuilder		2	
E. Travel and Transport Services	187 (7.55%)	382 (10.07%)	27 (10.46%)
1. blacksmith, smith, farrier	59	125	

Sector	Boston (1790)	Philadelphia (1774)	New York (1795)
2. carter, cartman, truckman	59	40	
3. chaise-letter	3		
4. coach-driver, coachman	6	6	
5. drover		1	
6. hack-driver	7		
7. innkeeper, innholder	24	73	
8. stable-keeper, livery-keeper	3	2	
9. tavern-keeper, taverner	26	97	
10. waterman, boatman, flatman		23	
F. Other Services	132 (5.33%)	121 (3.19%)	17 (6.58%)
1. barber, hairdresser	42	39	
2. chimney sweeper	6	1	
3. gravedigger		2	
4. lightman	7		
5. musician, fiddler	3	3	
6. servant, porter	63	70	
7. sexton	11	1	
8. razor grinder		2	
9. washerwomen		1	
III. Industrial	659 (26.6%)	1,017 (26.81%)	43 (16.67%)
A. Textile Trades	54 (2.18%)	110 (2.9%)	2 (0.77%)
1. duckcloth maker	24		
2. dyer, silkdyer, blue dyer	3	10	
3. fuller		4	
4. linen manufacturer, flax dresser		2	
5. spinner		1	
6. stocking weaver, knitter		59	
7. threadmaker		1	
8. weaver	3	32	
9. woolcardmaker, cardmaker	24		
10. woolcomber		1	

APPENDICES 213

Sector	Boston (1790)	Philadelphia (1774)	New York (1795)
B. Leather and Fur Trades	136 (5.49%)	385 (10.15%)	17 (6.58%)
1. currier		6	
2. harnessmaker, whipmaker		9	
3. hatter	29	72	
4. leather dresser, skinner	13	30	
5. leather merchant		1	
6. saddler, saddlemaker	6	32	
7. shoemaker, cordwainer	78	198	
8. tanner	10	37	
C. Food and Drink Processing	59 (2.38%)	56 (1.48%)	1 (0.38%)
1. brewer, beer house		19	
2. chocolate maker		3	
3. distiller	47	17	
4. miller, bran flourer, flour-maker	4	11	
5. sugarboiler, refiner, sugarbaker	8	6	
D. Shipbuilding and Fitting	213 (8.6%)	187 (4.93%)	12 (4.65%)
1. blockmaker	16	7	
2. boatbuilder		13	
3. caulker	14	14	
4. mastmaker	7	5	
5. oarmaker	1		
6. pumpmaker	4	2	
7. rigger	11	4	
8. ropemaker	42	13	
9. sailmaker	30	17	
10. sea cooper	16		
11. shipcarpenter, -joiner, -wright	72	112	
E. Metal Crafts (except blacksmiths)	80 (3.23%)	103 (2.72%)	4 (1.55%)
1. brassfounder, founder	15	4	
2. bucklemaker, buttonmaker		1	
3. clockmaker		8	

Sector	Boston (1790)	Philadelphia (1774)	New York (1795)
4. coppersmith	4	9	
5. cutler		10	
6. goldsmith	23	7	
7. gunsmith	1	5	
8. instrument maker	3	1	
9. locksmith		3	
10. nailor, nailsmith, nailmaker		7	
11. pewterer	6	3	
12. plane-maker, sawmaker		3	
13. silversmith	5	15	
14. tinner, tinker, tinman	15	20	
15. watchmaker	8	7	
F. Furniture Trades	35 (3.31%)	34 (0.9%)	2 (0.77%)
1. cabinetmaker	15		
2. carver	4	11	
3. chairmaker	11		
4. turner	1	17	
5. upholsterer, upholder	4	6	
G. Miscellaneous	82 (3.31%)	142 (3.74%)	5 (1.93%)
1. brickmaster		5	
2. brushmaker		4	
3. chaisemaker, coachmaker	16	29	
4. paperstainer, papermaker	3	4	
5. potter		24	
6. printer, engraver	17	21	
7. soapboiler, soap chandler	6	2	
8. whalebonecutter, combmaker, staysmaker	4	15	
9. wheelwright	8	20	
10. other trades	28	18	

Sector	Boston (1790)	Philadelphia (1774)	New York (1795)
IV. Commerce (Maritime) and Fisheries	635 (25.64%)	862 (22.73%)	60 (23.26%)
A. Mariners	231 (9.33%)	331 (8.73%)	24 (9.30%)
1. sea captain, master mariner	114	83	
2. mate	20	3	
3. pilot	2	22	
4. sailer, seaman, mariner	58	199	
5. fisherman	37	24	
B. Merchants and Support Staff	404 (16.31%)	531 (14.00%)	36 (13.95%)
1. accountant	3	1	
2. banker	1		
3. broker, scrivener	16	6	
4. chandler, ship chandler	17	15	
5. clerk, scribe	66	34	
6. cooper	70	142	
7. corn dealer, flour merchant		2	
8. merchant	206	329	
9. stevedore, trimmer		2	
10. underwriter	1		
11. wharfinger	24		
Categories I-IV Total	*2,477*	*3,793*	*258*
V. Unclassified			
A. Agricultural			
1. ditcher		1	
2. farmer, yeoman		111	
3. goat keeper		1	
4. gardner	15	17	
5. grazier		11	
6. welldigger		2	
B. Laborers (Unspecified)	157	614	
C. Unemployed/Retired	106		

Sector	Boston (1790)	Philadelphia (1774)	New York (1795)
D. Women Head of Household without occupation			206
1. widows		105	
2. other		72	
E. Males, without occupation			221
1. married man		635	
2. single man		612	
G. Illegible		40	

SOURCE: JACOB M. PRICE, "ECONOMIC FUNCTION AND THE GROWTH OF AMERICAN PORT TOWNS IN THE EIGHTEENTH CENTURY," *PERSPECTIVES IN AMERICAN HISTORY* 8 (1974): 177–85

Bibliography

Manuscripts

British National Archives
Treasury Papers

Historical Society of Philadelphia
Charles Stewart Letterbooks, 1751–63.
Daniel Clark Letter and Invoice Book, 1760–62.
Day Book Hampton and Norfolk, VA, 1748–50.
Duties Account Book, 1704–13.
John Stamper Letterbook, 1751–63.
Joseph Ogden Invoice Records, 1749–55.
Marshall Bills of Lading.
Murdock Receipt Book, 1765–71.
Orr, Dunlop, and Glenhope Letterbook, 1767–69.
Philip Francis, Invoice Book, 1771–72.
Port of Philadelphia Bills of Lading, 1716–72.
Port of Philadelphia Customs House Papers, 1704–89.
Port of Philadelphia Exciseman's Account Book, 1739–42.
Port of Philadelphia Register, 1741–42.
Port of Philadelphia Registry, 1682–86.
Robert Ellis Letterbooks, 1736–48.
Samuel Neave Almanac, 1738.
Ships Registered at the Port of Philadelphia before 1776: A Computerized Listing by John J. McCusker.
Tench Francis Invoice Book, 1759–61.
Uriah Woolsman Bills of Lading.

Library Company of Philadelphia
Account Books of Isaac Norris.
Allen and Turner Letterbook, 1755–64.
Jonathan Dickinson Letterbook, 1714–22.
Miscellaneous Bills of Lading.
Thomas Chalkley Account Book, 1718–27.

Lisbon Municipal Archive
Colecção Impostos.

Fundo Marco dos Navios.
Livro de Entradas do Marco dos Navios.

Massachusetts Historical Society
Account Book by Boston Merchant, 1736–41.
Amory Family Papers, 1697–1894.
Anonymous Sailor's Diary, 1733–36.
Benjamin Dolbeare Letterbook and Invoice Book, 1739–1811.
Benjamin Goodwin Account Books, 1767–96.
Benjamin Waterman Account Book, 1768–1842.
Benjamin Wheeler Papers.
Boston Shipping Firm Account Book, 1763–65.
British North American Customs Papers, 1769–72.
Bromfield and Clarke Family Papers.
Caleb Davis Papers, 1684–1831.
Captain John Nutt Invoice Book, 1772–84.
Charles Henry Frankland Diary, 1755–1813.
Charlotte Tirell Collection, 1690–1843.
Child Family Business Papers, 1765–1875.
Constant Freeman Account Books, 1768–74.
Dalton Family Papers, 1667–1906.
David S. Greenough Papers, 1631–1859.
Dering Family Papers, 1627–1898.
Dolbeare Family Papers, 1665–1830.
Edward Payne Shipping Record.
Ezekiel Price Papers, 1754–85.
Great Britain Commissioners of Customs Letterbook, August 7–September 17, 1770.
Hancock Family Accounts and Receipts, 1728–1829.
Higginson Family Papers, 1628–1902.
Hutchinson Family Papers, 1673–1769.
Jeffries Family Papers, 1622–1880.
John Erving Bills of Lading, 1732–48.
John Rowe Papers, 1765–91.
Lot Stetson Logbook, 1772.
Non-Importation Agreement, July 31, 1769.
Peter Faneuil Ledger.
Petition by Boston Merchants, April 1708.
Report on the State of Customs in the Port of Boston, 1768.
Revenge Sloop Papers, 1741–1801.
Samuel Bradford Papers, 1760–1818.

BIBLIOGRAPHY 219

Samuel Davenport Account Book, 1724–83.
Samuel P. Savage Papers, 1703–1848.
Ship Registers.
Slade–Rogers Family Papers, 1672–1933.
Thomas Nicholson Navigation and Logbooks, 1766–1813.

New York Historical Society
Alexander Watson Notebook, 1772–74.
Crean Bush Account Books, 1765–66.
Joseph Reed and Esther De Berdt Reed Papers, 1757–1874.
Philip John Schuyler Account Book, 1763–70.
Trade Book of the Sloop Rhode Island, December 1748–July 1749.
William Burnet Papers, 1720–42.
William Yarrington Diary, 1759–76.

Published Primary Sources

Allen, James. "Diary of James Allen, Esq. of Philadelphia, Counsellor-at-Law, 1770–1778, Part I." *Pennsylvania Magazine of History and Biography* 9, no. 2 (July 1885): 176–96.
Boston Records Commissioners. *A Report of the Records Commissioners of the City of Boston, Containing the Boston Town Records, 1770 through 1777*. Boston: Rockwell and Churchill, City Printers, 1887.
Boston Records Commissioners. *A Report of the Record Commissioners of the City of Boston, Containing the Selectmen's Minutes from 1736 through 1742*. Boston: Rockwell and Churchill, City Printers, 1889.
Boston Records Commissioners. *A Report of the Record Commissioners of the City of Boston, Containing the Selectmen's Minutes from 1764 through 1768*. Boston: Rockwell and Churchill, City Printers, 1889.
Boston Records Commissioners. *A Report of the Records Commissioners of the City of Boston, Containing the Selectmen's Minutes from 1769 through April 1775*. Boston: Rockwell and Churchill, City Printers, 1893.
Carter, Clarence Edwin, ed. *The Correspondence of General Thomas Gage with the Secretaries of State, 1763–1775*. 2 vols. New Haven: Yale University Press, 1931.
Cunningham, Anne Rowe, ed. *Letters and Diary of John Rowe: Boston Merchant, 1759–1762, 1764–1779*. Boston: W. B. Clarke Company, 1969 [1903].
Ford, Worthington C., ed. *Correspondence and Journals of Samuel Blachley Webb*. Vol. 1. New York: New York Times and Arno Press, 1969.
Gage, Thomas et al. *Letters to the Ministry from Governor Benard, General Gage, Commodore Hood, and also Memorials to the Lords of the Treasury from the*

Commissioners of the Customs with Sundry Letters and Papers Annexed to Said Memorials. Boston: Edes and Gill, 1769.

Minutes of the Common Council of the City of Philadelphia, 1704 to 1776. Philadelphia: Crissy and Markley, Printers, 1847.

Pruitt, Bettye Hobbs, ed. *The Massachusetts Tax Valuation List of 1771*. Boston: G. K. Hall and Company, 1978.

Edited Collections

Antony, Robert J., ed. *Pirates in the Age of Sail*. New York: W. W. Norton & Company, 2007.

Armstrong, Edward, ed. *Correspondence between William Penn and James Logan, Secretary of the Province of Pennsylvania, and Others, 1700–1750*. Vols. 1–2. Philadelphia: J. B. Lippincott and Co., for the Historical Society of Pennsylvania, 1872.

Barrett, Walter, ed. *The Old Merchants of New York City, 5 Volumes*. New York: Carleton, 1862.

Dickerson, Oliver Morton, ed. *Boston under Military Rule, 1768–1769 as Revealed in a Journal of the Times*. Boston: Chapman and Grimes, 1936.

Documents Relative to the Colonial History of the State of New York, 15 Volumes. Albany: Weed, Parsons and Company, 1853–87.

Greene, Jack P., ed. *Settlements to Society, 1607–1763: A Documentary History of Colonial America*. New York: W. W. Norton & Company, 1975.

Simmons, R. C., and P. D. G. Thomas, eds. *Proceedings and Debates of the British Parliament Respecting North America, 1754–1783*. Vols. 3–4. Millwood, NY: Kraus International Publications, 1984.

Truxes, Thomas M., ed. *Letterbook of Greg and Cunningham, 1756–57: Merchants of New York and Belfast*. Oxford: Oxford University Press on behalf of the British Academy, 2001.

White, Philip L., ed. *The Beekman Mercantile Papers, 3 Volumes*. New York: New York Historical Society, 1956.

Secondary Sources

Abu-Lughod, Janet. *Before European Hegemony: The World System A.D. 1250–1350*. Oxford: Oxford University Press, 1989.

Acemoglu, Daron, and James A. Robinson. *Why Nations Fail: The Origins of Power, Prosperity and Poverty*. New York: Crown Publishers, 2012.

Anderson, Fred. *Crucible of War*. New York: Alfred A. Knopf, 2000.

Andreas, Peter. *Smuggler Nation: How Illicit Trade Made America*. Oxford: Oxford University Press, 2013.

Andrews, John H. "Anglo-American Trade in the Early Eighteenth Century." *Geographical Review* 45, no. 1 (January 1955): 99–110.
Archer, Richard. *As if an Enemy's Country: The British Occupation of Boston and the Origins of Revolution.* Oxford: Oxford University Press, 2010.
Armitage, David, and Michael J. Braddock. *The British Atlantic World, 1500–1800.* New York: Palgrave Macmillan, 2002.
Aslanian, Sebouh David. *From the Indian Ocean to the Mediterranean: The Global Trade Networks of Armenian Merchants from New Julfa.* Berkeley: University of California Press, 2011.
Bailyn, Bernard, *Atlantic History: Concept and Contours.* Cambridge, MA: Harvard University Press, 2005.
Bailyn, Bernard. *The New England Merchants in the Seventeenth Century.* Cambridge, MA: Harvard University Press, 1979.
Bailyn, Bernard, and Lotte Bailyn. *Massachusetts Shipping, 1697–1714: A Statistical Study.* Cambridge, MA: Harvard University Press, 1959.
Banga, Indu, ed. *Ports and Their Hinterlands in India, 1700–1950.* New Delhi: Manohar, 1992.
Barrow, Thomas C. *Trade and Empire: The British Customs Service in Colonial America, 1660–1775.* Cambridge, MA: Harvard University Press, 1967.
Baskes, Jeremy. *Staying Afloat: Risk and Uncertainty in Spanish Atlantic World Trade, 1760–1820.* Stanford: Stanford University Press, 2013.
Baxter, W. T. *The House of Hancock: Business in Boston, 1724–1775.* Cambridge, MA: Harvard University Press, 1945.
Beckert, Sven. *Empire of Cotton: A Global History.* New York: Alfred A. Knopf, 2015.
Bentick-Smith, William. "Nicholas Boylston and His Harvard Chair." *Proceedings of the Massachusetts Historical Society*, 3rd series, 93 (1981): 17–39.
Bethencourt, Francisco, and Diogo Ramada Curto, eds. *A expansão marítima portuguesa, 1400–1800.* Lisbon: Ed. 70, 2010.
Bezanson, Anne, Robert D. Gray, and Miriam Hussey. *Prices in Colonial Pennsylvania.* Philadelphia: University of Pennsylvania Press, 1935.
Blussé, Leonard. *Visible Cities: Canton, Nagasaki, and Batavia and the Coming of the Americans.* Cambridge, MA: Harvard University Press, 2008.
Borneman, Walter. *The French and Indian War: Deciding the Fate of North America.* New York: HarperCollins, 2006.
Braudel, Fernand. *The Mediterranean and the Mediterranean World in the Age of Philip II.* Translated by Sian Reynolds. 2nd ed., 2 vols. Berkeley: University of California Press, 1995.
Braudel, Fernand. *The Wheels of Commerce: Volume II.* New York: Harper and Row, 1979.
Breen, T. H. *The Marketplace of Revolution: How Consumer Politics Shaped American Independence.* Oxford: Oxford University Press, 2004.

Brewer, John. *The Sinews of Power: War, Money and the English State, 1688–1783*. Cambridge, MA: Harvard University Press, 1988.

Bridenbaugh, Carl. *Cities in Revolt: Urban Life in America, 1743–1776*. Oxford: Oxford University Press, 1955.

Bridenbaugh, Carl. *Cities in the Wilderness: The First Century of Urban Life in American, 1625–1742*. New York: Alfred A. Knopf, 1955 [Ronald Press, 1938].

Buchnea, Emily. "Transatlantic Transformations: Visualizing Change Over Time in the Liverpool–New York Trade Network, 1763–1833." *Enterprise and Society* 15, no. 4 (December 2014): 687–721.

Burton, Antoinette. *The Trouble with Empire: Challenges to Modern British Imperialism*. Oxford: Oxford University Press, 2015.

Cappon, Lester J. et al., eds. *Atlas of Early American History: The Revolutionary Era, 1760–1790*. Princeton: Princeton University Press on behalf of the Newberry Library and the Institute of Early American History and Culture, 1976.

Carp, Benjamin L. *Rebels Rising: Cities and the American Revolution*. Oxford: Oxford University Press, 2007.

Carter, S. B. et al., eds. *Historical Statistics of the United States: Earliest Times to the Present, Millennial Edition*. Cambridge: Cambridge University Press, 2006.

Chaudhuri, K. N. *Asia before Europe: Economy and Civilization of the Indian Ocean from the Rise of Islam to 1750*. Cambridge: Cambridge University Press, 1990.

Clark, Christopher. *The Roots of Rural Capitalism: Western Massachusetts, 1780–1860*. Ithaca, NY: Cornell University Press, 1990.

Clowse, Converse D. *Measuring Charleston's Overseas Commerce, 1717–1767: Statistics from the Port's Naval Lists*. Washington, DC: University of Press of America, 1981.

Colonial Society of Massachusetts. *Seafaring in Colonial Massachusetts: A Conference Held by the Colonial Society of Massachusetts, 21–22 November 1975*. Boston: Colonial Society of Massachusetts, distributed by the University Press of Virginia, 1980.

Costa, Leonar Freire, Pedro Lains, and Susana Münch Miranda. *An Economic History of Portugal, 1143–2010*. Cambridge: Cambridge University Press, 2016.

Craig, Michelle L. "Grounds for Debate? The Place of the Caribbean Provisions Trade in Philadelphia's Prerevolutionary Economy." *Pennsylvania Magazine of History and Biography* 128, no. 2 (April 2004): 149–77.

Crandall, Ruth. "Wholesale Commodity Prices in Boston during the Eighteenth Century." *Review of Economics and Statistics* 16, no. 6 (June 15, 1934): 117–28.

Cromwell, Jesse. *The Smuggler's World: Illicit Trade and Atlantic Communities in Eighteenth-Century Venezuela*. Chapel Hill: University of North Carolina Press for the Omohundro Institute of Early American History and Culture, 2018.

Cutterham, Tom. "The Revolutionary Transformation of American Merchant Networks: Carter and Wadsworth and Their World, 1775–1800." *Enterprise and Society* 18, no. 1 (March 2017): 1–31.

Davis, Mike. *Late Victorian Holocausts: El Niño Famines and the Making of the Third World*. London: Verso, 2002.

Davis, Ralph. *The Rise of the Atlantic Economies* Ithaca, NY: Cornell University Press, 1973.

De Zwart, Pim, and Jan Luiten van Zanden. *The Origins of Globalization: World Trade in the Making of the Global Economy*. Cambridge: Cambridge University Press, 2018.

Dickerson, Oliver Morton. *American Colonial Government, 1696–1765: A Study of the British Board of Trade in Its Relation to the American Colonies, Political, Industrial, Administrative*. New York: Russell and Russell, 1912.

Dickerson, Oliver Morton. *The Navigation Acts and the American Revolution*. Philadelphia: University of Pennsylvania Press, 1951.

Dincecco, Mark. *Political Transformations and Public Finances: Europe 1650–1913*. Cambridge: Cambridge University Press, 2011.

Doerflinger, Thomas M. *A Vigorous Spirit of Enterprise: Merchants and Economic Development in Revolutionary Philadelphia*. Chapel Hill: University of North Carolina Press, 1986.

Downs, Carolyn. "Networks, Trust, and Risk Mitigation during the American Revolutionary War: A Case Study." *Economic History Review* 70, no. 2 (2017): 509–28.

Du Rivage, Justin. *Revolution against Empire: Taxes, Politics, and the Origins of American Independence*. New Haven: Yale University Press, 2017.

Eloranta, Jari, and Jeremy Land. "Hollow Victory? Britain's Public Debt and the Seven Years' War." *Essays in Economic and Business History* 29, no. 1 (2011): 101–18.

Ferguson, Niall. *Empire: The Rise and Demise of the British World Order and the Lessons for Global Power*. London: Allen Books, 2002.

Ferling, John. *Almost a Miracle: The American Victory in the War of Independence*. Oxford: Oxford University Press, 2007.

Fichter, James R. *So Great a Proffit: How the East Indies Trade Transformed Anglo-American Capitalism*. Cambridge, MA: Harvard University Press, 2010.

Fisher, Darlene Emmert. "Social Life in Philadelphia during the British Occupation." *Pennsylvania History: A Journal of Mid-Atlantic Studies* 37 (1970): 237–60.

Flynn, Dennis O., and Arturo Giráldez. "Path Dependence, Time Lags and the Birth of Globalization: A Critique of O'Rourke and Williamson." *European Review of Economic History* 8, no. 1 (2004): 81–108.

Frank, Andre Gunder, and Barry K. Gills. "The Five Thousand Year World System: An Interdisciplinary Introduction." *Humboldt Journal of Social Relations* 18, no. 1, World-Systems Analysis (1992): 1–79.

Gardner, Leigh A. *Taxing Colonial Africa: The Political Economy of British Imperialism*. Oxford: Oxford University Press, 2012.

Gestrich, Andreas, and Margrit Schulte Beerbühl, eds. *Cosmopolitan Networks in Commerce and Society, 1660–1914*. London: German Historical Institute London, 2011.

Goldstein, Jonathan. *Philadelphia and the China Trade, 1682–1846: Commercial, Cultural, and Attitudinal Effects*. University Park: Pennsylvania State University Press, 1978.

Grubb, Farley W. "The Circulating Medium of Exchange in Colonial Pennsylvania, 1729–1775: New Estimates of Monetary Composition, Performance, and Economic Growth." *Explorations in Economic History* 41, no. 4 (2004): 329–60.

Haddad, John R. *America's First Adventure in China: Trade, Treaties, Opium, and Salvation*. Philadelphia: Temple University Press, 2013.

Haggerty, Sheryllynne. *"Merely for Money?" Business Culture in the British Atlantic, 1750–1815*. Liverpool: Liverpool University Press, 2012.

Haggerty, John, and Sheryllynne Haggerty. "The Life Cycle of a Metropolitan Business Network, 1750–1810." *Explorations in Economic History* 48, no. 2 (2011): 189–206.

Haggerty, John, and Sheryllynne Haggerty. "Visual Analytics of an Eighteenth-Century Business Network." *Enterprise and Society* 11, no. 1 (2010): 1–25.

Hancock, David. *Citizens of the World: London Merchants and the Integration of the British Atlantic Community, 1735–1785*. Cambridge: Cambridge University Press, 1995.

Hancock, David. *Oceans of Wine: Madeira and the Emergence of American Trade and Taste*. New Haven: Yale University Press, 2009.

Harrington, Virginia D. "The New York Merchant on the Eve of the Revolution." PhD diss., Columbia University, 1935.

Hartigan-O'Connor, Ellen. *The Ties That Buy: Women and Commerce in Revolutionary America*. Philadelphia: The University of Pennsylvania Press, 2009.

Hatfield, April Lee. *Atlantic Virginia: Intercolonial Relations in the Seventeenth Century*. Philadelphia: University of Pennsylvania Press, 2004.

Henretta, James A. "Economic Development and Social Structure in Colonial Boston." *William and Mary Quarterly* 22 (1965): 75–92.

Herrero Sánchez, Manuel, and Klemens Kaps, eds. *Merchants and Trade Networks in the Atlantic and the Mediterranean, 1550–1800*. London: Routledge, 2017.

Heyrman, Christine Leigh. *Commerce and Culture: The Maritime Communities of Colonial Massachusetts: 1690–1750*. New York: W. W. Norton and Company, 1984.

Hoare, Anthony G. "British Ports and Their Export Hinterlands: A Rapidly Changing Geography." *Geografiska Annaler: Series B, Human Geography* 68, no. 1 (August 2017): 29–40.

Hobson, J. A. *Imperialism: A Study*. Ann Arbor: University of Michigan Press, 1965.

Hodacs, Hanna. *Silk and Tea in the North: Scandinavian Trade and the Market for Asian Goods in Eighteenth-Century Europe*. London: Palgrave Macmillan, 2016.

Hodacs, Hanna, and Leos Müller. "Chests, Tubs, and Lots of Tea: The European Market for Chinese Tea and the Swedish East India Company, c.1730–1760." In *Goods from the East, 1600–1800: Trading Eurasia*, edited by Felicia Gottman, Hanna Hodacs, Chris Nierstrasz, Maxine Berg, 277–93. New York: Palgrave Macmillan, 2015.

Hoffman, Philip T. *Why Did Europe Conquer the World?* Princeton: Princeton University Press, 2015.

Hunter, Phyllis Whitman. *Purchasing Identity in the Atlantic World: Massachusetts Merchants, 1670–1780.* Ithaca, NY: Cornell University Press, 2001.

Innes, Stephen. *Creating the Commonwealth: The Economic Culture of Puritan New England.* New York: W. W. Norton and Company, 1995.

Jensen, Arthur L. *The Maritime Commerce of Colonial Philadelphia.* Madison: State Historical Society of Wisconsin, 1963.

Jones, Alice Hanson. *Wealth of a Nation to Be: The American Colonies on the Eve of Revolution.* New York: Columbia University Press, 1980.

Kamen, Henry. *Empire: How Spain Became a World Power, 1492–1763.* New York: Perennial, 2003.

Klooster, Wim. "Inter-imperial Smuggling in the Americas, 1600–1800." In *Soundings in Atlantic History: Latent Structures and Intellectual Currents, 1500–1830*, edited by Bernard Bailyn and Patricia L. Denault, 141–80. Cambridge, MA: Harvard University Press, 2009.

Knight, Franklin W., and Peggy K. Liss, eds. *Atlantic Port Cities: Economy, Culture, and Society in the Atlantic World, 1650–1850.* Knoxville: University of Tennessee Press, 1991.

Koot, Christian J. *Empire at the Periphery: British Colonists, Anglo-Dutch Trade, and the Development of the British Atlantic, 1621–1713.* New York: New York University Press, 2011.

Lamikiz, Xabier. *Trade and Trust in the Eighteenth-Century Atlantic World: Spanish Merchants and Their Overseas Networks.* Woodbridge: Boydell Press, 2010.

Lamoreaux, Naomi. "Rethinking the Transition to Capitalism in the Early American Northeast." *Journal of American History* 90, no. 2 (September 2003): 437–61.

Land, Jeremy. "Price of Empire: Britain's Military Costs during the Seven Years' War." MA thesis, Appalachian State University, 2010.

Land, Jeremy, and Rodrigo da Costa Dominguez. "Illicit Affairs: Philadelphia's Trade with Lisbon before Independence, 1700–1775." *Ler História* 75 (2019): 179–204.

Landes, David S. *The Wealth and Poverty of Nations: Why Some Are so Rich and Some so Poor.* New York: W. W. Norton and Company, 1999.

Lemisch, Jesse. *Jack Tar vs. John Bull: The Role of New York's Seamen in Precipitating the Revolution.* New York: Garland Publishing, 1997.

Lindert, Peter H., and Jeffrey G. Williamson. *Unequal Gains: American Growth and Inequality since 1700.* Princeton: Princeton University Press, 2016.

Liss, Peggy K. *Atlantic Empires: The Network of Trade and Revolution, 1713–1826.* Baltimore: Johns Hopkins University Press, 1983.

Lydon, James G. *Fish and Flour for Gold, 1600–1800: Southern Europe in the Colonial Balance of Payments.* Philadelphia: Program in Early American Economy and Society, Library Company of Philadelphia, 2008.

MacGill, Caroline E. and Balthasar Henry Meyer, eds. *History of Transportation in the United States before 1860.* Washington, DC: Carnegie Institution of Washington, 1917.

MacPherson, David. *Annals of Commerce, Manufactures, Fisheries, and Navigation with Brief Notices of the Arts and Sciences Connected with Them.* London: n.p., 1805.

Mancall, Peter C., Joshua L. Rosenbloom, and Thomas Weiss. "Exports from the Colonies and States of the Middle Atlantic Region 1720–1800." *Research in Economic History* 29 (2014): 257–305.

Matson, Cathy. *Merchants and Empire: Trading in Colonial New York.* Baltimore: Johns Hopkins University Press, 1998.

McCusker, John J. *Essays in the Economic History of the Atlantic World.* London: Routledge, 1997.

McCusker, John J. *Money and Exchange in Europe and America, 1600–1775: A Handbook.* Chapel Hill: University of North Carolina Press, 1978.

McCusker, John J. *Rum and the American Revolution: The Rum Trade and the Balance of Payments of the Thirteen Colonies.* New York: Garland Publishing, 1989.

McCusker, John J. "The Rum Trade and the Balance of Payments of the Thirteen Continental Colonies, 1650–1775." *Journal of Economic History* 30, no. 1 (March 1970): 244–47.

McCusker, John J., and Russell R. Menard. *The Economy of British America: 1607–1789.* Chapel Hill: University of North Carolina Press, 1985.

McCusker, John J., and Kenneth Morgan, eds. *The Early Modern Atlantic Economy.* Cambridge: Cambridge University Press, 2000.

Merritt, Jane T. *The Trouble with Tea: The Politics of Consumption in the Eighteenth-Century Global Economy.* Baltimore: Johns Hopkins University Press, 2017.

Metcalf, Thomas R. *Imperial Connections: India in the Indian Ocean Arena, 1860–1920.* Berkeley: University of California Press, 2007.

Michener, Ron. "Money in the American Colonies." *EH.Net Encyclopedia*, edited by Robert Whaples. June 8, 2003, revised January 13, 2011. http://eh.net/encyclopedia/money-in-the-american-colonies (accessed December 6, 2022).

Mishoff, Willard O. "Business in Philadelphia during the British Occupation, 1777–1778." *Pennsylvania Magazine of History and Biography* 61, no. 2 (1937): 165–81.

Mizushima, Tsukasa, George Bryan Souza, and Dennis O. Flynn, eds. *Hinterlands and Commodities: Place, Space, Time and the Political Economic Development of Asia over the Long Eighteenth Century.* Leiden: Brill, 2015.

Müller, Leos. *Consuls, Corsairs, and Commerce: The Swedish Consular Service and Long-Distance Shipping, 1720–1815.* Uppsala: Uppsala University Press, 2004.

Müller, Leos. "Svenska ostindiska kompaniet och den europeiska marknaden för te." In *Sverige och svenskarna i den ostindiska handeln II: Strategier, sammanhang och situationer*, edited by Bertil S. Olsson and Karl-Magnus Johansson, 237–61. Riksarkivet, Landsarkivet i Göteborg, 2019.

Nadri, Ghulam A. *Eighteenth-Century Gujarat: The Dynamics of Its Political Economy, 1750–1800*. Leiden: Brill, 2009.

Nash, Gary B. *The Urban Crucible: Social Change, Political Consciousness, and the Origins of the American Revolution*. Cambridge, MA: Harvard University Press, 1979.

Ng, Adolf K. Y. et al. "Port Geography at the Crossroads with Human Geography: Between Flows and Spaces." *Journal of Transport Geography* 41 (2014): 84–96.

North, Douglass C., John J. Wallis, and Barry R. Weingast. *Violence and Social Orders: A Conceptual Framework for Interpreting Recorded Human History*. Cambridge: Cambridge University Press, 2009.

Norton, Marcy. *Sacred Gifts, Profane Pleasures: A History of Tobacco and Chocolate in the Atlantic World*. Ithaca, NY: Cornell University Press, 2008.

Oakley, Eric. "Columbia at Sea: America Enters the Pacific, 1787–1793." PhD diss., University of North Carolina at Greensboro, 2017.

O'Rourke, Kevin H., and Jeffrey G. Williamson. "When Did Globalization Begin?" *European Review of Economic History* 6, no. 1 (2002): 1–18.

Papenfuse, Edward C. *In Pursuit of Profit: The Annapolis Merchants in the Era of the American Revolution, 1763–1805*. Baltimore: Johns Hopkins University Press, 1975.

Pares, Richard. *Yankees and Creoles: The Trade between North America and the West Indies before the American Revolution*. Cambridge, MA: Harvard University Press, 1956.

Pitkin, Timothy. *A Statistical View of the Commerce of the United States of America*. New York: James Eastburn and Company, 1816.

Price, Jacob M. "Economic Function and the Growth of American Port Towns in the Eighteenth Century." *Perspectives in American History* 8 (1974): 121–86.

Price, Jacob M. "The Economic Growth of the Chesapeake and the European Market, 1697–1775." *Journal of Economic History* 24, no. 4 (December 1964): 496–511.

Price, Jacob M. "A Note on the Value of Colonial Exports of Shipping." *Journal of Economic History* 36, no. 3 (September 1976): 704–24.

Price, Jacob M. "Quantifying Colonial America: A Comment on Nash and Warden." *Journal of Interdisciplinary History* 6, no. 4, Interdisciplinary Studies of the American Revolution (Spring 1976): 701–9.

Price, Jacob M. "What Did Merchants Do? Reflections on British Overseas Trade, 1660–1790." *Journal of Economic History* 49, no. 2, The Tasks of Economic History (June 1989): 267–84.

Rediker, Marcus. *Between the Devil and the Deep Blue Sea: Merchant Seamen, Pirates, and the Anglo-American Maritime World, 1700–1750*. Cambridge: Cambridge University Press, 1987.

Riello, Giorgio. *Cotton: The Fabric That Made the Modern World*. Cambridge: Cambridge University Press, 2013.

Rothenberg, Winifred Barr. *From Market-Places to a Market Economy: The Transformation of Rural Massachusetts, 1750–1850*. Chicago: University of Chicago Press, 1992.

Rutter, Frank R. *South American Trade of Baltimore*. Baltimore: Johns Hopkins University Press, 1897.

Schlesinger, Arthur Meier. *The Colonial Merchants and the American Revolution, 1763–1776*. New York: Longmans, Green and Company, 1918.

Schumpeter, Elizabeth Boody. *English Overseas Trade Statistics, 1697–1808*. Oxford: Oxford University Press, 1960.

Shepherd, James F. "Commodity Exports from the British North American Colonies to Overseas Areas, 1768–1772: Magnitudes and Patterns of Trade." *Explorations in Economic History* 8, no. 1 (June 1970): 5–76.

Shepherd, James F., and Gary M. Walton. "Estimates of 'Invisible' Earnings in the Balance of Payments of the British North American Colonies, 1768–1772." *Journal of Economic History* 29, no. 2 (June 1969): 230–63.

Shepherd, James F., and Gary M. Walton. *Shipping, Maritime Trade and the Economic Development of Colonial North America*. Cambridge: Cambridge University Press, 1972.

Shepherd, James F., and Samuel H. Williamson. "The Coastal Trade of the British North American Colonies, 1768–1772." *Journal of Economic History* 32, no. 4 (December 1972): 783–810.

Swingen, Abigail L. *Competing Visions of Empire: Labor, Slavery, and the Origins of the British Atlantic Empire*. New Haven: Yale University Press, 2015.

Thomas, Robert Paul. "A Quantitative Approach to the Study of the Effects of British Imperial Policy upon Colonial Welfare: Some Preliminary Findings." *Journal of Economic History* 25, no. 4 (December 1965): 615–38.

Truxes, Thomas M. *Defying Empire: Trading with the Enemy in Colonial New York*. New Haven: Yale University Press, 2008.

Tyler, John W. *Smugglers and Patriots: Boston Merchants and the Advent of the American Revolution*. Boston: Northeastern University Press, 1986.

United States Department of Commerce. *Historical Statistics of the United States from Colonial Times to 1970: Bicentennial Edition*. Washington, DC: US Government Printing Office, 1975.

Vickers, Daniel. *Farmers and Fishermen: Two Centuries of World in Essex County, Massachusetts, 1630–1850*. Chapel Hill: University of North Carolina Press, 1994.

Wallerstein, Immanuel. *The Modern World System*. 3 vols. New York: Academic Press, 1974, 1980, 1989.

Wallerstein, Immanuel. *World-Systems Analysis: An Introduction*. Durham, NC: Duke University Press, 2004.

Walton, Gary M. "New Evidence on Colonial Commerce." *Journal of Economic History* 28, no. 3 (September 1968): 363–89.

Weeden, William B. *Economic and Social History of New England, 1620–1789*. 2 vols. Boston: Houghton, Mifflin and Company, 1891.

Wharton, Samuel. "Observations on Consumption of Teas in North America." *Pennsylvania Magazine of History and Biography* 25, no. 1 (1901): 133–43.

Wilson, David. *Suppressing Piracy in the Early Eighteenth Century: Pirates, Merchants and British Imperial Authority in the Atlantic and Indian Oceans*. Woodbridge: Boydell Press, 2021.

Young, Alfred F. *Liberty Tree: Ordinary People and the American Revolution*. New York: New York University Press, 2006.

Zahedieh, Nuala. *The Capital and the Colonies: London and the Atlantic Economy, 1660–1700*. Cambridge: Cambridge University Press, 2010.

Index

Account books   19–20, 28, 52, 57, 60n88, 93, 95–96, 104, 105n19, 109, 112–113, 115, 115n, 140–141, 141n76, 148
  See also Credit; Loans
Admiralty Court   120, 156, 173, 178
  Vice Admiralty Court Act (1768)   171–172
  See also Townshend Acts
Advertisement   11n22, 53–54, 63–64, 64n100, 81–82, 97, 132
  See also *Boston Gazette*; Newspapers; *Pennsylvania Gazette*
Africa   15, 24, 92, 149
  and British colonies   7, 160
  European outposts in   22
  import of rum   92–93, 146, 160–161
  Royal African Company   36–37, 153
  share of tonnage clearing   106
  shipping industry investments   48, 160
  shipping profits   162
  slave trade   24
Agents   20, 25, 28–29, 41, 44, 44n33, 55, 57–59, 60, 62–63, 78, 78n18, 84, 102–103, 112, 123–125, 127–129, 129n32, 130, 135, 141, 146–147, 154, 157, 163–164, 168n44, 171, 174, 178
  See also Broker; Customs; Supercargo
Agreements   176
  Articles of Agreement   56–57, 175
  non-importation   29–30, 39–40, 40n19, 69, 102, 167, 175–177
  See also Merchants; Navigation Acts; Revenue Acts; Townshend Acts
Albany   23
Alcohol
  See Rum
American Revolution   1–2, 12, 14, 21, 39, 41, 128, 169n46, 179–180, 180n
  See also Independence
Amsterdam   10, 21, 24, 26, 37, 37n9, 42, 109–110, 124, 130, 132–133, 147, 156, 177, 181
Annapolis   25
Arrivals
  of goods   97, 117, 168
  of newcomers   40, 138
  of ships   11, 11n22, 32n54, 53–54, 63, 102, 117, 135, 168
    See also Advertisement; *Boston Gazette*; Departures; Newspapers; *Pennsylvania Gazette*
Assemblies   50, 66, 155
Atlantic
  approach   3
  economy   1–4, 9–10, 15–17, 19, 21, 33, 35n1, 70, 102, 127–128, 151, 158, 181, 184
  ocean   2–3, 7–8, 12, 16, 21–22, 24, 24n24, 25, 27, 34–36, 42, 62, 70, 90, 99–100, 120, 137, 150, 181
  world   3, 35–38, 64, 98, 103, 119, 127, 181
Autonomy   2–3, 6–7, 12, 124, 153
  See also Constraints; Independence; State capacity

Baltimore   25, 62, 64
Banking   35–36, 42, 50–51
  See Credit; Currency; Specie
Barbados   57, 61n89, 112, 114, 137, 139, 142, 147, 153, 168
Barcelona   27, 156
Beef   73, 86–87
  See also Livestock
Beekman, Gerard   43, 62, 109–111, 113, 140, 147
Belfast   57, 64, 129, 132
Bermuda   77, 107, 113–114, 139, 155, 162
Bills
  of Credit   167
  of Exchange   59, 64–66, 104
  of Lading   61, 61n90, 91n, 92, 112, 119, 169
    See also Credit; Currency
Books
  See Account books; Letter books
Borders   35, 112, 120, 122, 130, 135, 137, 154
Boston
  exports   18, 20–22, 28, 33, 70, 73, 82, 84–94, 99, 105, 108, 112, 116–117, 143
  imports   18–22, 28, 72–73, 82, 90–91, 94, 99, 108–109, 117
  merchants   1–3, 14, 17, 21, 25, 27–29, 31, 33–35, 37–39, 41, 43, 50–53, 56–58, 60, 67, 71, 78, 82, 85, 94–96, 100, 103–105,

INDEX 231

109–111, 115, 131, 135, 137, 139, 143n84,
  146, 151–152, 155–156, 161n23, 162–165,
  167–170, 176, 180
occupation   1, 8–9, 14, 17, 27, 43n32, 44,
  68, 74, 82, 108, 145, 178–179
port of   1–2, 11n22, 13, 15–20, 25–27, 33, 35,
  44–45, 47–48, 53, 61–63, 67, 71–72, 74,
  82, 90–91, 94, 99, 101, 111, 126, 128–129,
  141, 143–144, 157–161, 164, 166, 168–172,
  174–177
primacy   19–20
See also East Asian Goods; Manufactures;
  Salt; Sugar; West Indies
Boston Gazette   18, 53, 63, 117, 126, 131n43,
  132n44, 137, 139, 146
Boston Massacre   178
Boston Tea Party   82
Boylston, Thomas   135–136
Brazil   22, 32, 37, 138
See also Latin America; South America
Bread   68, 76, 85–87, 89–90, 107–108, 111, 112,
  114–115, 117, 140, 148, 150
See also Flour; Grains; Wheat
Bristol   16n2, 40
British America   1–2, 6–7, 9, 11–12, 17, 27, 29,
  31–32, 35n1, 38, 45–47, 62, 70–71, 73,
  78–79, 81–82, 84, 90–91, 103, 107–110,
  122–123, 127–128, 131, 135, 141–142, 150,
  153, 157, 161, 165–166, 168, 168n44, 169–
  170, 175–177, 180
scholarship on   4, 4n4, 12
British Empire   1–3, 6–10, 13–14, 30–31, 35,
  37, 66, 77, 101–102, 120, 123, 126, 146n91,
  150–152, 152n1, 153–154, 165, 167–168,
  180–182
British Isles   13, 33, 46, 57, 103–104, 115–118,
  120, 143, 150, 154, 166
Broker   44, 60–61, 85, 105
See also Agent
Brokering   35, 42

Cádiz   21, 26, 66, 91, 91n49, 132, 148
Canada   8, 21, 27, 145, 161n23
See also French Canada; Quebec
Canary Islands   132, 133n49
See also Tenerife
Candles   63, 86–88
Cape Verde   24

Capital
See Merchants
Captain   41, 59, 61, 61n89, 63, 63n98, 65,
  94–95, 112, 125–127, 135, 138, 140–141,
  156, 173
Cargo   11n22, 30, 42, 50, 52–54, 57–62, 65–
  67, 94, 120, 124–126, 129–130, 132–135,
  140–141, 141n76, 142, 143n, 146, 146n91,
  147, 149–150, 155, 164, 166, 169–170,
  172–173, 184
Caribbean   7, 12–13, 22, 24n24, 32n54, 36, 42,
  46–47, 49, 49n45, 50, 55, 62, 76, 91, 93–
  94, 101, 105, 111–113, 122, 122n6, 128, 131,
  137–138, 140–142, 146–147, 149, 153, 168
Carter, John   183
Cash crop   6, 9, 16, 112
See also Plantations
Catholic   21, 91
See also Protestant
Cayenne   140–141
Charleston   92, 110, 155, 171–172, 180
See also Refineries
Chesapeake   50, 89
China   103, 127, 161, 183–184
Clark, Daniel   28, 84, 92, 110
See also Account books
Clearances   18, 52, 113, 117, 117n, 118, 138–140,
  142–144, 146, 160, 169
See also Entries
Cloth   84, 96, 110
Clothing   72–73, 96, 110, 121, 136,
  161n23, 177
Cocoa   55, 76, 126, 141
Cod   8, 15, 21, 85, 91, 138, 140
  dried   58
  salted   8, 21–22, 76, 84, 90, 112, 143
Coffee   75–76, 166, 169, 172–173
Commissioners of Customs   31, 163–164,
  168, 171
See also Customs
Communication
See Networks
Communities
See Merchants; Networks
Competition
See Merchants; Networks
Concord   1, 19–20, 179
Connecticut   4, 8, 20–21, 47, 48n41

Constraints   3, 12, 12–14, 30–33, 37n7, 70–71, 73, 81, 99–103, 112, 119–120, 123–125, 127, 136, 150
  merchants circumvention of prohibitions   13–14, 30–31, 35, 37, 70, 78, 78n18, 99–100, 102–103, 120–121, 123–130, 133–138, 140–142, 146n91, 147–150
  See also Agreements; Navigation Acts; Revenue Acts; Smuggling
Consulate   184
Consumers
  as recipients of merchant costs   68, 170–171
  base   3, 16, 30, 34, 44, 54, 63, 65, 70–72, 72n6, 73, 76, 78, 82, 91, 99–100, 102, 105n19, 108–112, 115, 119–120, 131, 137, 152, 169, 171, 181
  demands   13, 37, 57, 62, 66, 70–71, 73, 76, 81, 85, 91, 94–99, 140, 183
  disregard for the origin of the products   127, 131, 168
  resistance to imperial control   1, 151, 157, 174, 177
  See also Merchants
Continental Congress   183
Convoy   29, 111, 168
Core   4–5, 17
  See also Periphery
Corn   86–87, 107, 148–150, 163
Coxe, Tench   41
Credit   2, 17–18, 27–28, 33, 35n1, 36–37, 40, 45, 52–53, 56, 58–60, 64–66, 69, 97, 104–105, 163, 167, 182
  See also Currency; Merchants; Shortage; Specie
Cunningham, Greg   37, 37n9, 57, 62, 82, 97, 130, 132
Cunningham, Waddell   37, 37n9, 57, 62, 78n18, 82, 97, 129–130, 132, 147
  See also Smuggling
Curaçao   24, 40, 114, 131, 139
Currency
  chronic shortage in British America   6, 13, 20, 28, 31–34, 37–38, 55, 64–66, 69, 119–120
  chronic shortage in Brazil   32
  circulation   32–33, 59–60, 65, 85, 95, 104, 141
  creation of   7, 32, 167
  coins   32
  paper bills   32, 51, 167
  See also Bills of Exchange; Specie
Customs
  agents   78, 78n18, 84, 102–103, 112, 123–125, 127–129, 129n32, 130, 141, 146–147, 157, 163–164, 171, 174, 178
  collectors   31
  houses   23, 31, 130, 133, 138, 149, 157, 168, 168n44, 174, 178
  officers   31, 120, 138, 155–156, 163, 172, 174

Daughters of Liberty   177
Davis, Caleb   21n12, 39, 58, 58n77, 62, 66, 85, 90–91, 95, 96n65, 136–137, 137n64, 138–140
  See also Davis, Thomas
Davis, Thomas   39, 42
Delaware   4, 48, 50
  See also Middle Colonies
Delaware River   11n22, 24–25, 131
Departures   11n22, 53, 62, 168
  See also Arrivals
Diaspora   35–36
Distilleries   51, 73, 85, 92–94, 96, 146, 170
  See also Refineries; Rum
Dolbeare, Benjamin   21n12, 56, 96, 96n65, 104n17
Dollar   64
  See also Currency; Specie
Drought   32, 136
Dublin   63
Dutch Empire   9–10
  colonies   10, 22, 147
  knowledge of the language spoken in the   37n9
  traders   9, 37, 40, 136
  West India Company   9
  See also New Amsterdam; New York
Duties   9, 31, 50, 67–68, 108, 123, 129, 134, 146, 146n91, 147, 167, 170–171, 175
  See also Constraints

Earthquake
  in Jamaica   42
  in Lisbon   149n104

INDEX 233

East Asia 13, 21, 34, 63, 70, 72–73, 81–84, 120, 124, 129, 131–136, 146–147, 161, 163, 169, 183–184
  See also Porcelain; Silk; Spices; Tea; Textiles
East India 8, 70, 82, 84, 133
East India Company 70, 84, 133, 133n53, 154, 171, 177, 179
East Indian goods 70, 72–73
Enforcement 2–3, 6, 31, 69–71, 101–102, 120, 123–125, 129, 136, 151–152, 154–157, 164, 167–168, 172–174, 176, 180
  See also Autonomy; Constraints; Independence; State capacity
England 4, 9–10, 13, 21, 24, 27–28, 30, 32, 39–40, 58, 70, 79, 82, 89, 95, 97, 100, 104, 113, 115, 115n48, 116, 119, 123, 126, 130, 136, 150, 152n1, 154, 154n7, 158–159, 163–165, 169, 171, 176
  See also British America; British Empire; British Isles; Great Britain
Entrepôt 3, 108, 117
Entries 18, 28, 43n32, 52, 69, 96, 109, 117, 117n, 118, 124, 131n43, 134, 138–141, 141n76, 142–144, 149–150, 160
Ethnic 36
Europe 4, 8, 15, 18, 21–22, 26, 39, 42n26, 48, 57, 63, 71, 73, 75–76, 81, 84–85, 88, 90, 96, 96n65, 108, 110, 112, 115, 118–119, 122, 124, 126, 136, 140n72, 143, 145, 147–148, 160, 162–163, 175, 183
Exchange 1–3, 13, 21, 33, 35, 40, 58–59, 64–66, 70, 76, 85, 91, 95, 101, 104, 109, 112, 122, 127, 143, 146–148, 163, 166, 168, 182, 184
  See also Trade
Export
  See Boston; New York; Philadelphia; Trade

Family firm *See* Firm
Faneuil, Peter 108, 142, 39, 43, 53, 55
Farming 9, 11n22, 15, 20–21, 24, 44, 50–51, 60, 85, 95, 104–105, 108, 112, 156, 170
Firm 28, 62, 80, 92–93, 109
  family-owned 40, 56, 59, 62, 82, 97
  See also Cunningham, Waddell; Cunningham, Greg
Fiscal capacity 6, 100, 154
  See also Currency; Specie

Fiscal systems
  See Constraints
Fishing 8–9, 22, 85, 88, 108, 112, 141, 145
  See also Cod; Fisheries
Fisheries 21, 76, 85, 108, 143
  See also Cod; Fishing; Salt
Flag 121, 125, 148, 183
  See also Flag-trucing; Prisoner exchange
Flag-trucing 131, 148, 166
  See also Flag; Prisoner exchange
Flaxseed 64, 86–87, 147
Fleet 15, 22, 27, 49, 85, 112, 125, 148
Flour 24, 26, 28, 53, 60, 76, 84–87, 89, 89n41, 90, 93, 97, 105, 107–115, 117, 133, 136, 140, 145, 147–150, 156, 163, 166
Foreland 15–17, 33, 55, 60
  of Boston 12, 21–22, 33
  of New York 12, 24, 33
  of Philadelphia 12, 33
  See also Hinterland
France 13, 26, 55, 126, 128, 135n57, 142, 147, 154n7, 165, 167
Francis, Philip 43
Francis, Tench 110, 130, 132–133, 147–148, 166
French Acadia 109, 142
French Canada 9, 22, 55, 108, 121, 141–142, 147, 165
French Empire 58, 121
Fur
  beaver pelts 9
  trade 9, 22, 40, 147, 161n23, 165
Furniture 73

General Loan Office 58–59
  See also Credit; Loans
Georgia 4, 47, 83, 92
  See also Lower South
German 40–42, 64, 132, 135n57, 167
Gibraltar 21, 136
Ginseng 147, 183–184
Globalization 2, 4–5
  See also Networks
Gold 138
  See also Silver
Grain 11–12, 19, 21, 23–26, 28, 30, 60, 62, 68, 76, 85–87, 89–90, 104–105, 108, 110, 113, 136–137, 147–149, 181
  See also Flour; Wheat

Great Britain   1–2, 4, 6, 18, 24, 30–31, 45–48, 51, 53, 56, 58, 63, 68, 71, 76–77, 81, 84, 88, 91, 93, 96, 98–106, 114, 116–117, 119–125, 131n40, 136, 140n72, 142, 144–145, 148, 150–154, 154n8, 158–160, 162, 165, 167, 173, 176–178, 180–183
See also England
Guilders   132–134, 141, 166

Halifax   27, 111, 172
Hamburg   132, 166
Hancock, John   39, 42, 56, 64, 103, 108, 135
Hancock, Thomas   42, 56, 108
Hinterland   2, 12–13, 15–16, 25, 27, 30, 54–55, 70, 73, 96–98, 105, 141–142, 181
  of Boston   17–22, 25, 27, 33, 67, 70, 73, 98, 181
  of New York   22–24, 27, 33, 50, 67, 70, 73, 147, 181
  of Philadelphia   21, 24, 27, 33, 73, 90, 98, 164, 181
  See also Foreland
Hispaniola   24, 138–139
Holland   54, 124, 163–164
Honduras   13, 138–139
Hoops
  See Iron
Hudson River   22–23

Iberia
  See Portugal;Spain
Import   9, 13–14, 18, 20, 22, 24–25, 28, 30, 32, 32n54, 47, 56–57, 60, 67–69, 70–78, 81–82, 84, 90–91, 93, 96, 99–100, 103–104, 107–110, 115, 115n48, 116, 119, 123, 129, 133n53, 138, 145, 146n91, 158–159, 163–165, 169, 170, 173, 176–177
Independence
  of British colonies   7, 48
  of the US from the UK   1–4, 14, 40, 146, 151–152, 177, 179, 182–184
  See also Autonomy; American Revolution
India   3, 16
Indian Ocean   3, 7, 14, 35–36, 127, 135, 146, 181, 183
Indigo   16, 84, 97, 166, 169
Insurance   20, 29, 51, 51n54, 61, 61n92, 62, 81, 104, 132, 134, 156

Investment   13, 16, 35, 43, 45–51, 67, 90, 123, 126, 160, 161n23
Invoice   28, 53, 58n77, 60–61, 61n91, 72, 76, 78, 80, 80n, 81–82, 84, 89n41, 91n, 92, 95–96, 104n17, 110–112, 114, 115n, 119, 130, 132–135, 138, 147
Ireland   30, 48, 61n89, 106, 115–116, 142–144, 148, 150, 160, 162
  See also Dublin
Iron   28
  bar   86–87
  hoops   90, 93, 138
  pig   86–87, 90
  See also Metal

Jamaica   40, 42, 57, 59, 63, 96–97, 113, 127, 139, 147, 153

Kingston   23

Latin America   138
  See also Brazil; South America
Letter books   37, 52–53, 60n88, 104n17, 115n48
  See also Greg and Waddell Cunningham
Letters   96, 105n19, 110–111, 126, 129–130, 132, 146, 146n86, 147, 164, 168n44, 178
  and routes for illicit trade   130, 132
  between merchants of Boston   52
  common content in   53–55, 58n77, 61–62, 78n18, 95–96, 104n17, 136, 155, 163–164
  written in Dutch   37, 37n9
  written in French   37
  written in Portuguese   37
  written in Spanish   37
  See also Greg and Waddell Cunningham
Linguistics
  as an integrating factor   35–37
Lisbon   21, 24, 26, 26n33, 63, 66, 97, 110, 115, 124, 130, 131n40, 132, 148–149, 149n104, 150, 155, 156, 160
Livestock   19, 105
Livres   141
  See also Currency
Loans   50, 58n80, 59, 65, 141, 141n76
Logwood   19, 130, 138, 156
London   8, 21, 24, 26, 29, 31, 35, 35n1, 45, 45n36, 46, 57, 59, 65, 76, 104, 104n17,

INDEX   235

  109, 115, 129–130, 156, 158, 161, 164, 168,
    168n44, 172
  rise as a global emporium   10, 10n20
  See also England; Great Britain
Long Island   20, 23
Lords of Trade   31, 158
Louisbourg   55, 108, 141
Lower South   4, 77
  See also Georgia; South Carolina

Madagascar   135, 146
  See also The Charles (ship)
Madeira   62, 70–71, 88, 110, 133,
    148, 161
  See also Wine
Maine   20–21
Málaga   21, 88, 91
Manchester   62–63, 97
Manufactures   9, 33, 40, 43, 50–51, 58, 60,
    72–73, 76, 78, 84, 88, 88n37, 90–91, 97,
    110–112, 119, 132, 135, 137, 142, 147, 156,
    168, 176
  See also Clothing; Furniture; Metal
Marblehead   61n89, 85
Mariners   30, 39, 44, 93
Markets   110, 113, 116, 120, 143, 181
  marriage as an access
    mechanism   40, 56–57
  public   67
  restricted access to   2, 9, 14, 20, 35–37, 68,
    99, 120, 179–183
  role of women in   97–98
  See also Merchants; Trade
Maryland   4, 25, 30, 47, 54, 83
  See also Upper South
Massachusetts
  See Boston
Master   59, 61, 124, 156, 174
Medfield   19
Mediterranean   27, 36
Mercantilism   14, 30, 71, 131, 154, 171, 176
  British policies   4, 10, 13, 34–35, 68–69, 71,
    81, 99, 119–120, 136, 180
  resistance to its policies   2, 6, 13–14, 34–
    36, 42n26, 103, 151–154, 176, 181–182
Merchants
  capital and credit   27, 32–33, 35, 35n1, 36–
    38, 40–42, 45–52, 56–59, 67, 69, 90–91,

  104, 104n17, 105, 105n19, 111, 113, 123, 146,
    149, 161n23, 163, 182–183
  competition and complementarity   2, 4,
    12, 27–30, 33–35, 37
  communities   13, 36–42, 42n26, 43–45, 51,
    63, 69, 124, 156, 177
  integration factors between   35–38
  participation in the slave trade   24n24,
    37n7, 146, 149
  partnerships   49, 52–53, 56–57, 123, 129,
    175–176, 183
  shipping protection   7, 36. *See also* Pirates
  See also Account books; Constraints;
    Consumers; Trade
Metal
  metalware   73, 132
  products   72–73, 90, 93, 138
  specie   33, 104
  See also Iron
Methuen Treaty   125
  See also Great Britain; Portugal
Metropole   2–3, 45–46, 69, 71, 104, 119, 122,
    128, 151–152, 180–181
Middle Colonies   4, 8, 11, 72n5, 75, 77–78, 81,
    88, 91, 98–99, 103, 160, 162
  See also Delaware; New Jersey; New York;
    Pennsylvania; Philadelphia
Middlemen   14, 24, 44, 59–60, 85, 133, 135
Military occupation   14, 36n7, 68, 142, 168,
    177, 179
  See also Boston Massacre; Troops
Mills   24, 51, 85, 89–91
  owners   60, 149
Mississippi River   165
Molasses   13, 22, 55, 58, 72–73, 75–76, 85,
    91–94, 96, 101, 107, 109, 112–114, 128, 139–
    140, 142, 146–147, 166, 169–170, 172–173
  See also Sugar; Rum
Môle-Saint-Nicolas   58, 138–140
Montreal   22–23, 141, 168
  See also Canada; Quebec
Morris, Robert   41, 59

Naval Stores Act   31
Navies
  British   7, 36n7, 58, 102, 107, 148, 155–156,
    167–168, 172–173, 175
  imperial   29

INDEX

Navigation Acts 13, 25, 29–31, 58, 101–102, 122–124, 129, 150, 152–153, 155, 161, 167, 169–171, 180
  See also Constraints
Netherlands 21, 54, 57, 128, 147, 161
Networks
  of commodities 2, 4, 13, 16, 20, 24, 38, 70–99, 105, 121–122, 168, 180–181
  of consumption and demand 94–99
  of merchants 1–4, 6–7, 10, 13–14, 16–19, 24, 27–30, 33–35, 35n1, 36–93, 100, 115, 115n48, 136, 142, 145, 147–149, 181–184
  See also Merchants
New Amsterdam 9
  See also Dutch Empire; New York
New England 4, 8–9, 11n22, 21, 46–47, 55–56, 63, 72n5, 75, 77–78, 81–83, 88, 90–93, 97–99, 103, 107–110, 112, 145, 147, 158–160, 162
New Hampshire 4, 8
New Haven 20, 23
New Jersey 4, 22–23, 25, 30, 48, 50, 54
New London 20, 23
New Orleans 24
New York
  exports 22–24, 28, 30, 33, 70, 73, 82, 84, 87–94, 99, 105, 108–110, 112, 116–117, 148
  imports 23–24, 30, 72–73, 82, 88, 91, 94, 99, 108, 117
  merchants 1–3, 10, 14, 17, 24, 27–31, 33–35, 40–41, 43–44, 50–51, 53, 57–58, 60, 71, 78, 82, 85, 93–95, 103–105, 110–111, 113, 115, 120, 129, 131, 137, 156, 158, 163–167, 169–170, 176, 184
  occupation 9, 20, 27, 43–45, 74, 82
  port of 1–2, 8, 13, 15–17, 25–27, 30, 33, 35, 40, 47, 49, 53–54, 59, 62, 67–72, 74, 82, 90–91, 93–94, 99, 101, 111, 126, 128–129, 141, 143–144, 147–148, 150–152, 155–156, 159–161, 163–166, 169, 171–172, 175, 177, 179–182
  See also East Asian Goods; Manufactures; Middle Colonies; Salt; Sugar
Newark 23
Newburyport 18, 20, 53, 176
Newcastle 25
Newfoundland 18, 21, 85, 108, 114, 145, 155

Newspapers 11n22, 52–54, 54n65, 63, 64n100, 82, 97, 117n, 132, 143, 178
  See also Advertisement
Nicholson, Thomas 42, 94, 112, 140–141, 146n91
Nodal center 2–4, 12–13, 15, 17, 27, 33, 51n54, 70, 117, 151, 171, 181–182
  See also Port Complex; World-systems theory
Non-importation agreement *See* Agreements
Norris, Isaac 41, 58, 58n80, 59, 72, 148
North America 1–2, 6, 8, 12–13, 18, 22, 30, 32–33, 36, 45n36, 47, 61, 64, 69, 78, 84, 89, 92–93, 96, 101–102, 104–112, 114–118, 123, 132, 135, 137, 141–143, 147, 165, 167–168, 180–182
North Carolina 4, 47, 65, 142, 174
  See also Upper South
Nova Scotia 8, 18, 21, 108

Oil
  Spanish 157
  train 107, 235–238
  whale 63, 86–88, 97, 138
Origin
  of cloth 84
  of imported and exported goods 28, 82, 118, 145, 160, 163, 188
  of ships 54, 61, 132–133, 138–139, 140n74, 160
Orne, Timothy 18, 50–51, 85
Outfit
  of privateers 125–126
  of ships 45, 53, 94, 135, 143n

Pacific Ocean 14, 184
Packet boat/ship 52, 62–63, 102, 111, 166
Paper currency
  See Currency
Paris 24
Parliament 30–31, 123, 158, 164, 174–175, 177–179
Partnership *See* Agents; Merchants
Peddling 35, 63
Pelt
  See fur
Pennsylvania 4, 11, 11n22, 24, 32–33, 47–48, 58, 58n80, 59, 83–84, 90–91, 105, 107,

133, 133*n*53, 136, 155, 159, 163, 166–167, 171
See also Middle Colonies
Pennsylvania Gazette   117, 149, 166
Pepper   63, 81–82, 97
Periphery   1, 5, 7, 165
Perth Amboy   23, 25
Philadelphia
  exports   11, 24–26, 28, 30, 33, 70, 73, 82, 84, 87–94, 99, 105, 108–110, 112–117, 148–149
  imports   28, 30, 72–73, 82, 88, 91, 93, 99, 108, 115, 117
  merchants   1–3, 14, 17, 24, 27–31, 33–35, 37–38, 41–44, 46, 51–53, 56, 58–60, 71–72, 78, 82, 85, 93–95, 100, 103–105, 110–111, 113–115, 131, 137, 141, 151–152, 158, 160, 163–167, 172, 181–182, 184
  occupation   11, 27, 43–44, 74, 82, 179–180, 182
  port of   1–2, 8, 12–13, 15–17, 25–26, 26*n*33, 27, 30, 33, 35, 45–50, 51*n*54, 52–53, 57–58, 61*n*92, 62–64, 64*n*100, 65, 69–70, 71–72, 74, 82, 90–91, 93, 99, 101, 111, 126, 128–129, 141, 143–144, 149–151, 155–161, 163–164, 168–175, 177, 179, 181
  See also Manufactures; Middle Colonies; Salt; Sugar
Pine   86–88, 107
Pirate   7, 29, 61, 63, 125–126, 135–136, 161
  See also Insurance; Privateer
Plantation   12, 16, 22, 30–31, 36*n*7, 91, 93–94, 101, 112–113, 122*n*6, 139, 147, 153, 158, 163, 165–166
  See also Slaves
Plantation Duties Acts   31
Porcelain   60, 63, 73, 131–134, 181
Pork   73, 86–87, 95
Port city
  See Boston; New York; Philadelphia
Port complex   1–2, 4, 12, 15–17, 19, 25, 27, 33, 35, 46, 54, 70, 85, 99, 102, 119, 126, 140*n*74, 142, 172
Porto   21
Portugal   13, 21, 26, 37, 73, 89–90, 110, 125–126, 142–143, 148, 149*n*104, 161, 163, 181
Potash   86–88, 88*n*37, 89, 107, 147

Prices   5, 11*n*22, 21, 23, 52, 53–55, 58, 61–62, 68–69, 69*n*, 75–76, 80–81, 84–87, 89, 93, 97, 110–111, 132, 136–138, 143, 147, 161, 166, 171
Price, Ezekiel   29, 61, 61*n*92, 156
  See also Insurance
Prisoner exchange   131, 166
Privateers   7, 20, 29, 125–127, 135, 166
  See also Insurance; Pirate
Profit   8–9, 22, 25, 28, 35, 38, 40, 50–51, 54–56, 62, 68, 71, 76–77, 85, 92–94, 97, 100, 102, 109–111, 113–114, 116, 119–120, 123, 126, 128, 135–137, 139–140, 146, 148, 153, 158, 161, 180, 182–183
Protest   1, 30, 39, 68, 69*n*, 82, 164, 174, 176, 179
  See also Constraints; Revenue Acts
Protestant   36
  See also Catholic

Quaker   39, 42, 42*n*26
Quebec   27, 32, 84, 110, 141, 168
  See also Boston; Halifax

Reais   130, 148
  See also Currency; Specie
Refineries   51, 85, 90–93
  See also Sugar
Retailing   35, 41
  shops   56, 72, 81, 97
Revenue Acts   1, 29, 102, 167, 169–170
  See Agreements; Constraints
Rhode Island   4, 8, 20, 50, 54, 109–110, 114, 126, 132, 135, 140, 172–173
Risk   10, 29, 36, 42, 49, 51, 53, 56, 61, 110–111, 120, 127, 130, 133, 135*n*57, 136, 181–183
  See also Constraints
Rotterdam   37, 78*n*18, 124, 130, 132, 147
Rowe, John   39, 179
Rum   13, 21–22, 55, 58, 61*n*89, 63, 72–73, 75–76, 76*n*13, 82, 85–87, 92–94, 96–97, 105, 107–110, 112–116, 128, 135, 146–147, 161, 181

Sailors   1, 9, 105, 124
Saint-Domingue   42, 58, 94, 113, 138–140, 161
Salem (Port)   15, 18, 20, 46, 50, 53, 85, 108, 118, 136, 140, 140*n*74, 143, 143*n*, 145, 171

Salt   12, 21, 63, 72–73, 75–76, 79, 90–91, 95, 110, 140, 143n84, 156
Salutary neglect   151–153
Seven Years' War   14, 24, 27, 32, 102, 121, 128, 131, 135n57, 148, 151, 165, 165n33, 167, 180
Shipbuilding   8, 44–45, 47–49, 85, 89
Shipping   7, 21, 28, 35, 41, 46, 48, 51, 66, 93, 96, 104–105, 109–110, 114, 132, 134, 160–161, 169, 181
Shopkeeper   44, 50, 54–55, 60, 63, 96–97
Shortage
   See Currency; Specie
Silk   12, 55, 73, 78–79, 81, 84, 136, 169, 181
Silver   16, 32n54, 64, 111, 126, 135, 138, 156, 184
   See also Currency
Slaves   22, 24n26, 37n7, 43, 94, 101, 112, 138, 146, 149, 153
   See also Plantation
Smuggling   3, 13, 20, 20n9, 52, 82, 102–103, 127–133, 133n53, 134–135, 138, 142, 146, 146n91, 147, 152–154, 154n8, 155–156, 163–165, 171–173, 178, 181
   See also Constraints
South America   9, 18, 22, 24n24, 32n54, 100, 128, 140, 184
   See also Brazil; Latin America
South Carolina   4, 47, 110, 155
   See also Lower South
Spain   21, 32n54, 37, 73, 85, 91, 110, 126, 128, 137, 139, 142–143, 145, 148–149, 168, 181
   See also Barcelona; Canary Islands; Tenerife
Specie   6, 13, 31, 33, 37, 55, 64–66, 71, 95, 100, 103–105, 119, 163, 182
   See also Currency
Spices   72–73, 82, 131–132, 181
St. Eustatius   131, 138–139, 161, 163
St. Kitts   93–94, 113, 139
Stamp Act   1, 169–170, 175
Staples Act   31
State capacity   6–7, 14, 38, 120, 151
   See also Currency
Staves   86–88, 93–94, 138, 148, 150
Sugar   13, 22, 40, 51, 55, 58, 63, 70, 72–73, 75–76, 79, 82, 85, 90–95, 97–98, 101, 107–110, 112–114, 128, 137–142, 146, 146n91, 147, 166–167, 169–173, 178

   See also Molasses; Plantations; Rum; Sugar Act
Sugar Act   108, 108n22, 169–173
Supercargo   41, 59, 184
Suriname   13, 24, 42, 94, 113, 140–141
Sweden   184

Tanneries   43n32, 51
Tar   12, 107, 179
Taxes   1–2, 6, 9, 12, 29, 31, 43n32, 43–44, 64, 102, 150, 154, 154n7, 163, 167–171, 178, 183
Tea   12, 40, 54, 60, 63, 70, 72–73, 76, 81–82, 95, 97–98, 127–128, 131–133, 133n53, 134, 146–147, 154, 154n8, 156, 163–164, 167, 171, 177, 179, 181, 183–184
   Chausson   133
   Chinese   12, 181
   Green   73, 84, 97, 133
   Black   133
   Bohea   63, 73, 97, 133, 156
   Oolong   73, 133
Tea party
   See Boston Tea Party
Tenerife   132, 133n49, 134, 161
   See also Canary Islands
Textiles   16, 72, 81–82, 84, 181
The Argo (ship)   161
The Charles (ship)   135
The Fame (Ship)   124–125, 155
Timber   20–21
Tobacco   71, 84, 89, 113–114
Tonnage   13, 19, 27–28, 43n32, 45–49, 49n45, 50–51, 53, 94, 104, 106–109, 109n28, 110, 117, 143, 150, 159–161, 166
Townshend Acts   29, 169–171
Trade
   coastal   11n22, 22, 35, 45, 50, 77–78, 78n18, 88, 89n44, 90, 92–94, 100–102, 104–105, 107–112, 115, 117, 119, 141, 143, 181
   illegal   10, 13, 26n33, 81, 103, 120, 124, 127–129, 131, 134, 143, 146–147, 153, 153n, 154, 156, 156n14, 158, 164, 166, 168, 173, 175
   illicit   3, 81, 103, 124–125, 127–131, 135, 140–141, 143, 146, 146n91, 147, 153, 155–156, 166, 168, 174–175
   imbalance of   45n36, 71, 76–77, 100, 103, 152, 152n

INDEX   239

inter-colonial   2, 11n22, 13, 30, 100–105, 109–110, 117, 119–121, 144, 150, 181
intra-imperial   2, 22, 29, 115n48, 116
legal   3, 6, 26n33, 120, 123–124, 130–131, 133n53, 134, 143
trans-imperial   2–3, 13, 21n12, 26n33, 70, 78, 97, 102–105, 108–117, 119–153, 165, 168, 180–181
routes   15–16, 41, 52, 119, 130, 149, 181, 183–184
See also smuggling
Treasury
  British   32, 164, 168n44, 174
Treaty of Paris   21
Troops   166, 171, 177–179

Upper South   4, 77
  See also Lower South; Maryland; North Carolina; Virginia

Virginia   4, 9, 32, 47, 54, 82–83, 96, 121, 163–165, 174
  See also Upper South

Wadsworth, Jeremiah   183
Wales   40
War   1–2, 6, 14, 24, 29, 32, 51, 121, 126–128, 131, 131n43, 135n57, 136–138, 151, 155, 165–167, 173, 177, 179–180, 182–183

See also American Revolution; Prisoners of War; Seven Years' War
Wealth   4, 11n22, 41, 43, 68, 105, 135, 181
Weather   11n22, 53, 63, 108, 112, 136
West Indies   8–9, 18, 22, 24, 24n24, 25–26, 39, 42, 46, 48–49, 55, 57, 59, 61n89, 73, 75–76, 84–85, 88, 90–94, 96–97, 100–101, 104–106, 108–109, 111–115, 115n48, 116–121, 126, 131n40, 137–140, 142–143, 146, 146n91, 147–148, 156–157, 160–162, 169, 182
Whale   91
  See also Oil
Wheat   11, 20, 24, 60, 62, 66, 84, 86–87, 89, 91, 95, 105, 107, 126, 150, 156
Wholesaling   35, 40–41, 50, 53–54, 68, 91, 97, 105, 147, 169, 171
Wine   12, 21, 55, 63, 70–72, 76, 82, 88, 91, 110, 118, 130, 141, 143, 169
Wine Islands   18, 107, 122, 125–126, 160
Women   43, 43n32, 81–82, 91, 97–98, 177
Wood   19, 21, 80, 86–88, 88n37, 93–94, 109, 138
  See also Potash
Wool Act   31
World-Systems Theory   4–5

Printed in the United States
by Baker & Taylor Publisher Services